It is, indeed, in every possible
respect, desirable that every
nation should possess one city in
which every interest of man and
of society is adequately
represented and cared for.
—Anonymous, 1856

City of the World!
(for all races are here,
All the lands of the earth
make contributions here)...
—Walt Whitman, 1865

CITY OF THE WORLD

NEW YORK AND ITS PEOPLE

By Bernie Bookbinder

Foreword by Sydney Schanberg

With color photographs by Harvey Weber
Research by Robert W. Snyder

Harry N. Abrams, Inc.
Publishers, New York

A New York Newsday Book

At first look, this may seem to be yet another picture book about New York. But the pictures are not glib or glossy and neither is the trenchant history of New York City that Bernie Bookbinder has written to explain them. His gritty chronicle forces us to look first at the immigrant waves that have built the world's most powerful urban center and then at the conflict and prejudiced attitudes with which those immigrants were—and still are—greeted.

We like to comfort ourselves with the warmth of the self-congratulatory concept known as the melting pot, but the author shows us with clarity of research and language just how fictional this notion is. It has not been a place, not New York City nor the country as a whole, where newcomers have received cordial welcomes and quickly blended in. It has been instead "a cauldron" where each group had to fight, often literally, to win a foothold.

That alone would not necessarily lead to any discouraging thoughts, for historically immigrants to every country have had to wage hard struggles to gain acceptance. What does discourage is the pattern of racism that emerges from Bookbinder's carefully sketched account of New York as America's gateway city. He shows, sadly, that while the other major immigrant groups were able eventually to overcome (though not erase) native prejudices and seize their share of America's success story, our black immigrants, most of whom were initially brought from Africa as slaves, have never managed to break down what the author calls "a marked affinity for European stock."

Through education and entrepreneurship, the Germans and Irish and Jews and Italians managed to enter the mainstream, though at differing speeds, depending on how closely each group mirrored the prevailing societal norms. But through it all, no matter what their achievements in literature or theater or science or sports, blacks have remained our outsiders—along with the Latinos, who came later on and are still joining us in large numbers.

Yet for all its sober truths, this book is not a grim or gloomy history of New York City. Its pages reverberate with the boisterousness and raw joy and pain and tumult of the town's brawling evolution. It closes, appropriately, with an appeal to our humaneness and common sense, asking us to recognize that very soon, if it has not happened already, a majority of New Yorkers will be non-white and that if we are to make the city even a halfway civilized place, the people we have kept as outsiders must finally be welcomed as equals.

We know from the daily headlines that racial strife is imbedded deep within this city's social system. The test will lie in our willingness and ability to cast aside the stereotyping by color and language that we have so long and so assiduously engaged in.

That is why this book is not just good reading, it is required reading.

—Sydney Schanberg

Contents

One cannot contemplate a New York City without the contributions of immigrants. From subways to skyscrapers, they literally have built the metropolis. In its factories and sweatshops, they have made goods for the world, and from its warehouses and wharves, they have stored and shipped them. They have given distinction to its universities and colleges, art to its museums, entertainment to its theaters, music to its concert halls and jazz clubs, literature to its libraries, and vitality and diversity to its life.

Lured by liberty or livelihood, more than twenty million have disembarked here: Irish and Germans in the mid-nineteenth century, eastern European Jews and Italians a half-century later, blacks and Puerto Ricans during the mid-twentieth century, and Asians and Latinos today. Some brought skills, some brought ideas, some brought brawn; all brought hope.

For most immigrants, the introduction to American ways began as soon as they got off the boat. Their initiators were, at best, uncaring, at worst, predatory. The Irish and Germans, having fled their homelands to escape famine, depression, or political unrest, quickly discovered exploitation. Some became the victims of dockside "runners," would-be helpers who took their money in return for providing them with nonexistent jobs, nonexistent accommodations, and nonexistent railroad destinations. Such unbridled free enterprise roused government to intervene, prodding it, finally, to take some responsibility for the protection and orientation of immigrants. City officials finally came to the rescue of new arrivals in 1855 by converting Castle Garden, reputedly the nation's largest auditorium, into the Emigrant Landing Depot, the first facility for processing immigrants.

New arrivals were taken directly from the dock to the depot so they could be oriented and assisted while insulated from the rapacious runners. There were no meaningful medical examinations but bathing was compulsory, and tubs, troughs, soap, and towels were provided. More important, accurate information, previously the rarest of items, was provided by clerks, along with railroad and canal tickets, which were sold at correct prices. Although no beds were available, there was room for sleeping, and as many as three thousand immigrants sometimes spent the night. Food could be purchased, the facility was heated in the winter and, in the summer, was cooled by a fountain. The immigrants were required to divulge their resources—in 1855, the average was $86—and state their destination, which two out of five said was New York City. While the Emigrant Landing Depot was surely less than it might have been, it was considerably more than had existed before and at least served to cushion immigrants temporarily from the exploitation, deprivation, and suffering that would soon befall them.

By 1890, when scandal forced the depot's closing, an estimated eight million immigrants, mostly Irish and German, had been processed there. Authority was transferred subsequently to the federal government, which used its Barge Office facilities until the opening of Ellis Island in 1892.

During the half-century of greatest immigration, a period that ended with World War II and involved mostly Jews and Italians escaping religious persecution or poverty, Ellis Island came to symbolize both the indifference and callousness that characterized the treatment of newcomers to America and their hopes for new lives in a new land. For most, Ellis Island proved a traumatic experience; a period of anxiety-ridden waiting after the squalor of passage and the exhilarating sight of the American mainland. Herded like animals ("You think you're in a zoo," one Ukrainian recalled), immigrants feared being denied admission for failure to pass tests certifying their means, morals, health, and political ideology. For many, ignorance of the English language may have been a blessing, for they were spared the humiliation of knowing what disabilities were indicated by the letters that medical examiners had chalked across their clothing. A quarter-million were sent back. Some three thousand others, bewildered, frightened, and depressed, took their own lives. The place became known as the "Island of Tears."

In three great waves spanning more than a century, immigrants and migrants poured into New York City, filling its streets, its tenements, its schools, its factories, sweatshops, labor unions, hospitals, cemeteries, and jails. Driven by fear, hunger, and hope, they found opportunity and exploitation, wealth and poverty, justice and discrimination. They brought diversity—ethnic, religious, and racial— but discovered that joining the mainstream proved far easier than swimming against the tide. Despite vast differences in culture, as these photographs illustrate, the newcomers generally shared a rural background that provided little preparation for the urban environment they would enter. Among the earliest New Yorkers were the English, who left quaint communities such as Manchester to establish themselves throughout the eighteenth century. First to arrive in the mid-nineteenth century were the Irish, from settlements such as those in County Mayo, and Germans, from more affluent villages in places like Bavaria. Around the turn of the century, Italians from the southern cities, such as Naples, and Jews, from eastern European settlements, such as Maciejowice, Poland, occupied the Lower East Side. During the mid-twentieth century, the migrants were Latinos and blacks, the former from Puerto Rico, the latter from tenant farms in the rural South.

Where they came from: Naples, Italy

This experience was not universal. As the steerage-borne immigrants would soon learn, the nation's consecration to the principles of democracy was not without exceptions. The indignities and discomforts of Ellis Island were spared those who traveled in better accommodations: They were processed aboard ship.

Yet the masses still came. That such large-scale immigration continued, even burgeoned, was an indication not only of the newcomers' intolerable past but of their vision of a bountiful future. Opportunity and freedom beckoned, and if the reality did not always match the expectation, it seemed far better than that which had been left behind. The gratitude of immigrants, preserved on film, in print, and in legend, has served to overshadow the scorn implicit in governmental policies and performance.

Such insensitivity was prophetic: The disdain of the official reception served as conditioning for the attitudes that awaited in the neighborhood and the workplace. For historically, New Yorkers have shown little enthusiasm over the arrival of newcomers and less over their decision to remain. Their appearance has been greeted more often with fear and resentment than with joy and appreciation. Aside from their families, the warmest welcome foreigners received probably came from the Statue of Liberty.

Perhaps that is why, in an effort to mitigate guilt and amend history, we have so glorified that statue, enshrining its spirit in our national mythology. Among America's best-remembered poetry is Emma Lazarus's sonnet, "The New Colossus," that adorns the pedestal and expresses the ideal. In the name of the "Mother of Exiles," it magnanimously invites to our shores the "tired...poor...huddled masses...wretched refuse...homeless, tempest tost."

Lazarus wrote "Colossus" in 1883. By 1894, after perhaps five million of the "tired, poor, huddled masses" had accepted the invitation, the noted author Thomas Bailey Aldrich composed a poem on the same subject. Entitled "The Unguarded Gate," it warned about "a wild, a motley throng...bringing with them unknown

gods and rites," speaking "strange tongues...accents of menace alien to our air."
And it appealed to the "*white* goddess" of Liberty to "stay those who to thy sacred
portals come to waste the fight of freedom...lest from thy brow the clustered stars
be torn and trampled in the dust." Directing his invective at the full range of recent
immigrants—"men from the Volga and the Tartar steppes, featureless figures of
the Hoang-Ho, Malayan, Scythian, Teuton, Kelt, and Slav"—Aldrich evoked the
image of the Goth and Vandal barbarians who sacked Rome and asked, "Is it well to
leave the gate unguarded?"

Whether the majority of New Yorkers shared the sentiments of Lazarus or of
Aldrich is unknown. But it is not difficult to believe that attitudes toward aliens
have been engendered at least as much by xenophobia or motives of exploitation as
by feelings of compassion. The cruel irony is that the exploiters were generally
descendants of the exploited, perpetuating a cycle of affliction that endlessly has
victimized the most vulnerable. Ignorant of the contempt in which their forebears
were held, too many immigrants' offspring have expressed similar hostility toward
contemporary newcomers. Still, immigrants endure, and many surely triumph.
Yet there remains a tendency to appreciate them not for the energy and variety
they have brought but instead for their ability to expeditiously become like those
they joined, to conform.

This was evident from the experiences of those who arrived in the earliest immigrant wave. When Irish and German Catholics landed in the 1840s, they found a
city that had begun as Dutch, had become English, and had retained the values of
Protestant industriousness and asceticism. Measured against those standards, the
Germans, whose skills and discipline meshed more readily with the city's commercial nature, gained easier acceptance than did the farm-oriented Irish. (This, despite the fact that the Germans spoke a foreign language.) Similarly, subsequent
waves would find the city's reaction to them based largely on how closely their
traits approximated the prevailing norm.

Above left:
Where they came from: Maciejowice,
Poland

Above:
Where they came from: Krzemieniec,
Poland

Overleaf:
Where they came from: Kazimierz
nad Wisłą, Poland

*Where they came from:
Ortenau, Germany*

The faculty to become "Americanized," to fit into the majority culture, has been perceived traditionally as a goal pursued consciously by an ethnic or racial group and, consequently, has been applauded. But for some groups the opportunity to fulfill the "American dream" has been primarily an accident of good or bad economic timing. And for others, particularly blacks, the criterion for full acceptance—skin color—is unattainable.

There is no doubt that discrimination—in housing, employment, and education—has oppressed blacks and Latinos longer and more forcefully than earlier newcomers. And it has done so during an era of greater enlightenment and awareness, making this bigotry all the more reprehensible. Nonetheless, it would be intellectually dishonest to ignore the cultural baggage different groups brought with them to New York and the extent to which their heritage and traditions accelerated or inhibited their success. Self-sufficiency, family cohesiveness, urban experience, and exposure to the discipline and incentives of the marketplace have proved critical factors contributing to immigrant achievement.

Meanwhile, the history of religious, ethnic, and racial relationships in New York City has more closely resembled a cauldron than a melting pot. Distaste, distrust, and fear of outsiders have simmered beneath a surface of acceptance, ever ready to boil over into hostility and even violence.

Thus, Protestants, Catholics, Jews, African-Americans, Irish, Germans, Italians, Poles, Native Americans, Latinos, Asians, West Indians, and others all suffered abuse and discrimination at the hands of an entrenched majority. In the nineteenth century the most obvious bigotry involved Protestants against Catholics, in the early twentieth century it was Christians against Jews, and since the mid-twentieth century it has been whites against blacks. While the earlier religious and ethnic conflicts have largely been ameliorated, the racial antagonism remains unresolved, continuing to haunt the city as it does the nation.

This happened despite the myth that the gatekeepers of the New World were inspired more by compassion and generosity than by self-interest and greed. Such beliefs were short-lived among the immigrants, who found sanctuary but little solace in the slums and ghettos and barrios of New York.

Although the targets of discrimination have changed over the years, its cause seems strikingly constant: the protection of entrenched power. Time and again, an earlier immigrant group, having painfully accrued authority, struck at the perceived threat posed by more recent arrivals. Because the patterns of immigration have shifted during the city's history, the form of prejudice has been determined by the nature of the newcomers, becoming either religious bias, ethnic bias, or racism.

Where they came from:
County Mayo, Ireland

Yet the justification has remained surprisingly similar: The victims invariably have been "unsanitary," "backward," "secretive," and "criminal."

When New York's Protestant majority feared displacement by the influx of Irish Catholics in the 1850s, for example, they saw the immigrants as barbarians who would overwhelm them with numbers, undercut their wages, and debase the way of life they had struggled to achieve. Tailoring their prejudice to their quarry, they distorted the hierarchical nature of Catholicism to project irrational fears of political domination by the Pope and circulated fraudulent propaganda that fed anxieties about secret rites and practices.

This bigotry found comfort in a nativist political movement that became the "Know-Nothing" party, an organization whose exponents included Samuel F. B. Morse, the inventor of the telegraph. Morse, articulating the anti-Catholic party line, asked, "How is it possible that foreign turbulence imported by ship-loads, that the ignorance in hundreds of thousands of human priest-controlled machines, should suddenly be thrown into our society, and not produce here turbulence and excess? Can one throw mud into pure water and not disturb its clearness?"

A half-century later, when the Irish Catholics had acceded to control of the city's government and the ships were unloading Jewish immigrants from eastern Europe, the response again was to foment hatred. This time the basis was more ethnic than religious, but that hardly mattered; one result has been described as the worst anti-Semitic police riot in American history.

The incident occurred on July 30, 1902, during the funeral of Rabbi Jacob Joseph, a revered religious leader who had been brought to America from Lithuania to inspire a renewal of faith among the recent arrivals. The riot, initially provoked by Irish workers at the R. Hoe & Co. printing press factory along the funeral route, exposed the blatant hostility of the Irish police toward immigrant minorities and clearly warned that organized, authorized violence was possible even in a democratic society. When the Jewish mourners reacted to verbal and physical abuse by storming the plant, police, led by Inspector Adam Cross, fell on them with night-sticks. "Kill those Sheenies!" Cross reportedly shouted. "Club them right and left! Get them out of the way!" The result was the injuring of more than two hundred Jews and, in what many regarded as the ultimate injustice, the arrest of eleven of them but of only one Hoe worker. This point was made by the *New York Times*, which editorialized, "The police, or a considerable portion of them, regard the Jews of the Lower East Side not as claimants for protection but as fit objects of persecution. These unhappy Jews are not only not protected by the police, they are in need of protection against the police."

Where they came from:
Manchester, England

Opposite above:
Where they came from:
Vicksburg, Mississippi

Opposite below:
Where they came from:
Bethany, Georgia

As a consequence of the handling of the riot and an attempted police cover-up, Cross was dismissed and Commissioner John N. Partridge resigned. But any belief that anti-Semitism had been eradicated from the police department was dashed six years later when a new commissioner, Theodore A. Bingham, announced that Jews constituted 50 percent of New York City's criminals. (In fact, Bingham's figure was more than double the proportion of crimes attributed to Jews, who actually were underrepresented in the criminal population.)

Tragically, police intervention on the side of persecutors, rather than their victims, has been no rarity in American *racial* relations. Too often, this has been the case in New York, as well. Only two years before the Rabbi Jacob Joseph outbreak, the city's police had joined white mobs in a two-day rampage against blacks that drew incensed criticism from a citizens committee. "They ran with the crowds in pursuit of their prey," the report stated. "They took defenseless men who ran to them for protection and threw them to the rioters, and in many cases they beat and clubbed men and women more brutally than the mob did."

Blacks, considered "outsiders" as much as any immigrants, have been more victimized by mob rule in New York than any other group. The worst case was the New York Draft Riot of 1863, the bloodiest civil disorder in American history and one that, in its origins, closely resembled the anti-immigrant hostilities.

The precipitating factor for the three-day frenzy that began on July 13 was a provision of the Civil War's Conscription Act permitting legal draft-dodging by the payment of $300. But the context was far broader: Times were hard for blacks and Irish and German immigrants, and demagogic Democrats, such as New York City Mayor Fernando Wood, had harangued that while drafted white workers were fighting to end slavery, freed blacks would steal their jobs.

Fired by fear and resentment, gangs of workers, most of them Irish, destroyed the draft headquarters, compelled factories to shut down, repelled police, set fire to the homes of the rich and a black orphan asylum, and vainly attacked the mayor's residence. Rampaging through the streets, segments of the mob seized armories, fought army units to a standstill, and battered, burned, or hanged any black they could catch. Finally, on the fourth day, Union soldiers returning from the battle of

Gettysburg put down the riot. The death toll was minimally placed at more than one hundred, with at least one thousand injured.

Regardless of the animosities that impelled them at the outset, it was undoubtedly racism that accounted for the ferocity and sadism of the rioters. The cruelty was unspeakable, as one firsthand account testified: "A crowd of rioters in Clarkson Street, in pursuit of a negro, who in self-defence had fired on some rowdies, met an inoffensive colored man returning from a bakery with a loaf of bread under his arm. They instantly set upon and beat him and, after nearly killing him, hung him to a lamp-post. His body was left suspended for several hours. A fire was made underneath him, and he was literally roasted as he hung, the mob reveling in their demoniac act."

The pressures of discrimination and poverty that afflict New York blacks have erupted in repeated outbursts of violence, looting, and destruction during the twentieth century. While earlier race riots had been initiated by whites against blacks, a pattern set in 1935 found blacks retaliating against white exploitation by assailing white-owned property and those assigned to protect it.

In 1935, economic conditions throughout the United States were bad; in Harlem, they were abysmal. Work was scarce enough, but idle blacks found themselves looking on in frustration and resentment as most of the stores they bought from refused to hire them, most of the labor unions that controlled employment refused to admit them, and most of the public works jobs in their own neighborhoods were denied them. Even attempts to demonstrate and boycott were thwarted by injunctions.

The atmosphere was so combustible that only a minor pilfering incident involving a black teenager was needed to detonate an outbreak that spread throughout the ghetto. A commission appointed by Mayor Fiorello La Guardia, blaming "insecurity produced by years of unemployment and deep-seated resentment against the many forms of discrimination," predicted that unless conditions were improved, future outbursts were likely.

The commission's warning soon became a reality. In 1943, when a white policeman attempted to arrest a black woman in Harlem, a black soldier intervened and another race riot was under way. Blacks assaulted white passersby, overturned parked cars, and threw bricks and bottles at police who responded to the riot call. While most of the fury was again directed at property, six persons were killed and more than five hundred injured.

It did not receive much attention at the time, but a social phenomenon that apparently surfaced during this period involved a new form of prejudice: black anti-Semitism. In several sections of New York, but particularly in Harlem, blacks had moved into neighborhoods formerly occupied by Jews. And while the Jewish tenants moved out, Jewish landlords and merchants often retained ownership of the tenements and stores. Traditional hostility between tenants and landlords over rents, services, and maintenance, exacerbated by racial tensions and the fact that, aside from police, Jews were the most visible whites in the ghetto, made them the target of black anger.

While New York has been spared mass violence for more than two decades, there is almost daily evidence that tensions among the city's races, religions, and nationalities remain volatile. And almost daily, demagogues disguised as leaders surrender to their own basest impulses and the susceptibility of the electorate by igniting bias and hatred to gain favor.

On the national level, government policies, until recently, rather than seeking to dispel prejudice and bigotry against immigrants, institutionalized such attitudes through legislation that admitted or excluded races and nationalities based upon popular hostilities and political expediency. Thus, in 1882, reacting to racist hysteria fed by economic pressures, Chinese were barred. In 1924, discriminatory national quotas were imposed, based on previous immigration patterns. These

obviously favored northern and western Europeans, especially the British, at the expense of southern and eastern Europeans, and, particularly, Asians and Africans. In 1952, Cold War paranoia led to the exclusion of Communist sympathizers. It was not until 1965 that the system was liberalized, to the benefit of both the immigrants and the nation, by admitting those possessing needed skills, regardless of their country of origin. Opportunities were extended in 1980 to assist refugees from southeast Asia and Cuba.

New York, as the nation's main port of entry, received the burden and the benefit of such policies, sometimes accommodating, sometimes obstructing, but always conscious of the strangers in its midst. And just as different immigrants, depending on when they came, why they came, and where they came from, found a different city, so have its natives. Some have found it fascinating. E. B. White thought it "a miracle that New York works at all." Some have extolled its diversity. Walt Whitman called it the "City of the world! (for all races are here, all the lands of the earth make contributions here.)" Some have found it intriguing. O. Henry called it "Bagdad-on-the-Subway" for its mixture of the magical and material.

But New Yorkers might most appreciate Washington Irving's appropriation of "Gotham," the name of an English village near Nottingham. Irving chose it because of the ingenuity of its residents. Learning that King John had contemplated their hamlet as the site of his castle and fearing tax increases and other undesirable consequences from the royal presence, they behaved crazily when the monarch came on an inspection tour, leading him to abandon his plan. The successful stratagem earned the saying: "More fools pass through Gotham than remain in it."

Quick-wittedness and imagination, "outsiders" readily learn, are requisites for success in New York. And their struggle to succeed has characterized New York City's history. The result has been a unique city but one built as much through conflict as concord. That productive turmoil is the territory this book seeks to explore by describing changes the immigrants underwent and changes they wrought in their struggle through the unknown. The focus is on the aspects of city life where the impact of immigrants and of ethnic and racial diversity is most readily discernible: in the economy, in politics, in education, and in popular culture. Utilizing the observations of contemporaries, the book tries to convey the city that the immigrants found and inhabited: the neighborhoods, the tenements, the foods, pastimes, fulfillments, fears, and frustrations.

No immigrant who came to New York between 1892 and 1954 is likely to forget Ellis Island, the "Island of Tears," where they wept from the joy of arrival, the fear of rejection, and the humiliation of inspection. The processing center is depicted in photographs taken during the first decade of the twentieth century at the height of its activity and show the eye examination (above), the quarantine station on Hoffman Island and the release of immigrants from quarantine (above right and opposite above right), the childrens' rooftop playground (opposite above left), and immigrants leaving Ellis Island for the mainland and a new life (opposite below).

While some depictions of the immigrant experience cite the significant accomplishments of first-generation and second-generation Americans as proof of the opportunities offered by the city and the nation, here attention is concentrated on the immigrants themselves. What happened to those confused, fearful, hopeful strangers best reflects the nature of New York and New Yorkers because a society's worth is revealed most clearly by the treatment of its least fortunate members. That may be the reason so many myths have been created glorifying the reception of foreigners to our shores. And so one goal of this book is to demythologize New York's history. For in order to constructively address the city's future it is necessary to honestly deal with its past.

From the beginning, the pattern was clear. Beleaguered and fearful in a New World, newcomers sought the comfort of the familiar. Clustered in enclaves where they clung to the language and customs of their homeland, they were perceived by the broader society as "strange," "dangerous," "undesirable." While their children will learn new ways and seek to move into the majority, the immigrants, with a foot in each world, stand alone, transfixed.

Discomfort and despair preceded the immigrants' arrival in New York. Few who endured the transatlantic voyage were not afflicted by it. The horrendous treatment of passengers was exposed by a remarkable Irish reformer named Stephen de Vere, who sailed in steerage from London in 1847 and reported his findings to the British House of Lords: "Hundreds of poor people, men, women, and children, of all ages, from the drivelling idiot of ninety to the babe just born, huddled together without light, without air, wallowing in filth and breathing a fetid atmosphere, sick in body, dispirited in heart, the fevered patients lying between the sound, in sleeping places so narrow as almost to deny them the power of indulging, by a change of position, the natural restlessness of the disease; by their agonized ravings disturbing those around, and predisposing them, through the effects of the imagination, to imbibe the contagion; living without food or medicine, except as administered by the hand of casual charity, dying without the voice of spiritual consolation, and buried in the deep without the rites of the church."

As the first sizable immigrant group to arrive, the "Famine Irish," fleeing starvation, poured into Manhattan below Canal Street and occupied whatever housing was available; invariably substandard, frequently abysmal. The worst of it was the Five Points, a festering slum centered at today's intersection of Baxter, Mulberry, and Worth streets, northeast of City Hall. Even the seasoned senses of Charles Dickens were repelled by what he observed during a visit in 1842: "Lanes and alleys, paved with mud knee-deep: underground chambers, where they dance and game; the walls bedecked with rough designs of ships, and forts, and flags, and American Eagles out of number: ruined houses, open to the street, whence, through wide gaps in the walls, other ruins loom upon the eye, as though the world of vice and misery had nothing else to show: hideous tenements which take their name from robbery and murder; all that is loathsome, drooping, and decayed is here."

The Five Points was notorious enough to become the subject of frequent newspaper articles and even something of a tourist attraction. Both the dilapidated buildings and their occupants were described luridly by journalists such as George Foster, who, after noting that the rotting wooden buildings were on the verge of collapse, observed that the occupants seemed likewise. "Nearly every house and cellar is a groggery below and a brothel above," he wrote in 1849. "In the doors and at the windows may be seen at any hour of the afternoon or evening, scores of sluttishly-dressed women, in whose faces drunkenness and debauchery have destroyed every vestige of all we expect in the countenance of women, and even almost every trace of human expression."

Rock bottom in the Five Points was the Old Brewery, an abandoned eighteenth-century plant converted into a brothel, cache for stolen goods, and reputed living quarters for more than one thousand "thieves, murderers, pickpockets, beggars, harlots, and degenerates of every type." The Old Brewery's legendary notoriety led to its purchase in 1852 by the Ladies' Home Missionary Society and replacement with the Five Points Mission "in order to change it from a pest-house of sin to a school of virtue." To raise funds for the project, the society conducted candle-lit tours of the vacated structure, leading thousands of respectable city residents through the winding corridors and decrepit stairways that only recently had housed their fellow New Yorkers. "The company thronged several of the apartments," reported the *Daily Tribune*, "where miserable men, women and children yet remain, and moodily submitted to the gaze of the strangers in that community of degraded outcasts."

Unlike the high-rise tenements of a later era, nineteenth-century slums were often ramshackle structures that had outlived their appeal for all but the homeless.

Opposite:
New York's size and diversity have doubtless contributed to its being a city of neighborhoods. Almost from the beginning, newcomers from Europe clustered together protectively in enclaves where they could associate with others of a similar language and background. Neighborhoods offered familiar faces, rituals, customs, food, and even clothing, making them the focal point of immigrants' social life. They spawned block parties with games, ethnic delicacies, music, and, as this photo taken in the Kingsbridge section of the Bronx in 1931 shows, dancing.

Of all the city's early slums, Five Points, just north of the present City Hall, was considered the worst. And the most notorious building in Five Points was the Old Brewery. Home, although the word is hardly appropriate, to an estimated one thousand people, the onetime plant served as a brothel, storage place for stolen goods, and hideout for criminals of every type. The Old Brewery underwent conversion again in 1852, when the Ladies' Home Missionary Society bought it and made it a mission. Funds were raised by conducting guided tours of the crumbling structure.

The tours focused attention not only on the terrible conditions under which many New Yorkers were living but the scandalous exploitation of other impoverished immigrants by landlords and their agents. Apart from the squalid Five Points, newcomers inhabited what were called "reconstructed tenant houses," actually former one-family dwellings converted to accommodate as many occupants as could be squeezed in. As the immigrant tide swelled, landlords began constructing tenements specifically for them. Often, these were built in rear lots, behind existing structures, where space, light, and air were minimal. Every portion of the tenements was utilized, including the basements, which were dark, stifling, and filled with seepage from sewers and privies.

Landlords frequently leased these tenements to agents, who then sublet the premises for whatever profit they could make. In 1857, a state investigating committee, after inspecting some of the dwellings, said of such an agent: "He measures rooms, and estimates—not their capacities for accommodating human life in health and comfort—but their capability of containing human life to pay the rent."

The unimaginable overcrowding, the absence of proper sanitation, the infestations of vermin all contributed to terrible epidemics of cholera, typhoid, and typhus, which swept through the slums with predictable regularity during the mid-century decades. The greatest number of deaths were recorded during the periods of greatest immigrant influx, and, unsurprisingly, the Irish were the principal victims. More than four out of five Bellevue Hospital admissions were foreign-born and more than 85 percent of them were Irish. In 1857, immigrants and their children accounted for three out of five cancer deaths, a majority of tuberculosis fatalities, and most of the infant mortality, which that year represented nearly two-thirds of the total deaths in New York City.

Such scourges no doubt help to explain why a substantial number of Irish left the city. A study by historian Jay P. Dolan found that more than half of the Irish immigrants who arrived in New York between 1850 and 1875 departed. Those who remained, according to John Hughes, who became bishop of New York's Catholic diocese in 1842 and knew them well, were "the destitute, the disabled, the broken-down, the very aged and the very young, for want of means or through want of inclination to go further."

Although their circumstances were truly abominable, particularly in the eyes of native New Yorkers, the Irish had fled a land stricken by famine and poverty. "It is but truth to say," Hughes conceded, "that their abode in the cellars and garrets of New York is not more deplorable nor more squalid than the Irish hovels from which many of them had been 'exterminated.'" For the Irish who stayed in New York, the Catholic church was a formidable ally, although more out of habit in many cases than piety. The recent arrivals clutched Catholicism almost as much for its association with Ireland as for its spiritual value. According to Hughes: "It is only when he has the consolation of his religion that he feels comparatively happy in his new position. If on the Sunday he can be present at the holy sacrifice of Mass, if he can only see the minister of his religion at the altar and hear the word of God in the language to which his ear was accustomed from childhood, he forgets that he is among strangers in a strange country."

Religious ritual was just one of the Old World traditions that immigrants embraced as a defense against the unfamiliar New World. The retention of their culture—customs, holidays, foods, and dress—lent stability to their lives and distinctiveness to their neighborhoods. For Irish Catholics, the church filled social needs, too, although sometimes with difficulty.

With death a commonplace event, funerals took on greater significance. Traditionally, in Ireland, wakes had combined mourning and merrymaking, and the popular custom was readily transplanted to America despite clerical disdain. After holding a wake at home, mourners would follow the body of the deceased to the cemetery in a procession that reflected the family's status, based upon the number of carriages involved. The spirit of free enterprise soon pervaded this ritual as companies were formed to provide "for rental, everything needed for a successful funeral—scarves, crepe, and gloves together with carriages and hearses."

But the church was displeased. Bishop John Dubois, Hughes's predecessor, was only the first to complain that the funerals resembled festivals with "frequent drinking instead of holy water, distasteful conversation instead of prayers."

The Irish enthusiasm for drinking and, occasionally, fighting was transported across the Atlantic from the permissive, rough-hewn society they had known in Ireland. And saloons, which were ubiquitous within the Irish wards, served as poor men's social clubs, where news could be gleaned and gossip spread. Native New Yorkers tended to view this behavior with aversion, and vilification of the Irish as drunkards and brawlers generally came from genteel American-born Protestants who had little taste for liquor themselves and whose sense of propriety reflected their own refined upbringing. Many of our conceptions of city life during the mid-nineteenth century are based on the diaries of George Templeton Strong and Philip Hone, both elitist conservatives who scarcely concealed their disapproval of immigrant and working-class people.

For example, in 1857, when Strong encountered a group of Irish women keening over the accidental deaths of two laborers, he reported: "It was an uncanny sound to hear, quite new to me. Beethoven would have interpreted it into music worse than the allegretto of the Seventh Symphony. Our Celtic fellow citizens are almost as remote from us in temperament and constitution as the Chinese."

While immigrant beliefs and behavior drew snide comments from nativist aristocrats, nativist masses were considerably more aggressive. In 1842, tensions between Protestants and Catholics ran high over the issue of school funding and boiled over on election day as mobs went on a rampage in the heavily Irish Sixth Ward, gutting a hotel used as a polling place. According to the *New York Herald*, "The Sixth Ward Hotel was turned inside out. Bishop Hughes' premises were assaulted and other dwellings in the Ward more or less injured by stones and brickbats. The military were ordered out about 9 o'clock in the evening and their presence alone saved the Cathedral [Old St. Patrick's] and other churches of the Catholics from being destroyed by this mob. Fifty-six of the rioters were arrested...."

As election day approached two years later, Hughes decided to forestall any repetition. He organized three thousand armed Catholics, who stood guard around church property. The mobs appeared carrying signs that inveighed against "Popery" but did not attack. However, their candidate, James Harper, who founded the publishing firm that became Harper & Row, was elected mayor.

Shortly after, anti-Catholic rioting erupted in Philadelphia and threatened to break out in New York as nativist leaders planned a mass demonstration at City Hall. Hughes called on Catholics to stay home while warning city officials that "if a single Catholic Church is burned in New York, the city will become a second Moscow." Robert Morris, the lame-duck mayor being replaced by Harper, asked: "Are you afraid that some of your churches will be burned?" "No, sir," Hughes replied, "but I am afraid that some of yours will be burned. We can protect our own. I come to warn you for your own good." The rally was called off.

By the end of the Civil War, Irish Catholics had become numerous enough to warrant serious attention by New York's political apparatus, which was under the control of Democratic Tammany Hall. This became clear in 1871, when Irish Protestants were very nearly prevented from celebrating their historic 1690 victory over Catholics at the Battle of the Boyne. To be sure, the previous year's parade

The mass arrival of immigrants from famine-ridden Ireland during the mid-nineteenth century produced a vicious backlash in the city from the entrenched Protestant majority. Typical of the anti-Irish sentiment is this Harper's Weekly *cartoon satirizing St. Patrick's Day behavior. In it, Thomas Nast, who later gained fame for his attacks on corrupt Tammany Hall leader William Marcy "Boss" Tweed, portrayed the Irish celebrants as apelike brutes.*

had claimed five lives, and, in 1871, the Ancient Order of Hibernians had vociferously announced its intent to break up any Protestant celebration of Catholic humiliation.

The Orangemen immediately sought protection from Police Superintendent James J. Kelso, who not only turned them down but forbade them to parade because to do so would *cause* violence. This decision was widely construed as a capitulation to Catholicism, an interpretation enthusiastically seconded by one Hibernian leader as "the greatest concession ever given the Irish." However, on the day before the event was to have taken place, Governor John T. Hoffman overruled Kelso with the support of Mayor A. Oakey Hall and offered protection to the marchers.

Consequently, on July 12, 161 Orangemen turned out and were guarded by 800 policemen and 2,200 state militiamen. The protection was so overwhelming, reporters noted, that the presence of the marchers was discernible only through their banners. The paraders proceeded down Eighth Avenue, which was lined with menacing crowds, when, at the corner of 24th Street, a half-dozen shots were fired from a tenement. The troops, who had been marching with their loaded muskets at half-cock, poured hundreds of rounds into the crowd and up and down adjacent streets until "the sidewalks ran with blood, and a more ghastly mosaic work could not be fancied than the white flags partially covered over with human gore." Reports varied, but there were approximately fifty persons killed, including two militiamen, and about one hundred wounded.

Although Orangemen continued to celebrate their victory in subsequent years, the bloodshed in 1871 apparently chilled further confrontations. For a few years, heavily guarded processions marched uneventfully. Beginning in 1875, the Irish Protestants abandoned the city streets and withdrew to picnic groves on the banks of the Hudson to commemorate the Battle of the Boyne. This tacit surrender marked the ascendancy of Irish Catholics, a phenomenon given architectural form in 1879 with the opening of St. Patrick's Cathedral, an event of transcendent significance since it symbolized the emergence of a poverty-stricken minority in the very center of Protestant wealth and exclusivity. The cathedral is now the seat of the wealthiest archdiocese in the United States.

The ascension of the Irish in New York was accomplished with much greater

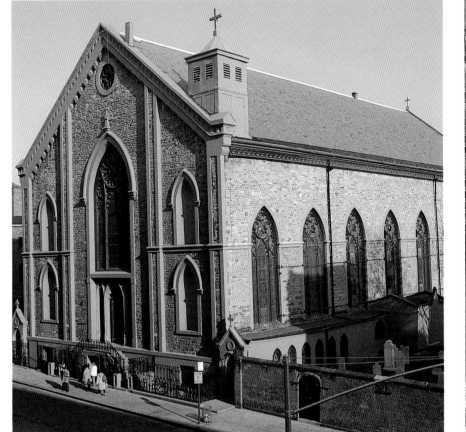

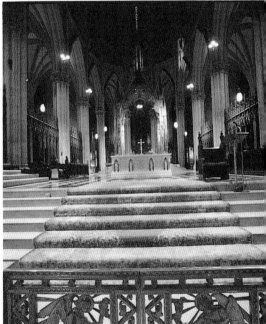

Immigrant survival in New York was abetted significantly by the efforts of earlier arrivals. Oswald Ottendorfer, a successful German-American, was responsible for the Ottendorfer branch of the New York Public Library at 135 Second Avenue. The oldest branch library in Manhattan and the first built specifically as a library, it was turned over to the city in 1884, even before its completion. Over the door of the library is the inscription: Freie Bibliothek u. Lesehalle (Free Library and Reading Room). Ottendorfer's desire to help fellow immigrants adopt American ways led him to select the first volumes, which he divided equally between German and English titles.

Social clubs were organized along class, as well as ethnic, lines, and at the turn of the century, facilities such as these German club rooms at the corner of Sand and Van Duzer streets catered to a middle-class clientele.

difficulty and pain than was that of German immigrants, who arrived at roughly the same time. Despite their different language, the Germans' skills, diligent work habits, and urban backgrounds, compared to the Irish, made them more acceptable to New Yorkers.

The Germans settled south of 14th Street on the Lower East Side and by the 1850s had formed their own community, called *Kleindeutschland* or *Deutschlandle*, meaning "Little Germany," where, according to German author Karl Theodor Griesinger, "The height and detail of the houses, the inhabitants, and their language and customs differ greatly from those of the rest of New York." *Kleindeutschland*'s population, comprising about two-thirds of New York's 120,000 Germans in the antebellum period, were drawn from all parts of Germany, he reported, although Bavarians predominated.

For these transplanted Europeans, Griesinger suggested, life went on largely as before. "Bakers, butchers, druggists—all are Germans. There is not a single business which is not run by Germans. Not only the shoemakers, tailors, barbers, physicians, grocers, and innkeepers are German, but the pastors and priests as well. There is even a German lending library where one can get all kinds of German books. The resident of *Kleindeutschland* need not even know English in order to make a living, which is a considerable attraction to the immigrant."

Griesinger alludes to the belief of many German immigrants that they left behind a more sophisticated and tolerant society than the one they found in America. As a fun-loving people they resented the restraints imposed by the dour reformers who set New York's moral tone. What tensions arose between the Germans and native New Yorkers dealt mainly with their differing attitudes toward drink and toward Sunday; the former behaved exuberantly, the latter piously.

To the Germans, Sunday meant relaxation: picnicking, dancing, singing, and drinking beer. "There are more inns in *Kleindeutschland* than in Germany," Griesinger stated. "Every fourth house is an inn, and there is one for every two hundred people. To the stranger, coming for the first time into the section, it would appear that there was nothing but beer saloons. Actually an immense quantity of beer is consumed.

"On Sunday the movement in the streets is like that in a dovecote. People go from the inn to the church and back to the inn again. Everybody wears his Sunday clothes and is in high spirits. In the afternoon, on days when the weather is good, almost everybody leaves town and goes on a picnic. On Sunday night there is still more merriment in *Kleindeutschland*. The inns are crowded, even with women. There is music, in spite of the laws against making noise on Sunday."

Griesinger could not resist stressing the difference in the Sunday ambience of "Little Germany" and the native American neighborhoods. "What a contrast it presents to the American sections," he wrote, "where the shutters are closed, and the quiet of a cemetery prevails!" Even the *Volkstheater* was open, where there were comedians whose "ribald songs receive the enthusiastic applause of the audience. The people enjoy themselves immensely; the entertainment costs only ten cents, and one gets a free beer now and then. Such is the way Sunday is celebrated in *Kleindeutschland*."

It was not only their attitude toward Sunday, however, that distinguished many of the German newcomers from the American mainstream. Stirred by the ferment of the 1848 Revolution and the socialist ideas of philosophers such as Karl Marx, some brought an antipathy toward capitalism that found expression in a variety of cooperative endeavors. As skilled tailors and piano, furniture, and cabinet makers, the German immigrants organized and joined associations that formed the foundation of the American labor movement. As intellectuals, they were active in promoting utopian schemes and even advocating terrorism as a means of establishing proletarian rule.

Consequently, the beerhalls and coffeehouses of *Kleindeutschland* resounded to the clash of economic and political ideologies and the crackle of organizational zeal. At a time when capitalism was expanding rapidly, many of the Germans were promoting radical alternatives. The impetus for change came from Forty-eighters, reformers, socialists, and freethinkers, the latter a group who opposed all organized religion and were involved in ongoing conflicts with native Americans *and* religious Germans, both Catholic and Protestant.

In their often furious debates, epithets such as "infidel" and "atheist" were hurled by conservatives, while the radicals charged their opponents with being "barbarians" who needed to be "enlightened" and rescued from their "primitive forest of churches and dogma."

The German immigrant community was not only divided between believers and nonbelievers but between Catholics and Protestants, most of whom were Lutherans. Although not as obvious to outsiders and certainly not as violent as that between Irish Catholics and Protestants, the religious schism among the German newcomers was significant and affected their involvement in such organizations as the Turnverein (literally "gymnastic society"), the popular clubs that extolled liberalism, reform, and physical culture.

Turnverein celebrations, featuring gymnastics, singing, dancing, and beer drinking, drew excited crowds to places such as the Harlem Pleasure Gardens, where, in the spring of 1856, 12,000 New Yorkers, according to the *Tribune*, gathered to enjoy themselves: "The pleasures of the festival consisted in an enormous straining of enormous muscles on the part of the Turners, who had gymnastic apparatus erected for their accommodation; in listening to very tolerable music from a number of German bands, and to an intermittent thunder-storm of singing from a dozen German song-societies; in irregular waltzing on rather rough grass-plots; in watching eighty starred policemen and a number of shadows eagerly initiating themselves into all German customs, as they had little else to do; in sitting on the grass and talking to one's friends—German women are not afraid to sit on the grass—in looking on generally, and last and greatest in drinking lager-beer.... The amber nectar flowed in a thousand streams. It was estimated that

Although Germans came to New York along with the Irish during the first great immigration wave of the mid-eighteenth century, their skills and industriousness won them earlier acceptance into the mainstream. A remnant of the significant German involvement in the city's life exists in the form of the German-American Shooting Club on St. Mark's Place.

The opening of the Eldridge Street Synagogue (above and above right) in 1887 reflected the flood of eastern European Jews, who were looked down upon by coreligionists who earlier had come from Germany.

Looking more like the Middle East than the middle of Brooklyn, the world headquarters of the Lubavitcher Chassidic Movement at 770 Eastern Parkway, in Crown Heights, is the site of the celebration of the Jewish holiday of Succoth (below right). Rabbi Menachem M. Schneerson, known to his followers as the "Rebbe," distributes honey cake to a member of the devout congregation. The Rebbe's public addresses, called Fabrengens, are delivered on special occasions and telecast throughout the world.

everybody who attended the festival, from the Mayor to the hand-organ man's monkey, drank from two to twenty glasses. Policemen were conspicuous for their constant and untiring devotion to it."

The Turner movement in the United States blossomed with the arrival of the Forty-eighters, who had a profound impact on the German community through not only the Turnverein and their vibrant political clubs but through their involvement in the German-language press. Edited and staffed by political refugees from Germany, these outspoken daily and weekly newspapers kept up a running barrage of opinion and commentary about the key issues of the day: opposition to slavery, support of women's rights, atheism, and socialism.

The foreign-language press, in fact, has always played a vital role in sustaining immigrant life in New York. Less than a half-century later, the same Lower East Side stoops and benches that held German readers of *Staats-Zeitung* were supporting Jewish subscribers to the *Forward*.

While a significant number of Jews had come to New York with their Protestant and Catholic German countrymen during the mid-nineteenth century, their numbers swelled after the 1881 assassination of Czar Alexander II brought a new and vigorously anti-Semitic regime into power in Russia. The following year, the so-called "May Laws" closed most professional, industrial, and agricultural pursuits to Jews and limited their rights to settle in cities and practice their religion. During the next decade, about 150,000 Jews left Russia; 90 percent of them came to America, and an overwhelming proportion remained in New York.

This influx of eastern Europeans created a dichotomy within Manhattan's existing Jewish community. The earlier arrivals from Germany, having achieved some measure of economic success and social acceptance, had moved uptown, adopted American ways, and tended to identify with Reform Judaism. The newcomers flocked to the Lower East Side, where they retained their European ways and Orthodox religion. This clash of cultures was epitomized in 1887 at the opening of the Eldridge Street Synagogue, described by the *Israelite*, a newspaper published by uptown German Jews, as "the first great house of worship built by eastern European Jews in this country." After references to "loud talking" and "running to and fro," the newspaper stated that "our downtown brethren have not the slightest notion of what is the meaning of decorum in the house of God. This may no doubt be attributed to the fact that they visit it too often and consider it almost their second home."

As might be expected, contempt for the eastern Europeans was not limited to their coreligionists. Journalists and others who helped shape public perceptions of the immigrants were hardly reticent, as a typical article from a 1902 issue of *Leslie's Weekly* makes evident: "Those of the poorer classes are often grimy and strangely and shabbily dressed, although numbers of the women wear bright and picturesque costumes. These include Italians, Russian Jews and several other nationalities. They appear generally to be of a low order of knowledge, if not intelligence, as well as of physical development. The better class, comprising natives of Great Britain, Germany, and Scandinavia, frequently are as well attired as are average Americans. Better developed physically, and mentally superior to the former class, they are more desirable acquisitions to American citizenship."

Such denigrating attitudes were commonplace at the outset of the twentieth century, by which time the Irish had become relatively well integrated into American society and had established a secure hold on New York politics and law enforcement. Jews in the Lower East Side were well aware of the influence of the Irish through the newspapers and, more to the point, through street confrontations or run-ins with cops on the beat, as well as such events as the police riot that occurred during the funeral of Rabbi Jacob Joseph.

Nevertheless, as Jews became assimilated into the fabric of the city, they, like other ethnic groups from preceding generations, penetrated all facets of municipal government, including the police department. The twentieth century did not witness any repetition of the 1902 riot, although Jews were often subjected to isolated incidents of harassment and assault. Anti-Semitic activity was significantly increased during the rise of Adolf Hitler in the 1930s and '40s with the advent of street-corner agitators from such right-wing and pro-Nazi organizations as the Christian Front and Christian Mobilizers.

This period was also marked by the emergence of the Rev. Charles E. Coughlin, a Catholic radio priest with a vast national following who, though always careful to rely on innuendo, undoubtedly contributed to the spread of anti-Semitism as well

One of the most persistent forms of intolerance—anti-Semitism—has often surfaced in New York, the city with the world's largest Jewish population. Even during World War II, when Americans of all faiths were united against the virulent anti-Semitism of Nazi Germany, Jewish merchants in New York were victims of blatant bigotry.

as lending it seeming respectability. Through his publication *Social Justice*, Coughlin circulated the discredited "Protocols of the Elders of Zion," a fraudulent document that purportedly was a Jewish-Communist blueprint for world domination. While Coughlin was frequently criticized and eventually silenced by his superiors, he got enthusiastic support from the *Brooklyn Tablet*, the official archdiocesan newspaper. And in Irish-Jewish neighborhoods, such as Washington Heights, his message was translated by rabid adherents into insults, vandalism, and beatings.

The absorption of Jews into New York life was accompanied by their dispersion throughout the city and even into the suburbs, freeing much of the Lower East Side to shelter the next wave of newcomers. Yet, like a first love, the memory of crowded streets and overcrowded tenements lingered; the recollections are preserved in more than a dozen Yiddish-language newspapers that collectively were read by an estimated 600,000 New Yorkers in the early twentieth century. Most popular was the *Forward*, which under its innovative editor, Abraham Cahan, not only chronicled Jewish life, published Jewish literature, and promoted humanistic socialism but, through its *Bintel Brief* column, advised perplexed or dejected immigrants about how to cope with the frustrations of life in America.

Bintel Brief, literally "Bundle of Letters," by presenting the problems of Jewish newcomers and the guidance of an experienced and sympathetic "American," provides a fascinating insight into universal conflicts of faith, assimilation, and loyalty faced by aliens in a strange land. A compilation of letters and responses entitled *A Bintel Brief*, and edited by Isaac Metzker, affords an intimate look inside the tenements and sweatshops, in fact, into the very bedrooms of *Forward* correspondents. The letters reveal households riven by such timeless human frailties and cruelties as seduction, infidelity, desertion, and violence.

The responses are often surprising, sometimes reflecting compassion, sometimes hardheaded advice, sometimes impatience. The following letter deals with a situation common to most immigrants: the incompatibility of past and present. The answer is far more pragmatic than might be expected.

Esteemed Editor:

I hope that you will advise me in my present difficulty.

I am a "greenhorn," only five weeks in the country, and a jeweler by trade. I come from Russia, where I left a blind father and a stepmother. Before I left, my father asked me not to forget him. I promised that I would send him the first money I earned in America.

When I arrived in New York in 1906 I walked around for two weeks looking for a job, and the bosses told me it was after the season. In the third week I was lucky, and found a job at which I earn eight dollars a week. I worked, I paid my landlady board, I bought a few things to wear, and I have a few dollars in my pocket.

Now I want you to advise me what to do. Shall I send my father a few dollars for Passover, or should I keep the little money for myself? In this place the work will end soon and I may be left without a job. The question is how to deal with the situation. I will do as you tell me.

ANSWER: The answer to this young man is that he should send his father the few dollars for Passover because, since he is young, he will find it easier to earn a living than would his blind father in Russia.

In New York, many immigrants encountered social freedom they had never experienced before, a freedom that led to relationships that violated traditional behavioral codes. Occasionally, Jewish men and women who had fallen in love with Christians asked whether they should marry. Generally, the editor begged off in such situations, ruminating that a similarity of religion hardly guaranteed marital happiness.

The stress and instability of immigrant life, particularly in the overcrowded tenements of the Lower East Side, together with the dilution of traditional disciplines,

The conversion of the Jewish Daily Forward building at 175 East Broadway to a Chinese church graphically illustrates the change that has overcome this portion of the Lower East Side, New York's traditional immigrant enclave. The building, also the former headquarters of the Workman's Circle (Arbiter Ring), gained fame as the home of the publication that, under the direction of editor Abraham Cahan, provided news and guidance to generations of Jewish immigrants in the first half of the twentieth century. The Forward (Forverts in Yiddish) and Workman's Circle are now located at 45 East 33rd Street.

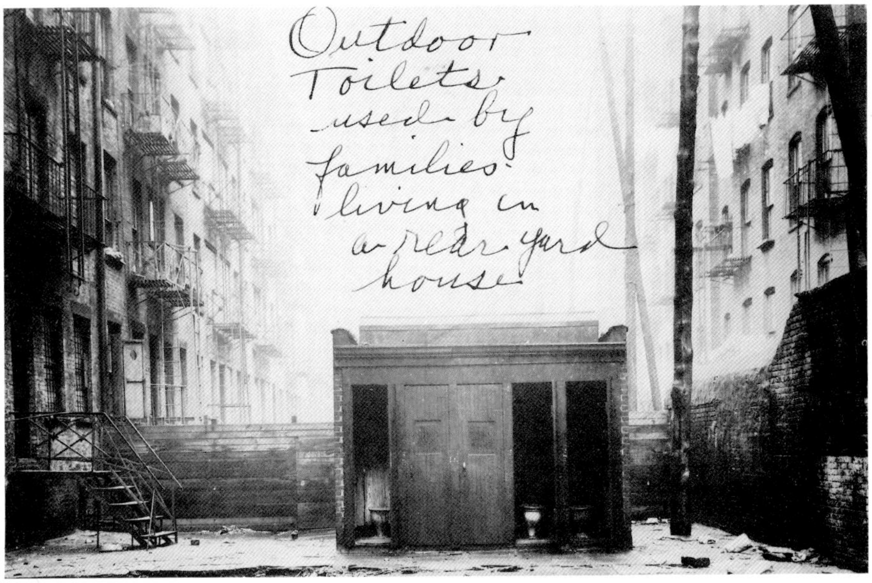

Outdoor Toilets used by families living in a rear yard house

At the beginning of the twentieth century, indoor plumbing was not standard equipment in New York tenements. Instead, tenants were compelled to walk to outdoor wooden privies, a chilling prospect on winter nights.

placed a heavy burden on intimate relationships. This led to an inordinate amount of domestic discord, incest, prostitution, infidelity, and desertion. *Bintel Brief* recorded such calamities and tried to deal with them.

While Cahan could be sympathetic when the circumstances called for understanding, he had little use for what he considered foolishness or nonsense.

Dear Editor:

I am a young man of twenty-five and I recently met a fine girl. She has a flaw, however—a dimple in her chin. It is said that people who have this lose their first husband or wife. I love her very much. But I'm afraid to marry her lest I die because of the dimple.

ANSWER: The tragedy is not that the girl has a dimple in her chin but that some people have a screw loose in their heads.

A not uncommon concern among the impoverished immigrant community was the enticement and threat of prostitution. Many *Bintel Brief* writers detailed their experiences in being lured or forced into the bordellos that abounded in lower Manhattan. Typical was the letter of a young woman who, worn out by life in a sweatshop, sought a matchmaker who told her that, "pretty girls could wallow in pleasure if they made the right friends." She wrote, "What I lived through afterwards is impossible for me to describe. The woman handed me over to bandits, and when I wanted to run away from them they locked me in a room without windows and beat me savagely."

The editor responded that "such letters from victims of 'white slavery' come to our attention quite often, but we do not publish them. We are disgusted by this plague on society, and dislike bringing it to the attention of our readers. But as we read this letter we felt we dare not discard it, because it can serve as a warning for other girls. They must, in their dreary lives, attempt to withstand these temptations and guard themselves from going astray."

Life on the Lower East Side was very much a product of the tenements, where constricted space contributed unintentionally to bringing families closer together emotionally, as well as physically. Samuel Chotzinoff recalled that "privacy in the home was practically unknown. The average apartment consisted of three rooms: a kitchen, a parlor, and a doorless and windowless bedroom between. The parlor became a sleeping-room at night. So did the kitchen when families were unusually large."

Ironically, the prototype of this cramped, stifling life-style was a tenement design entitled "Light, Air, and Health." Conceived by James E. Ware, the plan won a contest sponsored by *The Plumber and Sanitary Engineer* trade journal in 1879 along with the epithet "dumbbell tenement," derived from its shape as seen from above (each floor was pinched in at the middle to facilitate narrow air shafts between adjacent buildings). The award, which in the opinion of architects, as well as tenants, set back the cause of comfortable urban housing by decades, was dismissed by Dr. A. N. Bell, editor of the *Sanitarian*, as an "ingeneous design for a dungeon."

The buildings lacked heat, hot water, and private bathrooms (there were usually two public toilets on each floor, a substantial improvement from outdoor privies). The rents were often unaffordable, so many tenants sublet rooms to lodgers, compressing family members into even tighter quarters. There were also unexpected guests. Irving Howe writes of the recurrent fear of one youth that he would return from school to find "that his cot in the dining room would again be occupied by a relative just off the boat from Europe and given shelter by his parents." Of far greater concern was the danger of fire. The design, construction, and overcrowding of the tenements conspired to promote the rapid spread of flames; occupants were in constant jeopardy in these firetraps.

Under such circumstances, it is not difficult to understand why the immigrant Jews sought relief outside the home: in cafés, in dance halls, and in the Yiddish theater. The cafés were a remnant of the Old World that survived the trip to the Lower East Side relatively intact. These "coffee-and-cake parlors," as they were sometimes known, provided immigrant artists and thinkers (and those who thought they were) with a poor man's drawing room and a curious audience of observers and *kibitzers*. Politics, philosophy, art, and culture were debated endlessly for the price of a cup of coffee or piece of pastry.

In *World of Our Fathers*, Irving Howe describes the experiences of an immigrant Jew from Boston named Keidansky who decided to vacation in the Lower East Side cafés where "people feel free, act independently, speak as they think, and are not ashamed of their feelings." He was not disappointed. "Why," he later told friends in Boston, "I have gotten enough ideas on the East Side to last me for ten years." One observation alone would appear to have made the trip worthwhile: "Everywhere you meet people who are ready to fight for what they believe in and who do not believe in fighting."

Despite their serious preoccupations, the Jews enjoyed a good time. Although never inclined toward saloons or other drinking establishments favored by the Irish and German immigrants, they were not averse to spending time in dance halls. Such places proliferated with the arrival of Jewish immigrants, and by 1907 there were thirty-one dance halls in the ninety blocks between Houston and Grand streets, east of Broadway, or, reported Howe, eliminating parks and empty lots, "a dance hall for every two and a half blocks! Here, in 'the winter picnic-grounds of our district,' fraternal societies staged their 'balls,' families celebrated weddings, and young people came in large numbers for an hour or two of dancing. . . . Long a favorite among Jews even in the old country, dancing became for the younger immigrants one of the few easily accessible pleasures: it enabled them to meet other young men and women, it brought a few moments of release."

For first-generation American Jews, the children of immigrants reared in the New World amid Old World traditions, the Lower East Side was a strange and wonderful territory, a wilderness no less formidable nor promising than that explored by pioneers a century earlier. The lasting value of that experience is lyrically conveyed through Howe's recollections:

Right:
Among the most colorful traditions immigrants brought to America were the outdoor markets that clogged their Lower East Side neighborhoods. On Hester Street, in the heart of the Jewish sector, anything and everything was for sale, including eggs, pots, pans, and used clothing. The narrow streets of the Lower East Side are still jammed on Sundays when merchandise is sold from stands and pushcarts.

Opposite and below:
Despite the best efforts of educators, social workers, recreation directors, and cops, New York City's kids have adopted the streets for work and play.

The streets were ours. Everyplace else—home, school, shop—belonged to the grownups. But the streets belonged to us. We would roam through the city tasting the delights of freedom, discovering possibilities far beyond the reach of our parents. The streets taught us the deceits of commerce, introduced us to the excitements of sex, schooled us in strategies of survival, and gave us our first clear idea of what life in America was really going to be like.

We might continue to love our parents and grind away at school and college, but it was the streets that prepared the future. In the streets we were roughed by actuality, and even those of us who later became intellectuals or professionals kept something of our bruising gutterworldiness, our hard and abrasive skepticism. You could see it in cab drivers and garment manufacturers, but also in writers and professors who had grown up as children of immigrant Jews.

The streets opened a fresh prospect of sociability. It was a prospect not always amiable or even free from terror, but it drew Jewish boys and girls like a magnet, offering them qualities in short supply at home: the charms of the spontaneous and unpredictable. In the streets a boy could encircle himself with the breath of immigrant life, declare his companionship with peddlers, storekeepers, soapboxers. No child raised in the immigrant quarter would lack for moral realism: just to walk through Hester Street was an education in the hardness of life. To go beyond Cherry Street on the south, where the Irish lived, or west of the Bowery, where the Italians were settling, was to explore the world of the gentiles—dangerous, since one risked a punch in the face, but tempting, since for an East Side boy the idea of *the others*, so steadily drilled into his mind by every agency of his culture, was bound to incite curiosity.

The Italians, too, had a strong sense of territoriality, but it seemed to apply as much to fellow Italians from different regions as to non-Italians from anywhere. Paralleling the emigration of eastern European Jews, southern Italians and Sicilians began arriving in New York in the 1880s and occupied an area—"Little Italy"—to the west of the Jews. As Thomas Kessner points out in *The Golden Door*, "Like most foreigners they preferred to live among their own. In setting up their 'Little Italy' they carefully retained their Old World subdivisions. The local traditions and hatreds of numerous *paesi*, like the pungent cheeses which the Italians brought with them, proved sufficiently hardy to cross the sea and retain their original sharpness."

The neighborhoods were as clearly drawn as the regions they represented: the *Napoletani* occupied Mulberry Street, and Mott Street between East Houston and Prince; the *Basilicati* lived on the other side of Mott; the *Siciliani* held out on Prince Street; the *Calabresi* on Mott, between Broome and Grand; and people from Apulia could be found on Hester Street.

The basic distinction was between north and south, with northern Italian immigrants eager to retain the social superiority they had asserted in Italy. But since there were few northerners among the great mass of Italians who came to New York toward the end of the nineteenth century, the antagonisms were almost exclusively among those from the south. "Every Italian child was conditioned at an early age," explained author Michael La Sorte, "to distrust 'strangers' and to accept as immutable certain beliefs about regional differences in behavior and temperament. You trust members of your own family first, relatives second, *paesani* third, other Italians a distant fourth, and everyone else not at all."

Leonardo Sciascia, a writer, recalled that Sicilians such as his father knew that all the Calabresi "were small and swarthy. My uncle said that all Calabresi have hard heads. The people of Sardinia are treacherous, the Romans rude, and the Neapolitans are a bunch of beggars."

Regional hostilities were not unique to Italians, but the intensity of these feelings governed many of the important aspects of their lives and even were seen as having slowed their progress by limiting their opportunities. "It is inconceivable," wrote Antonio Margariti, after describing a near-fatal clash, "that two men from the same part of Italy could hate each other so much rather than liking and supporting one another in this strange land."

The so-called "birds of passage" syndrome—which held that a substantial proportion of Italians, as well as some other immigrants, viewed America as a temporary money-making venture rather than a permanent home—also was a significant factor in shaping the newcomers' life-styles. For example, it resulted in a disproportionate number of young men, which, in turn, created a need for different living arrangements, such as boardinghouses. It was not uncommon for Italian families to take in several compatriot outsiders. This often became a necessity when new arrivals from Italy encountered signs on "American" boardinghouses stating, "We do not rent to Negroes or Italians." Given the regional antipathies, however, it was important to match housekeepers and boarders, and the failure to do so frequently produced friction and occasionally violence. When things went well, the relationship between a housekeeper and her boarders almost approached a familial one, with the housekeeper becoming a surrogate mother. The surplus of young, vigorous Italian men accentuated other needs, too, and reportedly swelled the activity, if not supply, of prostitutes.

Italians, like Jews, clung tenaciously to their Old World cuisine and made consuming it a significant social event. Sunday was always the most important day of the week because Sunday dinner brought together family, friends, and *paesani* to gorge, absorb the week's gossip, and resume old arguments. Besides celebrating Italian holidays in traditional style, immigrants often lent a distinctive touch to American festivities. Geno Baroni recalled that in the midst of a heated debate about blacks in America, "Momma came into the room and said: 'Stop your arguing. We're all Americans. It's Thanksgiving. Eat your spaghetti.'"

When residents of Little Italy sought entertainment, they might patronize the theater or one of its particularly Italian components, a puppet show. The latter often featured a battle between armored Christian knights and Saracen warriors. Live theater was distinctive, too, and catered to the characteristics of the audience, as journalist Hutchins Hapgood noted in 1900: "Quick to respond to the emotional situation, they do not need realistic settings and devices to make them feel the illusion of the stage. That they ignore what are really trivial incongruities points to feeling and imagination, and in aesthetic competency puts them far ahead of those blasé rounders on Broadway who watch closely the mechanics of the scene. It is, indeed, the human drama only in which the Italians are absorbed."

Their passion set the Italian immigrants quite apart from the native Americans, a difference recognizable to both groups. "The Italians were most struck by the coldness of Americans," wrote La Sorte, "their inability or unwillingness to display public emotion." An astounded Pasquale D'Angelo wrote, "They will go to a funeral of their best friend and keep a straight face. I believe they are ashamed if in a moment of forgetfulness they've turned to look at a flower or a beautiful sunset."

The richness of Italian culture was evident in the enthusiasm of the people for *festas*, or feast days, the exuberant celebrations that honored regional patron saints. The Danish-born journalist Jacob Riis, who gained a reputation as a reformer by exposing immigrant living conditions, described the San Donato festival in 1899 for *Century Magazine*. Riis and then-Police Board President Theodore Roosevelt were chatting at police headquarters when they saw a street procession and followed it into a backyard.

It was a yard no longer, but a temple. All the sheets of the tenement had been stretched so as to cover the ugly sheds and outhouses. Against the dark rear tenement the shrine of the saint had been erected, shutting it altogether out of sight with a wealth of scarlet and gold. Great candles and little ones, painted and beribboned, burned in a luminous grove before the altar. The sun shone down upon a mass of holiday-clad men and women, to whom it was all as a memory of home, of the beloved home across the seas; upon mothers kneeling devoutly with their little ones at the shrine, and upon children bringing offerings to the saint's glory....
The fire-escapes of the tenement had, with the aid of some cheap muslin draperies, a little

Above and overleaf:
Little Italy, which has retained much of its flavor, as well as a predominantly Italian-American population, for about a century has also retained Mulberry Street as a principal thoroughfare. Largely occupied by Napoletani (Neapolitans), whose gregarious, zestful nature gave the area its ambience, Mulberry's outdoor markets, with their fresh fruit, vegetables, meat, and seafood, provided delights for the eye, nose, and ear.

The joy of eating, especially with one's family, has always been part of being Italian. The Di Constanzo family observes an annual tradition by dining together in their Mulberry Street restaurant on New Year's Eve. It was the end of 1942 and the United States was immersed in World War II, as the flag and photograph attest.

tinsel, and the strange artistic genius of this people, been transformed into beautiful balconies, upon which the tenants of the front house had reserved seats. In a corner of the yard over by the hydrant, a sheep, which was to be raffled off as the climax of the celebration, munched its wisp of hay patiently, while bare-legged children climbed its back and pulled its wool....

The musicians, issuing forth victorious from a protracted struggle with a fleet of schooners in the saloon, came out, wiping their mustachios, and blew "Santa Lucia" on their horns. The sweetly seductive melody woke the echoes of the block and its slumbering memories. The old women rocked in their seats, their faces buried in their hands. The crowd from the street increased, and the chief celebrant, who turned out to be no less a person than the saloon-keeper himself, reaped a liberal harvest of silver half-dollars. The villagers bowed and crossed themselves before the saint, and put into the plate their share toward the expense of the celebration. Its guardian made a strong effort to explain about the saint to Mr. Roosevelt.

"He is just-a lik'-a your St. Patrick here," he said, and the president of the Police Board nodded. He understood.

Their insularity made all immigrants vulnerable to deception by more experienced countrymen, and Italians, further isolated from the "Americans" by a language barrier, were hardly immune to such victimization. Confused by American customs and fearful of strangers, they put an often naive trust in their *paesani*. This confidence was a foundation for the *padrone* system, under which immigrant laborers were hired, transported, housed, fed, and—frequently—exploited. It also gave rise to Italian banks, which flourished in Little Italy despite periodic embezzlements, thefts, and swindles.

Camillo Cianfarra, who clerked for an Italian bank, described its functions as having "to receive the letters from Italy and forward them to the worker's new address; to furnish paper, envelopes, stamps, and pencils; to send fancy cards to sweethearts and families on Easter and Christmas; to lend money; to write tickets for those who wished to join relatives in America; to pick them up at the docks; and

to respond punctually to written requests." Some of the banks were chartered and others were not; in a variety of ways they differed from the standard American institutions. Where American banks tended to be impersonal but efficient, the Italian banks were warm in ambience, haphazard in operation. Rules were flexible, based on circumstances. Bankers might be in one location one day, another the next. Sometimes interest was paid on deposits, sometimes depositors paid a fee. And the bankers felt no inhibitions about speculating with their depositors' funds, occasionally risking substantial amounts.

Fear of dealing with authority, an attitude that survived the transatlantic journey, made Italian immigrants especially subject to extortion by fellow Italians, although the extent of organized "Italian" crime seems to have been greatly exaggerated by the New York press. Criminals exploited fears as written notes— demanding money and threatening bombing or death for nonpayment—allegedly from the "Black Hand," a secret society that functioned in Italy, were placed in mail slots or under doors in Italian neighborhoods.

Reacting to some bombings and other forms of violence, newspapers, in particular the *New York Times*, succeeded in gaining creation of a special police unit in 1906 to deal with "Italian crime." Headed by Detective Lieutenant Joseph Petrosino, the unit conducted extensive investigations, which, according to historian Richard Gambino, found "that the criminals in the Italian immigrant culture were petty hoodlums who victimized their own people and that the thugs acted as common criminals either alone or with a few accomplices and not as members of an organized and disciplined illegal society." Although Petrosino was gunned down in Palermo, Sicily, in 1909 while pursuing the possibility of an international criminal syndicate, his findings were confirmed by an investigation that found that twenty-nine of thirty cases attributed by the press to the Black Hand were actually the work of others.

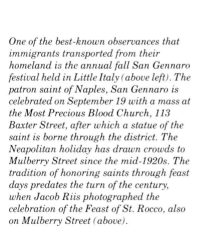

One of the best-known observances that immigrants transported from their homeland is the annual fall San Gennaro festival held in Little Italy (above left). The patron saint of Naples, San Gennaro is celebrated on September 19 with a mass at the Most Precious Blood Church, 113 Baxter Street, after which a statue of the saint is borne through the district. The Neapolitan holiday has drawn crowds to Mulberry Street since the mid-1920s. The tradition of honoring saints through feast days predates the turn of the century, when Jacob Riis photographed the celebration of the Feast of St. Rocco, also on Mulberry Street (above).

Overt racism was part of the street scene in pre-World War I Harlem. Here, a "To Let" sign advertised apartments "For Respectable Colored Families Only."

Italian immigrants, not only victimized but defamed by crime, were also stereotyped as indolent and lacking in ambition. The Congregational Home Missionary Society, in what presumably was a "sympathetic" leaflet, stated, "The Italians of the tenements and slums—those of them who will work—always select that class of occupation which offers the least resistance."

But despite its viciousness, the sting of ethnic or religious derogation never approached the magnitude of racism, particularly as it affected New York's black population. Scattered in several neighborhoods for more than two centuries, blacks moved, or more likely were driven, from Five Points, Greenwich Village, and West Side ghettos called the Tenderloin and San Juan Hill (the last, named for the Spanish-American War battlefield, was a sardonic reference to the interracial conflicts that wracked the area). By the turn of the twentieth century, blacks were beginning to move into New York in increasing numbers from the rural South, a migration prompted both by racist legislation in the southern states and a search for a better life in the industrialized North. With them they brought a new ingredient, a different culture. Nurtured in the backwoods and farmlands below the Mason-Dixon line, it distinguished them from urban blacks as well as from the European immigrants. Racial relations in the city, never good, became further strained with this influx.

At about this time, subway lines were extended northward into Harlem, bringing that well-to-do suburban settlement within easy commuting time of the downtown business districts. The desirability of Harlem as an upper-middle-class residential area became obvious, and developers rushed to provide attractive housing. "The newly built elevator apartment houses, many equipped with servants' quarters, rented for prices that could be paid only by the wealthy," wrote Gilbert Osofsky in his classic study, *Harlem: The Making of a Ghetto.* "The most magnificent was a group of spacious, luxurious brownstones built on One Hundred and Thirty-eighth and One Hundred and Thirty-ninth Streets in 1891." Designed by the notable architect Stanford White and described as "distinctive as a suburban colony but with all the advantages of city life," the remarkable complexes consisted of 116 houses of from 10 to 16 rooms.

Promoters and speculators fueled a boom. But they overbuilt, priced themselves out of the real estate market, and wound up with the inescapable bust. Almost overnight, the Harlem foreseen as an elite white enclave had a new destiny. Lenders stopped advancing money to West Harlem speculators and even foreclosed on mortgages. By 1905, with the collapse at its depth, imaginative black realtors took over and initiated the process that would alter Harlem's constituency for generations.

Over the next two decades, the accelerated migration of blacks from the South and West Indies, the discriminatory policies in the rest of Manhattan, and the availability of housing in Harlem created a vast ghetto. In the timeworn tradition of American race relations, as the blacks moved in, the whites moved out, and Harlem changed, was transformed into something different, special. Both a refuge and a pulpit, it became a magnet: "The Negro Capital of the World."

From throughout the nation and the Caribbean, Harlem attracted the best-educated, the most-gifted, the elite. Soon it was seen as a cultural oasis, a territory where creative blacks could interact, could assert their blackness free from white values and judgments. And for a brief time—a decade beginning about 1925—it provided a unique opportunity for what W.E.B. Du Bois termed the "Talented Tenth" to demonstrate their accomplishments. They called their era the Harlem Renaissance.

An extraordinary period by any measure, it involved such outstanding and diverse black political and social leaders as Harvard-educated philosopher Du Bois, and his opponent in the struggle for black advancement, Booker T. Washington;

Music, mournful or joyous, has been a staple of black religious observance since slavery. When blacks moved up from the rural South and into Harlem in the early twentieth century, they brought the tradition with them. Outdoor revival meetings, characteristic of the countryside, became commonplace in uptown Manhattan.

Despite hardships and discrimination, black families gained middle-class status and more in the years following World War I. This Harlem apartment in 1918 possessed such accoutrements as a fireplace and picture-decorated mantel.

During and after World War I, many blacks came to New York from the rural South in search of jobs and political and social equality. Their search proved largely unrewarding, as they encountered many of the same barriers in the North. And in the cities, racial violence erupted periodically. Blacks in New York organized to gain justice through peaceful means, sometimes employing mass demonstrations, such as this march protesting a 1917 St. Louis riot.

The Harlem Renaissance of the 1920s became far more than a cultural revolution, although it attracted black writers, poets, painters, and musicians from throughout the country and even the world. It had a marked influence on black consciousness and pride. And it led to black affluence and the opportunity to demonstrate black taste. As a result, some of New York's choicest neighborhoods were reachable by the "A" train.

Marcus Garvey, the charismatic proponent of black nationalism, and pioneer labor leader A. Philip Randolph; such writers and poets as James Weldon Johnson, Langston Hughes, Countee Cullen, George S. Schuyler, Alain Locke, Claude McKay, Zora Neale Hurston, and Jean Toomer; such dramatic performers as Paul Robeson and Ethel Waters and such musicians as Duke Ellington, Fats Waller, and Fletcher Henderson.

They represented diversity in terms of ends and means, to be sure, but there was a consensus, too, that the chance to end racism was at hand. Johnson believed that "nothing can go farther to destroy race prejudice than the recognition of the Negro as a creator and contributor to American civilization." From a less naive perspective, Hughes added, "Harlemites thought the millennium had come. They thought the race problem had at last been solved through Art...."

But there was excitement and promise. And it was captured by David Levering Lewis in *When Harlem Was in Vogue:* "Almost everything seemed possible above 125th Street in the early twenties for these Americans who were determined to thrive separately to better proclaim the ideals of integration. You could be black and proud, politically assertive and economically independent, creative and disciplined—or so it seemed. Arna Bontemps and fellow literary migrants made a wonderful discovery. They found that, under certain conditions, it was 'fun to be a Negro.' "

Style has been a Harlem hallmark, but it probably reached its heights during the 1920s, as these women testify.

The aura of the Harlem Renaissance beckoned to the downtown cultural establishment. "It was a period when, at almost every Harlem upper-crust dance or party," Hughes recalled, "one would be introduced to various distinguished white celebrities there as guests. It was a period when almost any Harlem Negro of any social importance at all would be likely to say casually: 'As I was remarking the other day to Heywood—' meaning Heywood Broun. Or: 'As I said to George—' referring to George Gershwin. It was a period when local and visiting royalty were not at all uncommon in Harlem."

Among the most avid white negrophiles was Carl Van Vechten, a midwestern critic, photographer, and novelist, who quickly established a symbiotic relationship with the "New Negroes," promoting their works to leading editors and publishers, and immersing himself in what he saw as an exotic culture. Van Vechten embellished his role by throwing lavish downtown soirees. In *This Was Harlem*, by Jervis Anderson, black journalist George S. Schuyler recalled what it was like:

The literary lights, the stars of the ballet, the kings and queens of the theatre, the painters, sculptors and editors who had attained envious preeminence frequented Van Vechten's salons on West 55th Street and later on at Central Park West; and to this company Van Vechten introduced their darker opposite members. Here they rubbed shoulders, sipped cocktails, nibbled *hors d'oeuvres*, conversed, sang and danced without self-consciousness. What was at first an innovation and a novelty soon became commonplace, an institution.

Such salons in the early twenties were rare to the point of being revolutionary. At the time it was most difficult for Negroes to purchase a ticket for an orchestra seat in a theatre, even in Harlem, and it was with the greatest difficulty that a colored American in New York could get service in a downtown restaurant. Except at Coney Island, beaches were closed to Negroes and few were the other places that would tolerate their patronage....

Most of the white people of Van Vechten's circle knew Negroes only as domestics and had never had them as associates. It was extremely daring for a white person to dine publicly with a Negro, and certainly to dance with one; but if those of the upper crust could be weaned over to such social acceptance, it was likely that a trend would be started which would eventually embrace the majority of those whites who shaped public opinion and set the social pace.

To this laudable endeavor Carl Van Vechten and his famous actress wife, Fania Marinoff, devoted themselves as assiduously as any sincere revolutionists could....

Van Vechten's quid pro quo, his black guests discovered in the summer of 1926, was a novel entitled, somewhat indelicately, *Nigger Heaven*. It was superficial, controversial, and extraordinarily successful. Dealing with a cultured Harlem couple, it enabled white readers to visit the cabarets and parties, meet the hostesses and hookers, and indulge themselves in fantasies involving the proscribed uptown life-style.

Du Bois made his reaction clear in a review in *The Crisis*, the organ of the National Association for the Advancement of Colored People (NAACP), of which he was editor: " 'Nigger Heaven' is a blow in the face... an affront to the hospitality of black folk and to the intelligence of white... the phrase 'Nigger Heaven,' as applied to Harlem is a misnomer.... But after all, a title is only a title, and a book must be judged eventually by its fidelity to truth and its artistic merit. I find this novel neither truthful nor artistic.... It is a caricature. It is worse than untruth because it is a mass of half-truths...."

Other blacks, many of them friends, including James Weldon Johnson, responded more favorably. But perhaps a typical Harlemite's reaction came from Johnson's secretary, Richetta Randolph. "To the end," she wrote in a vain appeal to her employer, "I had hoped for something which would make me feel that he had done Negro Harlem a service by this work.... What Mr. Van Vechten has written is just what those who do not know us think about all of us.... I am serious when I say that I think only you can redeem Mr. Van Vechten by writing something to counteract what he has done."

In a sense, reaction to *Nigger Heaven* exposed the cleavage between the world of Harlem's high-flying "Talented Tenth" and the other hard-pressed 90 percent. For the overwhelming majority, daily life was hardly heavenly. Living costs, traditionally higher in poorer neighborhoods, were especially so in Harlem, where tenants, who invariably earned lower wages, were socked with higher rents than their white counterparts. Even the most conservative studies indicated that while working-class whites were spending one-fifth of their incomes on housing, blacks had to shell out at least one-third. To deal with such problems, Harlem residents devised their own solutions. One was the "Hot Bed System," in which mattresses would be taken over by new sleepers as soon as their occupants awoke and left, and another was the "Rent Party."

Although rent parties originated in the South, they were institutionalized in Harlem, where topflight musicians were eager to pick up a few extra dollars giving dancers and listeners their money's worth. With the price of admission ranging from a dime to a dollar, this was not difficult. Anyone who paid was welcome, since the money went for the needy tenants' rent; other funds were raised through the sale of food and (particularly during Prohibition) drink and perhaps a cut from the dice and card games. Well-organized, these frequent affairs were advertised through the distribution of printed cards that announced "whist parties" or "social matinees."

In *Music on My Mind*, pianist Willie "The Lion" Smith recalled that "they would crowd a hundred or more people into a seven-room railroad flat and the walls would bulge—some of the parties spread to the halls and all over the building. All the furniture was stashed in another apartment except the chairs and beds...."

The rent party was the place to go to pick up on all the latest jokes, jive, and uptown news. You would see all kinds of people making the party scene; formally dressed society folks from downtown, policemen, painters, carpenters, mechanics, truckmen in their workingmen's clothes, gamblers, lesbians, and entertainers of all kinds. The parties were recommended to the newly arrived single gals as the place to go to get acquainted....

Of course, there were also parties where there was such a racket all night long that the neighbors called the cops to quiet the joint down, and these would usually end with the law having a ball for themselves.

While Harlemites were ready to party on Saturday night, they also were prepared to pray on Sunday morning. The church, the wealthiest and most stable black institution, moved uptown, too, during the opening decades of the twentieth century. Church membership in Harlem doubled and tripled along with the population, and sometimes as many as five services were held on the Sabbath.

Many black churches found the trip to Harlem rewarding materially as well as spiritually, for their downtown properties brought top prices while land and buildings uptown were considerably cheaper. Whenever possible, black congregations purchased Harlem churches from departing whites, and when they couldn't, they built their own. St. Philip's Protestant Episcopal Church, for example, sold its property on West 25th Street for $140,000 in 1909 and its cemetery two years later for $450,000. When a white congregation of the same denomination in Harlem declined to sell its church to the blacks, St. Philip's commissioned black architect Vertner Tandy to design a $200,000 early Gothic structure on West 134th Street in 1911. The same year, St. Philip's transacted the largest black real estate deal in the city's history to that point by purchasing a row of ten new apartment houses on West 135th Street, between Seventh and Lenox avenues, for $640,000.

One of Harlem's major institutions, Abyssinian Baptist Church, did not put down its uptown roots until 1923, when it occupied a new $300,000 building on West 138th Street, although its notable pastor, the Rev. Dr. Adam Clayton Powell, Sr., later stated that he had been aware "as early as 1911 that Harlem would be the final destination of the Abyssinian Church." For blacks, religious experience went beyond belief and prayer; it had significant social value and, because of the interests and dynamism of some of its clergy, political dimensions, too. In the case of Powell, his sermons were important enough to attract the interest of white journalists, as this report from Konrad Bercovici indicates: "The pastor, a tall, colored man, with a thunderous voice and big curly head of hair, looks very much like the picture of Alexandre Dumas. . . . This church, like most other Negro churches, is really more than a church. It is a social center. At a service on a Sunday, the pastor comments upon the political events that have taken place during the week, and sways the audience to his view by his thunderous oratory. He speaks as much of earthly events as he praises the Lord. Not a thing that has happened in the world escapes him; and he is not afraid to denounce the things he does not agree with."

Outspoken blacks, especially if their targets were white, could generally rely on support in Harlem. But no one was prepared for the phenomenal popularity of a young Jamaican named Marcus Garvey and his Universal Negro Improvement Association (UNIA). Founded in Harlem in 1917, Garvey's movement tapped the postwar frustration and disillusionment of American blacks who, "ready for any program that would tend to restore even a measure of their lost dignity and self-respect," enthusiastically embraced his exhortations to black nationalism. Stirring race consciousness in black audiences in Harlem and throughout the nation, Garvey rapidly built a vast grass-roots following that shared his dream of going "Back to Africa." After 25,000 delegates jammed Madison Square Garden in 1920 to attend the first International Convention of the Negro Peoples of the World, Mary White Ovington, a white NAACP director, exclaimed that Garvey was "the first Negro in the United States to capture the imagination of the masses" because he had inspired the most menial black laborer to believe "that when night came he might march with the African army and bear a wonderful banner to be raised some day in a distant beautiful land."

But Garvey's magnetism provoked fear among white conservatives (the FBI assigned a black agent to watch UNIA headquarters) and created concern among black integrationists (Du Bois called him "the most dangerous threat to the Negro race"). His flamboyance and imagination, which led him to make himself the "Provisional President of Africa," wear garish uniforms, and appoint African knights, dukes, and duchesses, were ridiculed by the white press. And his failure to properly supervise the sale of stock in his Black Star Line Steamship Corporation resulted in his arrest on mail fraud charges. The forces arrayed against Garvey proved too

One of America's most remarkable leaders, West Indian Marcus Garvey, founder of the Universal Negro Improvement Association and the "Back to Africa Movement," struck a responsive chord among blacks equaled perhaps only by the Rev. Martin Luther King, Jr. Garvey's personal magnetism, embellished by his garish costume, fanciful titles, and message of black superiority, inspired a sense of dignity and purpose that drew followers by the millions. Blacks from all classes and backgrounds, including the Garveyite pictured above, joined his movement and poured money into the ventures he headed. White ridicule of Garvey only strengthened his appeal to blacks, who kept their faith long after he was imprisoned in 1925 and deported two years later.

Built in 1923, the Abyssinian Baptist Church on 138th Street, between Lenox and Seventh avenues, became a sounding board for two dynamic pastors, Adam Clayton Powell, Sr., and his son, the charismatic congressman, Adam Clayton Powell, Jr.

powerful, and, by 1925, his movement collapsed following his imprisonment and deportation. Yet, there was no doubt that he had kindled an undeniable spark of racial pride that would surface again forty years later in the Black Power movement.

As the '20s began to fade, so too did the Harlem Renaissance. The death in 1931 of A'Lelia Walker, heiress to a cosmetics fortune and the black social arbiter of the era, heralded the end of that unrivaled epoch. Langston Hughes recalled, "That spring for me (and, I guess, all of us) was the end of the Harlem Renaissance. We were no longer in vogue, anyway, we Negroes. Sophisticated New Yorkers turned to Nöel Coward. Colored actors began to go hungry, publishers politely rejected new manuscripts, and patrons found other uses for their money.... The generous 1920s were over."

The arrival of the '30s, and the Great Depression, dealt a severe blow to New Yorkers. In Harlem, the impact on blacks was devastating. For another ethnic group that was to occupy territory in Harlem adjacent to the blacks, it was an equally harsh time. But it also marked a beginning. "By 1929," wrote noted Puerto Rican socialist and nationalist Bernardo Vega in his classic *Memoirs*, "the old neighborhood on the East Side (along Third Avenue, between 64th and 106th streets), made up mostly of *tabaqueros* (cigar workers), had moved up toward Harlem and El Barrio was finally consolidated as the heart of the Puerto Rican community in New York."

El Barrio, the Puerto Rican quarter, was concentrated in those days between 110th and 116th streets, from St. Nicholas to Madison avenues in Manhattan, and while the bulk of Puerto Ricans now live in the Bronx, East Harlem "continues to be the area most completely associated with the Puerto Rican community...in a way that no other area of the city has been."

As Vega watched, "El Barrio took on its own distinctive features. There arose a culture typical of that common experience of people fighting for survival in the face of hostile surroundings.... Small pharmacies and *botanicas* sprang up throughout the neighborhood. There wasn't much difference between one and the other—*boticas* and *botanicas*. Both dealt in herbs like lemon verbena, sage, and rue, and they even carried pieces of the Devil's-claws. Doctors, witches, druggists, mind readers,

An enduring part of Spanish Harlem is La Marqueta, the formerly open-air, now enclosed, marketplace by the viaduct at Park Avenue, between 111th and 116th streets. Presently operated by the city, La Marqueta has been a focus in El Barrio *for most of the twentieth century, providing Puerto Ricans and others with exotic foodstuffs of every description.*

dentists, spiritualists, palm readers, all shared the same clientele. Misery always seems to breed superstition, and when there is no hope of getting out of a life of poverty, dreams are the only consolation left. This helps explain the role of religion, in all its popular forms. It also helps explain why there was so much gambling, as is always true of destitute communities. And, of course, there was dancing."

It was not until after World War II, however, that Puerto Ricans came to New York in large numbers, filling apartments in East Harlem vacated by Italians and Jews and spilling over into the South Bronx and parts of Brooklyn. By that time, the conditions that facilitated the earlier mass migrations were in place. Economic conditions were poor in Puerto Rico, relatives were waiting on the mainland, transportation was cheap, and jobs were available. Further, as citizens, Puerto Ricans were free to come and go as they wished.

Despite these factors, few welcome mats were put out by New Yorkers. The newcomers found themselves assailed by the same kinds of hostilities and suspicions that had been heaped on their predecessors. The press was among the most vituperative. It was unnecessary to read beyond some of the headlines, such as the one over a 1940 *Scribner's Commentary* article that stated, "Welcome Paupers and Crime: Puerto Rico's Shocking Gift to the U.S."

Perhaps the most persistent concoction—which simultaneously denigrated both Puerto Ricans and a supportive left-wing congressman—was one charging that they were being brought to New York and put on welfare by Representative Vito Marcantonio in order to get their votes. The arrival of Puerto Ricans in large numbers during the early 1950s coincided with the era of Cold War tensions, and Marcantonio (who, among other things, was the only congressman to actively oppose United States involvement in the Korean War) was an easy target of the Red-baiting press. In 1950, for example, the *Daily Mirror* editorialized that "Marcantonio's principal strength comes from hordes of Puerto Ricans enticed here from their home island, for the value of their votes, and subjected to pitiful poverty, which Marcantonio has done nothing to alleviate—except force thousands on city relief." Actually, relatively few Puerto Ricans voted (until 1964, they were required to pass a literacy test in English in order to register), and their electoral impact in Marcantonio's district was never significant.

While such disparagements were hardly novel for new arrivals, bigotry and prejudice struck Puerto Ricans with particular force because their multiracial island culture was so free of it. "The irony of the Puerto Rican's situation," a 1964 study by the Puerto Rican Forum declared, "is that he has *not* come to escape—as so many Europeans did—oppression, discrimination, or breakdown of his society; he has, in fact, come *to* it. For most Puerto Ricans, life in New York is their first contact with a social system that puts them on the very bottom rung of the ladder."

Herman Badillo, the former congressman, Bronx borough president, and deputy mayor who is generally regarded as the city's most conspicuous Puerto Rican, said that "skin color matters in the United States in a way that it doesn't in Puerto Rico." As a result, he said, it's easier for white Puerto Ricans to move ahead in New York and "it's impossible to elect a black Puerto Rican." Badillo, who came to East Harlem in 1941 as a twelve-year-old, recalled the color barriers that defined daily life for his people. He said, for example, that restaurants assigned white Puerto Ricans to work as busboys but kept black Puerto Ricans in the kitchen.

State Supreme Court Justice John Carro, who arrived in El Barrio from Puerto Rico in 1937, confirmed the cultural shock of discovering bias and intolerance. "It seemed to me that I came here to encounter racism and prejudice . . . in Puerto Rico, all these things were foreign to me." East Harlem was a patchwork of racial and ethnic "turfs," he recalled. "If you crossed Lexington you were beaten up by the Italians and if you crossed Fifth Avenue you were beaten up by the blacks."

For protection and camaraderie, Carro, who later became a street worker and policeman, joined youth gangs. There were gangs on every block and fights within the Puerto Rican community as well as outside it. As a schoolboy with little command of English, he said that he often found himself in fights with black youths without even knowing why. And when he went to the neighborhood's Jefferson Pool, he twice was almost drowned by Italians. The gang syndrome was so widespread, the judge said, that parents and adult relatives took it for granted. "They thought that belonging was part of Americanizing," he said.

The significance of ethnic self-consciousness and cohesiveness among Puerto Ricans as an aid to survival amid New York City's perils and squalor was evident throughout Piri Thomas's best-selling autobiography, *Down These Mean Streets*. Thomas, like Irving Howe, stressed the importance of street life: "Hanging around on the block is a sort of science. You have a lot to do and a lot of nothing to do. In the winter there's dancing, pad combing, movies, and the like. But summer is really the kick. All the blocks are alive, like many-legged cats crawling with fleas. People are all over the place. Stoops are occupied like bleacher sections at a game, and beer flows like there's nothing else to drink. The block musicians pound out gone beats on tin cans and conga drums and bongos. And kids are playing all over the place— on fire escapes, under cars, over cars, in alleys, back yards, hallways."

While the streets are the site of much Puerto Rican social activity—a logical carryover from the function of the plazas in their native island—"hometown clubs" located in storefronts or basements have long been popular in El Barrio. Tying the migrants to one another and to Puerto Rico through common geography, the organizations—similar to the Jews' *landsmanshaftn* (see page 139) and the Italians' social clubs—now represent each of that country's seventy-seven cities and towns. Carro recalled how casually they originally were formed. "All you needed was two or three people to get together," he said. "You'd just meet in someone's house at first, and later maybe collect dues and rent a storefront." The societies play an important part in members' lives, providing far more than simply a place to pass

time. "On Sunday in New York," the Puerto Rican Forum reported, "one can wander into hundreds of 'hometown club' meetings, where members gather from every part of the city to spend their leisure day together, eating, playing cards, making plans for future activities, or talking over old—and new—times. These and other similar groups have helped the family in its role to cushion the individuals in the face of adversity." However, in the 1960s, according to Yolanda Sanchez, president of the National Latinas Caucus, an attempt to knit the clubs into a political base by forming a "congreso de pueblos" was thwarted by infighting, much as regional differences diluted the influence of Italian immigrants.

For Puerto Rican immigrants, an important symbol of their island heritage and a tangible reminder of the rural and urban markets they had known at home is La Marqueta, the colorful city-owned establishment under the railroad viaduct on Park Avenue, between 111th and 116th streets. More than a fixture, it has served as a reflection of East Harlem's ethnic history. It was there when Bernardo Vega arrived in 1916:

> On Park Avenue was an open-air market where you could buy things at low prices. Early in the morning the vendors would set up their stands on the sidewalk under the elevated train, and in the afternoon they would pack up their goods for the night.... Many of the Jews who lived there in those days were recent immigrants, which made the whole area seem like a Tower of Babel. There were Sephardic Jews who spoke ancient Spanish or Portuguese; there were those from the Near East and from the Mediterranean, who spoke Italian, French, Provencal, Roumanian, Turkish, Arabic, or Greek. Many of them, in fact, could get along in five or even six languages. On makeshift shelves and display cases, hanging from walls and wire hangers, all kinds of goods were on display. You could buy everything from the simplest darning needle to a complete trousseau. For a quarter you could get a used pair of shoes and for two or three cents a bag of fruit or vegetables.

One pioneer settler named Raquel Rivera recalled the scene in *From Colonia to Community*, by Virginia E. Sanchez Korrol: "In the twenties and thirties the *Marqueta* was almost all Jewish. What happened was the Jews began to sell Puerto Rican products like *platanos* and other items. Eventually, Puerto Ricans took over the stalls but in the early times it was run by others, Jews, Italians.... Everyone communicated very well. I would see the 'storekeepers' put your purchases in a little basket, weigh it and say 'un dollar' or 'two dollars,' (holding up two fingers), whatever it cost. Actually, I didn't do any shopping myself, but I accompanied my aunt who did shop. The Jewish vendors always knew a few words in Spanish: *si, bueno, barato* and so on."

In 1939, *The WPA Guide to New York City* updated the scene that it said "expresses most vividly the Latin-American character of the locality." Now, it reported, "its block-long, steel-and-glass sheds replace the old pushcart market.... Many tropical fruits grown in the various homelands of the inhabitants of Spanish Harlem are in season displayed here.... From the spice stalls women pick twenty or thirty different varieties which are mixed and stuffed into one bag. Fish of all kinds are on display, including huge tuna sold in slices.... The women shoppers move about with dignity: fair-skinned Creoles with dark eyes, lean-faced, copper-complexioned Spanish Indians, sensitive-looking West Indian Negroes. Voices are musical, and bargaining is done in a friendly spirit. The first price asked is always more than the Puerto Rican vendor expects to receive: *regatear* (to bargain) is the custom in his country."

But to Piri Thomas, a decade or two later, La Marqueta held far less appeal. "It splat out on both sides of the street and all the way up the middle, and there wasn't anything you couldn't buy there. It was always packed with a mess of people selling or buying, and talking different languages. Most of the vendors were Jewish, but they spoke Spanish like Puerto Ricans." When he shopped with his mother, Thom-

Puerto Ricans, following the traditions of other newcomers, have enriched New York's culture with their customs. Here, congregants celebrate the Fiesta del Reyes in colorful costumes at St. Brigid's Church, Avenue B and Tompkins Square Park, in 1957.

as recalled, the merchants would reprimand her for squeezing the vegetables, and, intimidated, she would buy those she had handled:

It was more fun to go with Poppa to the Market. He fought down to the last penny and sometimes came out winning. The vendors seemed to enjoy the hassling. In a bag of apples they would put four good apples on top of a pile of soon-to-rot ones. Poppa called this selling irregular goods at first-class prices. He fought to get first-class goods at the price of irregulars.

Poppa discounted the vendors' friendly "*Como estas?*" He said that "How are you?" were the first Spanish words the vendors learned so they could win the peoples' confidence and gyp them in their own language. I wondered if Poppa didn't like Jews the way I didn't like Italians.

As this anecdote indicates, the immigrant experience has its ignoble underside, a defensiveness that responds to prejudice by expressing bias, that reacts to rejection by debasing outsiders. Newcomers quickly learn that while New Yorkers may point with pride to their city's ethnic variety, immigrants continue to be relegated to the least desirable neighborhoods. The Lower East Side, for example, has served for more than a century as a catch basin for New York's foreign poor, and the same neglected tenements once inhabited by Jews and Italians are occupied today by Chinese and Puerto Ricans. Thus, the pattern of ethnic enclaves is perpetuated. By manipulation, by tradition, by choice, ever-new sounds, sights, and smells appear, adding to the city's diversity and contributing to its multitude of competing interests.

The history of New York City politics can be divided into three eras: before, during, and after Tammany Hall. The periods coincide roughly with the ebb and flow of immigration, but that is no coincidence. For Tammany, which became synonymous with urban bossism and corruption, was a machine that helped make Americans out of Europeans, voters out of aliens, and, frequently, something out of nothing.

The archetypical American political organization, Tammany democratized politics by wresting the political process from the grip of the elite and making it accessible to the masses. The Hall survived for almost a century, despite the almost universal opposition of reformers and moralizers and its own scandalous behavior because it spoke a language the voters understood best. Had it occurred to Tammany's leaders to give New York a motto, it surely would have been "Quid Pro Quo."

Of course, Tammany did not invent politics nor even introduce politics to New York City. Before Tammany, for almost two centuries, New York, whether a colony or a state, whether under a Dutch or British or American flag, was distinguished by the competition and conflict of divergent interests: familial, ethnic, religious, economic, and ideological.

What Tammany did was play a major role in shaping "modern" politics, in which public policy evolves through the clash of group interests as interpreted by political parties. It did this by helping to alter the nature of politics from a lofty *noblesse oblige* concept pursued by powerful families for the presumed benefit of all to what is practiced today.

New York City's political history began when it was called New Amsterdam and was governed by the Dutch. Then, as now, governments offered incentives to businessmen, and so the Netherlands legislature, called the States-General, granted a trading monopoly to the Dutch West India Company as an inducement to colonize the New World. The merchants set up shop on Manhattan Island, and the city began its existence in the 1620s as, literally, a company town.

By modern American standards, New Yorkers in 1664, when the English took over and renamed the city, were politically powerless, although no more so than many of their contemporaries around the globe. Eventually, however, the English, who, unlike the Dutch, exercised authority through political rather than economic agents, gradually relaxed the reins.

In 1686, Governor Thomas Dongan, an Irish Catholic appointed by the Catholic Duke of York, responding to New York City's leaders, granted a charter that guaranteed the city's "privileges, liberties, franchises, rights, royalties, free customs, jurisdictions, and immunities." By granting a measure of local autonomy and voting rights, the Dongan Charter assured the Dutch, who still comprised a majority, of a significant function in the city's political affairs.

However, the amity heralded by these concessions was shattered a few years later when, in 1688, London merged New York, New Jersey, and New England into the Dominion of New England, minimizing the influence of the Dutch, whose numbers were concentrated in New York alone. This decision, which disaffected the Dutch leaders, was to have a profound effect on New York's political history for it fed Leisler's Rebellion and marked the inception of "interest" or "party" politics in America.

Jacob Leisler was a wealthy, cantankerous, and aggressively Protestant merchant whose prestige as a member of New York's Dutch community had been diminished considerably under English control. In 1689, word reached America that Catholic King James II had been deposed by the Glorious Revolution and replaced by his Protestant daughter, Mary, and her Dutch Protestant husband, William of Orange. For New York, this event seethed with religious, ethnic, economic, and political implications. Triumphantly, Leisler and his son-in-law, Jacob Milbourne,

Opposite:
In addition to serving as the city's executive and legislative seats (by housing the office of the mayor and the chambers of the City Council and Board of Estimate), City Hall, between Broadway and Park Row, functions as New York's ceremonial site: The bodies of Abraham Lincoln and Ulysses S. Grant laid in state and heroes such as aviator Charles Lindbergh and astronaut John Glenn were received here. Behind City Hall is that monument to corruption, the New York County Courthouse, known more familiarly (and appropriately) as the Tweed Courthouse, which cost city taxpayers about $8 million more than it should have as a consequence of Boss William Marcy Tweed's involvement in its construction. The bulky marble version of a Palladian villa serves as well as an indirect monument to the immigrant waves that Tweed mobilized as voters through his Tammany Hall political machine.

declared their allegiance to "the Protestant religion and His Royal Highness the Prince of Orange" and with their Dutch followers proclaimed the liberation of the colony from "tyranny, popery, and slavery."

For almost two years, until March 1691, Leisler ran the province, largely because of a delay by the Crown in reestablishing the provincial government. It took fully sixteen months for Henry Sloughter, the new governor named by King William, to arrive in New York after his appointment. Sloughter's first act was to demand that Leisler and Milbourne yield authority, but they resisted long enough to enable Sloughter to charge them with treason. They were tried, convicted, hanged (in what is now City Hall Park), and beheaded.

The harshness of the penalty (a lesser charge of sedition was seen as more appropriate) triggered a reaction in both New York and London that culminated in a parliamentary review of the case, a reversal of the verdict, and a posthumous apology. While the redress came too late for Leisler and Milbourne, their defiance created a political schism in New York that divided the city between pro-Leislerians and anti-Leislerians, the Dutch and the English, and the less affluent and the elite. These divisions represented the stumbling forerunner of party politics in America.

The reverberations of the Leisler affair echoed for decades and contributed significantly to the colony's reputation for factional, hard-fought politics. Legislative battles were waged between merchants and landed gentry, upriver interests and New York City, Dissenters and Anglicans. One notable controversy concerned attacks on Governor William Cosby that led to the libel trial of John Peter Zenger in 1735. Although the importance of the case itself in terms of press freedom in colonial New York has been exaggerated, the arguments and agitation it provoked helped spread the contention that government was the servant of the people and that open criticism of magistrates was a legitimate way to hold them accountable. Subsequent years saw spirited campaigns for election to the Assembly and, ultimately, conflicts over whether and how to oppose British colonial policies.

The late eighteenth century saw two significant events: the Revolutionary War and the founding of the Tammany Society. While the connection is tenuous (Tammany was formed after the war to reinforce antimonarchial attitudes), the Revolution created new leaders, as well as new political and social forces, that nourished the city's appetite for factionalism and made it ripe for Tammany's advent.

By mid-century, antipathy toward Britain was beginning to politicize all levels of New York society, eventually creating a new generation of leaders, such as Alexander Hamilton and Aaron Burr, who would remain a force in city politics after the Revolution. Each month brought conflict closer and the city's populace was volatile, but after the Redcoats quickly won the Battle of Long Island in the late summer of 1776, the British occupied Manhattan for the remainder of the seven-year Revolution, causing Patriots to flee the city and Tories to seek protection within it. The occupation effectively ended political ferment within New York City for the duration.

After the Treaty of Paris concluded the war, the British troops finally departed in November 1783, turning over to General George Washington a city that had been devastated by major fires in 1776 and 1778, a city stripped of trees and of pride, and a city abused and despoiled during the cruel and grueling occupation. Washington remained for a few weeks and bade farewell to his officers at Fraunces Tavern.

Although he left in glory as the heroic military leader of the American Revolution, Washington would return to New York some five years later to achieve the pinnacle of his political career as the chief executive of the new nation. On April 30, 1789, Washington stood on the open second-floor balcony of Federal Hall, the former City Hall, which only two months earlier had become the first Capitol, took the oath of office, and was inaugurated President of the United States.

For five years, from 1785 to 1790, New York City served as both the capital of the

state and of the nation. And in its latter capacity, with both Congress and the President in residence, it became the political and social center of the New World. Some of the most revered figures in American history strolled the sidewalks of New York in those heady days: President and "Lady Washington," as she was sometimes called; Vice President John Adams, Secretary of State Thomas Jefferson, House Leader James Madison, Senators James Monroe and John Hancock, Treasury Secretary Alexander Hamilton, Chief Justice John Jay, Attorney General Edmund Randolph, and Aaron Burr.

The rough-and-tumble politics that characterized the prewar period resumed in the nineteenth century but with a new cast and new political parties. And as the eighteenth century wound down, the organization that would epitomize such activity came into being as a relatively innocuous national patriotic and fraternal order. It was named after the Delaware Indian chief, Tammany or Tamenend, sometimes termed "Saint Tammany," to mock such Tory associations as St. George's and St. Andrew's. In New York, the Tammany Society, or Columbian Order, was formed about 1786 and incorporated three years later. Dedicated to protecting the new nation against monarchial rule, the society adopted a Native American image, utilizing pseudo-Indian nomenclature and rituals. It called its steering committee the "Council of Sachems," members referred to each others as "braves," and the clubhouse, built in 1812, was officially designated as the "Wigwam," although everyone knew it as "Tammany Hall."

Tammany entered the scene when politics was still largely an endeavor indulged in by gentlemen from notable and powerful families and helped transform it into the kind of widespread affair that exists currently. In its early days, although Tammany was very much the domain of the well-to-do and socially prominent, suspicions of the monarchy and aristocracy led most members to align themselves against the Federalists, whose policies seemed too evocative of Toryism.

The Tammanyites' anti-Federalist stance put them behind Jefferson in his historic struggle with Hamilton for control of the infant nation's direction. The philosophic difference between these two brilliant leaders was rarely more elegantly expressed than in the following exchange. Hamilton, in articulating his Federalist

The pristine grandeur of the Governor's Room seems out of place among the often nefarious political activities that have surrounded it in City Hall. Decorated with portraits of notables, including war heroes and governors, as well as George Washington's desk, and the 1789 inaugural flag, the room, once used by governors, is now used to host receptions and is open to the public.

beliefs, said of Jefferson's supporters, "Your *people*, sir, are a great beast. They seldom judge or determine correctly." Jefferson's response was eloquent: "Sir, if we think the people not enlightened enough to exercise their power with a wholesome discretion, the remedy is not to take power *from* them, but to enlighten them with education. Preach, my dear sir, a crusade against ignorance."

Tammany, too, professed an affinity for "the people" and, despite its later history of depredation and well-earned reputation for greed, generally could be found on their side. One of its first opportunities arose against Hamilton, who, in addition to contending with Jefferson on the national scene, frequently found himself at odds in New York with a Jeffersonian ally named Aaron Burr. Like Hamilton, Burr was a lawyer, a politician, and a well-known figure in the city. Although Burr was not a member of Tammany, he recognized its organizational talents and utilized its support to win city and state legislative elections in 1800 against Hamilton and Jay.

The rivalry between Burr and Hamilton, which went back to the Revolution when both had served as aides to Washington, simmered for many years at the bar and in politics, and while they behaved civilly toward one another in public, feelings between them were undoubtedly rancorous. Hamilton repeatedly frustrated Burr's ambitions, and after a series of political and personal reverses, Burr sought vengeance, demanding a duel when Hamilton failed to apologize for a critical reference that had appeared in the press. Hamilton was fatally wounded in the July 1804 encounter in Weehawken, New Jersey. Burr fled the scene and the region—he was indicted for murder in both New York and New Jersey—and abandoned any likelihood of a future in New York City politics.

The death of Hamilton, who had played such a commanding role in post-Revolutionary New York, predeceased by a few years the Federalist era. It also marked the beginning of a new era of growth, for between the censuses of 1800 and 1810, New York surpassed Philadelphia to become the largest city in the United States. Heralding this spirit of progress, a competition had been held in 1802 to design a new City Hall. When the winning entry was completed in 1811 at its present site in leafy City Hall Park, the building stood at the northern end of developed Manhattan, a fact that led cost-conscious Mayor DeWitt Clinton to construct its north side in cheap brownstone in the belief that nobody would view it from that perspective.

Clinton, who first became mayor in 1803, went on, as has no modern counterpart, to become governor in 1817, where he achieved fame for himself and fortune for New York City by developing the Erie Canal. DeWitt was a member of a notable family; his uncle, George Clinton, had been elected governor in 1801 as a Jeffersonian, or Democratic, Republican to help fulfill that party's accomplishment of simultaneously heading the nation, under President Jefferson, and New York City, under Mayor Edward Livingston, as well as the state.

DeWitt Clinton, a Democratic Republican like his uncle, a resourceful politician, and one of the earliest officeholders to recognize the effectiveness of patronage, battled for years within the party against Tammany, particularly over the issue of the canal. Tammany, never known to confuse the relative priorities of principle and expediency, opposed the canal until it became aware of the project's popularity, whereupon it championed the cause as if it were its own.

The decline of the Federalists precipitated an internal struggle for control of New York State's only remaining party, the Democratic Republicans, between two factions: Clintonians, who followed the governor, and Bucktails, his opponents, named after the deertails Tammany sachems wore in their hats at meetings. This struggle soon metamorphosed into a virtual vendetta between Clinton and Martin Van Buren, an Upstater whose short stature and political expertise won him the nickname "The Little Magician."

Their conflict lasted for almost a decade before Van Buren won. But his more lasting triumph was as an innovator who not only created an effective political machine but revolutionized American politics by legitimatizing political parties.

Before Van Buren, parties were considered self-serving groups led by selfish men; entities that violated the spirit of harmony espoused by the Founding Fathers. But according to Van Buren and his Albany Regency (a term describing the machine he left in control of New York State politics while he served in the United States Senate), political parties fulfilled the democratic ideal by enabling the people to participate in government and checked abuses of power by subordinating individuals to party discipline.

Van Buren's decisive victory against Clinton was fought over the Constitutional Convention of 1821, an overdue conclave sought by the Bucktails to update the state's anachronistic laws but opposed by the Clintonians as a threat to their incumbency. Although governor, Clinton was unable to thwart the drive for reform, and the convention succeeded in extending suffrage to virtually all white males and amending other statutes to significantly curtail the power of the elite. When adopted in 1822, the new constitution contained the means for radically altering politics throughout the state by opening up the process to mass participation.

The most immediate beneficiary of the changes was Van Buren, who, after winning election to the Senate, utilized the efficiency of his Albany Regency to become governor in 1828 and succeed Andrew Jackson as president in 1836. "The Little Magician" recalled this in his *Autobiography*, pointing out that "I left the service of the State for that of the Federal Government with my friends in full and almost unquestioned possession of the State Government in all its branches, at peace with each other and overflowing with kindly feelings towards myself, and not without hope that I might in the sequel of good conduct be able to realize similar results in the enlarged sphere of action to which I was called."

Ultimately, however, it was Tammany that shrewdly manipulated the reforms to organize the electorate, consolidate its own power, and perpetuate its existence long after Van Buren and the Regency had faded from the political tapestry. To be sure, it was circumstance that unlocked the door, but it was cunning, drive, and instinct that let Tammany in.

In the middle decades of the nineteenth century, two major factors converged to provide Tammany with its opportunity. The first was the flood of immigrants, mostly Irish, who poured into New York City after 1840; the second was the city's total inability to cope with this onslaught. Tammany moved to fill this need. It befriended the immigrant, smoothed his way, gave him a job, and helped him become a citizen. The latter service was not totally altruistic: Citizens could vote, and vote they did, for whomever their patrons in the Hall suggested.

Although twentieth-century Tammany has projected an unmistakably Irish image, there was nothing ethnic about the earlier Hall. Those who ran it and those whom it supported for public office were neither foreigners nor Catholics; they were native-born Protestants. Yet even as Tammany's pragmatism allowed it to overlook probity when the need arose, so could it overcome bigotry when the prize was right. And as the newcomers jammed New York's docks and then its tenements and wards, what the Hall's leaders saw were not tens of thousands of despised Irish-Catholic or German aliens but rather that number of votes (and, given the Hall's talented ward captains, generally a few more). Still, in those days, for all its opportunism, Tammany's focus did not extend past the next election; not until after the Civil War and the accession of William Marcy (Boss) Tweed was there recognition that supporters would vote throughout a lifetime and even beyond, for political loyalty was bequeathed like an inheritance to the next generation.

Tammany's cultivation of the immigrant was highly organized and effectively executed. Throughout the city, meetings were held to acquaint foreigners with the Hall's attributes. Generally, the speakers were role-model immigrants, who were admired by their audiences and who spoke their language, literally as well as figuratively. In the always unfamiliar and usually hostile new environment, Tamma-

The Tammany Tiger, portrayed by political cartoonist Thomas Nast as a predatory Democratic beast, began life as the symbol of Americus Engine Company Number 6, the "Big Six" volunteer unit that gave William Marcy Tweed his first opportunity to demonstrate leadership. The tiger, the creation of Joseph H. Johnson, a noted artist who also was a member of the engine company, was adopted as the emblem of Tammany. The city's fire departments, which provided extensive social connections for the working class, became nineteenth-century spawning grounds for politicians.

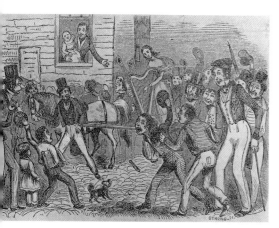

Politics has often been a dirty business in New York, and always a colorful one. Excitement ran high, as illustrated by this portrayal of an 1845 rally in the Sixth Ward, and frequently tempers did as well.

ny glowed like a welcoming beacon to the recent arrivals. And for all this friendship and advice and employment the immigrants were asked merely to vote—at least once in each election.

Although Tammany had no monopoly on election fraud, which was commonplace and characteristic of all political organizations at the time, it had no peers at "getting out the vote." An 1845 investigation into irregularities provided the following derisive description: "The morning of the election was a busy time at the Alms House. Officers hurrying to and fro—getting together inmates of the establishment, clad in their new dresses—distributing to them tickets to vote and tickets for grog—putting into their hands nice pieces of silver coin, that they might solace themselves after the arduous labor of depositing their ballots."

While Tammany, after sizing up the potential value of the immigrant vote, sought ardently to woo the newcomers, the Whig party saw its opportunity in the opposite direction. Organized in the first quarter of the nineteenth century in opposition to the Jacksonian Democrats, the Whigs united nationally around commercial and financial interests. In New York City, the Whigs emerged as a major threat to the Democrats around 1840, when they made clear their appeal to conservative, nativist sentiments. This strategy won them a significant victory at the polls in 1844 when James Harper, a founder of the future Harper & Row publishing firm, was elected mayor. But Harper's popularity was short-lived (his promises of reform failed to materialize), and while the Whigs remained active for the next decade, the wisdom, or shrewdness, of Tammany's judgment in aligning itself with immigrants was seemingly confirmed.

Tammany's strength was due in large measure to its ongoing efforts; for the Hall, politics was a full-time job, not merely an election-time campaign. In plying its trade, Tammany utilized three vital, all-male institutions: the police force, the volunteer fire departments, and the saloons. The police, who represent power in any society, were an invaluable political asset in the lawless, venal New York City of the mid-nineteenth century. And they also represented an ideal vehicle for dispensing patronage, particularly for new arrivals. In 1855, the chief of police, himself an English immigrant, reported that one-third of the city's force was foreignborn, and of these, three-quarters were Irish. The practice was to assign the immigrant officers to patrol immigrant areas, doubtless to ensure that voting frauds could be perpetrated without interference.

Voting the dead and voting more than once in the same election was so routine that politicians, such as Tammany's Gulian Verplanck, discussed it openly. "It is not only true that Mr. H. voted for the whole Jackson ticket in the 5th ward," he wrote in connection with the 1828 elections, "but did it *twice* running, and then observed that he was now going over to Hoboken, but to-morrow would vote in the first ward, for all the Jackson ticket except Alderman Cebra, whom he could not swallow."

Preelection events included the release of prisoners from Blackwell's Island so they could vote. On occasion, fraud was so widespread as to be mathematically provable: In 1868, for example, the actual vote in one ward exceeded the number of eligible voters by 8 percent. George Templeton Strong, whose diary provides a colorful record of the observations and thoughts of an upper-class nineteenth century New Yorker, wrote, after visiting City Hall in 1838, that "it was enough to turn a man's stomach—to make a man abjure republicanism forever—to see the way they were naturalizing this morning at the Hall. Wretched, filthy, bestiallooking Italians and Irish, and creations that looked as if they had risen from the lazarettos of Naples for this especial object: in short, the very scum and dregs of human nature filled the clerk of Common Pleas office so completely that I was almost afraid of being poisoned by going in."

In those precivil-service days, law enforcement was incredibly politicized: Police

Crime control has been a concern of New Yorkers for more than a century, and demands for a police presence made the cop on the beat an important neighborhood figure. Here, an arrest on Mulberry Bend in the early twentieth century provides a diversion, if not a lesson, for street children.

officers were appointed by aldermen who were themselves elected. Thus, the police were directly linked to the political process and dependent for their livelihood on the outcome of elections. It was also a time before discipline, or even a uniform, was required. In 1853, when Mayor Jacob Westervelt succeeded in putting uniforms on policemen, the move was hailed by the *Evening Post* not so much because it would induce police to "watch society" but because it would enable society to "watch them."

While the police force provided jobs for the faithful and protection for the corrupt, the volunteer fire departments offered a unique opportunity for young men to demonstrate their organizational talents. The departments, which sponsored frequent picnics and other festivities, served as social clubs with lenient membership requirements that would readily accept immigrants and afford them the status withheld by society at large. The foremost graduate of the volunteer fire department school of politics was Boss Tweed himself, as well as two successors to Tammany leadership, "Honest John" Kelly and Richard Croker.

In fact, Tweed's involvement as foreman of the "Big Six," or Americus Engine Company Number 6, which he had helped organize in 1848, later inspired scathing *Harper's Weekly* cartoonist Thomas Nast to use a tiger, the company's emblem, as a symbol of Tammany's ravenous destructiveness. As the company's young, muscular leader, Tweed, a chair and brush manufacturer, soon gained a reputation for his forcefulness and political connections. When the Americus Company was charged with attacking Hose Company Number 31 on the way to a fire—a not infrequent occurrence in those days among zealous volunteers—the report of a Common Council committee's decision to oust Tweed was mysteriously altered to call only for his brief suspension.

However, Tweed was somewhat less successful in his dealings with the voters. His first venture into elective politics failed when, in 1850 at the age of twenty-seven, he ran as a Democrat for assistant alderman from the Seventh Ward and lost to a Whig. The following year, wiser if sadder, he ran again against the same Whig for the higher office of alderman and won after persuading a friend to split the Whig vote by running as a Temperance candidate. Moreover, third-party aspirants helped Democrats win fifteen of twenty seats on the Board of Aldermen. Since the Common Council was composed of the twenty plus twenty assistant aldermen, their number and behavior soon made them known as "The Forty Thieves."

While Tweed became the quintessential Tammany leader, he did not fit the Tammany stereotype of an Irish Catholic from humble beginnings. Born April 3, 1823, to a middle-class, Protestant, third-generation Scottish family, Tweed neither smoked nor drank; he did, however, possess other attributes of political immortality: gregariousness, reliability, drive, daring, a remarkable memory, sagacity, and total amorality. At about three hundred pounds, he was also unmistakable.

A fast learner, as were his fellow Tammany councilmen, Tweed quickly joined in voting to cancel some of the most lucrative projects initiated by the preceding council, thus enabling the newcomers to reward their friends. Among the gifts were ferry and railroad franchises, leases and outright sales of city-owned piers and markets, and whatever public works contracts they could think of. This, of course, in addition to shamelessly padding the payroll. In the two years before they were turned out of office by the voters, "The Forty Thieves" managed to increase municipal expenditures by $8 million, or 37 percent, and hiked the tax rate by more than 25 percent. The *Tribune* described them as "the most debased, corrupt and disgraceful body of men ever invested with legislative power, at least in this country."

While most of the former "Thieves" withdrew from public view, no doubt to enjoy their newly acquired wealth, Tweed lingered, having been elected to Congress in 1852 (while retaining his seat on the Common Council). Bored with national affairs, he left Washington in 1855 to seek reelection as alderman but lost and soon found his as yet limited influence within Tammany dwindling. When Tweed's early political fortunes seemed to sag, another ambitious Tammany brave appeared to seek power within the party and the city. His name was Fernando Wood, and he had entered politics through one of that era's most popular routes: the saloon.

The corner saloon was the urban counterpart of the rural general store: It was the focus of neighborhood activity, the place where gossip was exchanged, favors sought, deals made, and intelligence gleaned. It was also a meeting place for politicians and a hangout for toughs, whose valued skills played such vital roles in political campaigns. Running a saloon, or even tending bar, gave one access to information and contacts, and a clever operator with political aspirations, such as Wood, found it an ideal launching pad.

Born in 1812, Wood bought his first saloon when he was only twenty and began a fast-rising political career four years later when he joined the Tammany Society. He served one term in Congress, but failing to gain renomination in 1842, he spent the rest of that decade in business, making and accumulating money. By 1850, Wood was financially secure enough to reenter politics full time, and, although he picked the wrong year to run for mayor (Democrats lost throughout the state and city), he tried again four years later and, in an election typically tainted by charges of fraud, won. His popularity with immigrant voters, particularly the Irish, was credited for the victory; in fact, the Irish Sixth Ward cast four hundred more votes for him than it had registrants.

Wood's tenure—which extended over three terms, interrupted by a brief Reform regime—was noteworthy for his efforts to centralize authority in the mayor, which gained him the title "Fernando the First" from his critics. Whether his motives were sincere or self-serving is unclear, but his goal triggered a power struggle with the Republican Legislature for control of the city that led the legislators to halve Wood's second term and culminated in a bizarre riot between two police forces, the city's traditional Municipals and a new Metropolitan department created by the state.

The term-cutting was a reaction to Wood's flagrant corruption following his reelection in 1856. The Legislature reduced the mayor's tenure to one year, compelling him to run again in 1857, a race he lost. However, the traditional two-year term was reinstituted for the 1859 election, which Wood won.

The clash occurred on June 16, 1857, after a city street commissioner appointed by Republican Governor John King sought to take office in City Hall and was thrown out by Wood's Municipal police. When one of the governor's Metropolitans then sought to arrest Wood for inciting a riot, and he too was thrown out, the governor sent a force of two hundred Metropolitans to do the job. They were met at the steps of City Hall by a superior force of Municipals, a battle ensued, and before they withdrew, more than twenty Metropolitans were injured. Ten regiments of the state militia were ordered to the scene, but Wood submitted to arrest before further disorders could occur. For the next few weeks both forces patrolled the city's streets, occasionally helping to free suspects arrested by their rivals. The issue was resolved the following month when the state's highest court upheld the Metropolitan Police Act and Wood disbanded his Municipal force.

The fruits of the Metropolitans' victory were somewhat less than sweet, however. On the Fourth of July, the "Dead Rabbits," a vicious Irish gang partial to Wood, assaulted some Metropolitans and then attacked a saloon frequented by their traditional nativist rivals, the "Bowery Boys." Two days of rioting followed, during which thousands joined in clubbings, knifings, and shootings that claimed at least ten lives and injured one hundred. When the Metropolitans proved incapable of restoring order, two militia regiments had to be called in. Reaction to the Metropolitans' conduct during the outbreak was so negative that some even urged statehood for the city as a means of ridding it of the state force.

Wood's defiance of the state and of the Republicans won him admiration and support from many city Democrats, although the press and some Tammany factions, for different reasons, felt his administration was ruinous. No sooner had the city recovered from the shock of the police riot than it was struck by economic disaster. The Panic of 1857 threw thousands of New Yorkers out of work in the fall of that year, but Wood, who suffered from no shortage of ideas and innovations, proposed a New Deal-type recovery program decades before Franklin Delano Roosevelt was even born. Wood urged the Common Council to speed up a battery of public works projects to put the unemployed back on the job and suggested that they be paid in foodstuffs (flour, cornmeal, and potatoes) at municipal expense.

Appealing to the public over the heads of the aldermen, the mayor reiterated the portion of his disputatious inaugural address that contained a radical attack on capitalism: "Do not let us be ungrateful as well as inhuman. Do not let it be said that labor, which produces every thing, gets nothing and dies of hunger in our midst, while capital, which produces nothing, gets every thing, and pampers in luxury and plenty."

Now the press found Wood dangerous as well as incompetent and, in conjunction with Tammany elements, including Tweed, worked successfully against his reelection. A wealthy manufacturer and Democrat named Daniel F. Tiemann, running as a reformer on a fusion ticket, eked out a victory over Wood, who, in what was to become a New York tradition, denied a second term to the reformer in the following (1859) election.

Wood, regarded by some as the most professional and sophisticated mayor—as well as the most corrupt—the city had seen to that time, remained an unflagging proponent of home rule for New York and an implacable foe of the Republican-controlled State Legislature that sought to deny it.

In 1861, during his final mayoral term, he seriously advocated that the city secede from the Union and become the "Republic of New York," on the grounds that the city "may have more cause of apprehension from the aggressive legislature of our own state than from external dangers.... Our city occupies the position of a

The height of Tammany's power and the depth of its ignominy probably occurred under the aegis of Boss Tweed, the corpulent, teetotaling boss who ran the organization and city with equal arrogance until his 1873 conviction on a multitude of corruption charges involving graft, bribery, embezzlement, and larceny. His less avaricious political skills were directed at maintaining the organization's impressive strength at the polls, a talent validated by his own election to the state senate after his scandalous behavior had been exposed.

conquered province entirely dependent on the will of a distant, and to our wants and wishes, an indifferent and alien government." He probably was the first and surely was the most forceful city official to recognize and articulate the discord between rural, Protestant, nativist, Republican Upstate and urban, Catholic, immigrant, Democratic Downstate, a conflict that continues into the present.

One of the city's most complex and controversial leaders, Wood was undone to a large extent by overweening ambition and hypocrisy. Dissatisfied with merely holding the support of immigrants, he made a bid for the aid of their opponents as well, secretly joining the anti-immigrant "Know-Nothing" party. This move, when it became public knowledge, cost him the backing of immigrants and jeopardized his standing with Tammany. He was further damaged in the years preceding the Civil War by his staunch—and unpopular—position in support of the South and slavery. After failing reelection in 1861, Wood's influence ebbed in the city proper, although he stayed in politics, spending most of his remaining twenty years serving in Congress.

While out of the foreground during Wood's mayoral reign, Tweed was hardly out of the picture. Through observing Wood's operations, he learned how public jobs and contracts were bought and sold and, perhaps more important, came to comprehend something that Wood never understood: A successful politician can cheat the public but must never double-cross his cronies.

Moreover, through a twist of fate, Tweed got help from a most unexpected source: the Republican State Legislature. In 1857, he won a seat on the Board of Supervisors, a relatively unimportant post traditionally under the control of the mayor. However, as an outgrowth of its ongoing conflict with Wood, the Legislature that year made the board bipartisan, removed the mayor from it, and substantially increased its power.

As it turned out, Tweed could not have created a better opportunity for himself. For thirteen years, until 1870, he served on the board and was four times its president. For Tweed, the board offered an apprenticeship in corruption: He formed alliances with other key supervisors and brazenly charged those seeking the board's assistance a 15 percent "commission." He also used his committee posts to hone his larcenous skills, on one occasion buying benches for $5 apiece from a building undergoing conversion and selling them to the county for $600 each.

Although thinking up new schemes to defraud the public consumed a good deal of his time, Tweed did not neglect his political career. In 1861 he became chairman of the New York County Democratic Central Committee, a position less potent than it might seem but one that gave him a chance to demonstrate his administrative talents, such as turning off the lights when an opposing faction within Tammany sought to nominate a rival candidate. By 1863, Tweed's diligence paid off when he became the first in Tammany's history to be named both chairman of its General Committee and Grand Sachem. To complete his conquest, Tweed was named Deputy Street Commissioner that year, giving him control of the city's largest work force, a vast source of patronage, and the means to deal with builders and contractors.

While some wars are born of idealism, most end in cynicism, a condition that seemed to envelop the nation following the terrible trauma of the Civil War. In Washington, it was manifest in the corruption of the administration of Ulysses S. Grant; in New York, it was immortalized by the Tweed Ring.

By the time he organized the wholesale pillage of New York, Tweed had seemingly accomplished a life's work: Aside from the power and social access implicit in his political positions, he was wealthy and lived well with his family in exclusive Murray Hill. His money-making talents were prodigious. With the help of Judge Barnard and, conceivably, even some schooling, Tweed was admitted to the bar in 1860 in time to represent the Erie Railroad of Jay Gould and James Fisk during their celebrated war with Commodore Cornelius Vanderbilt, an assignment that earned him more than $100,000. He had the acumen to purchase control of the New York Printing Company, which not only handled all the city's printing but also that of any major company that did business with the city, including railroads, ferry lines, and insurance firms. And he had the foresight to buy a marble quarry in Massachusetts that would later supply all the stone for that most extraordinary memorial to crooked government, the New York County or Tweed Courthouse on Chambers Street.

Not even football coach Knute Rockne, when he put together Notre Dame's famed "Four Horsemen" backfield, demonstrated the Boss's skill in assembling the Tweed Ring. For craftiness and cunning, there was Peter Barr (Brains) Sweeny, the city chamberlain or treasurer; for political clout and unquestioning loyalty, there was Richard (Slippery Dick) Connolly, the comptroller; for flair and style, there was Abraham Oakey (The Elegant Oakey) Hall, the mayor; and for scheming and arrogance, there was William Marcy (Boss) Tweed, the public works commissioner, state senator, and chairman of the state finance committee.

Among them, and with the assistance of Governor John T. Hoffman, Judges George Barnard, Albert Cardozo, and John H. M'Cunn, and an army of payroll-padders, no-shows, ward heelers, hangers-on, clerks, doorkeepers, messengers, and manure inspectors, the Tweed Ring, during its brief, five-year tenure, stole so much money from the City of New York that experts still argue over whether it was closer to $30 million or $200 million.

If the scope of the Ring's operations was incomprehensible, the cast of characters was no less fantastic. Their activities suggest a Broadway production, a hardly inappropriate analogy since Hall was not only a playwright but an actor who appeared in his own works during his mayoral stint. A former district attorney no less, Hall prided himself on his wit, which was generally limited to low-level puns, and his attire, the color of which he sought to match to the occasion (he wore only green on St. Patrick's Day). He apparently was regarded with a mixture of admiration and affection by most of his constituency and an inordinate proportion of editorial writers. One journalist who was not impressed, however, was Thomas Nast, the *Harper's Weekly* political cartoonist. When Nast's pen led the overmatched mayor to ridicule him as the "Nast-y artist of Harper's Hell Weekly—a Journal of Devilization," Nast responded with the searing epithet "Mayor Haul."

Cataloguing even a portion of the Ring's larcenies would fill a book and does: Alexander B. Callow's fascinating political biography, *The Tweed Ring*. But the story of the Tweed Courthouse provides an instructive example of the magnitude, brashness, and style of the Boss and his cohorts. The tale begins in 1858, when the city stipulated that a county courthouse be designed and constructed in City Hall Park at a total cost, including furnishings, of not more than $250,000. By 1871, when the roof fell in, so to speak, on the Ring, more than $13 million had been spent on the still-unfinished structure.

Even a diligent study of the courthouse project would likely fail to turn up any form of fraud *not* perpetrated by the Tweed gang. The tone was set at the outset when Connolly told contractors that this time the kickback to the Ring would be 65 percent. This ensured an astronomical cost to the public as contractors resorted to higher mathematics to calculate sufficiently enriching returns for themselves. Apparently, the task was not beyond them. For example, Andrew Garvey, who won the job of "plastering" the marble and iron building, charged almost $3 million, including more than $1 million for "repairs." One year, investigators found, he billed the city $500,000 for plastering and an additional $1 million for repairing the same work.

Carpenters and plumbers were correspondingly rewarded, while suppliers' charges seemed limited only by their imaginations. Furniture, carpets, and shades

Bitter ridicule was political cartoonist Thomas Nast's weapon for attacking Boss Tweed and his cronies during an extended campaign that helped arouse public indignation. This example, which appeared in Harper's Weekly *in September 1871, indicates Nast's cynical expectation that the depredators may well survive. Beneath the recognizable features of the Tweed Ring and the remains of such victims as law, justice, liberty, and the New York City Treasury, the caption states: "A group of vultures waiting for the storm to 'blow over'—'Let us prey.'"*

Tammany Hall, a latter-day symbol of urban bossism and corruption, was, to be accurate, not a political machine but a structure, the headquarters of the Tammany Society. Originated as a patriotic organization after the Revolutionary War, Tammany became a city power in the mid-nineteenth century when it recognized the political capital to be made by cultivating New York's immigrant masses. In a period of limited social welfare programs, Tammany provided advice, benefits, and jobs in return for votes. The quality—and integrity—of its leadership varied, but its army of precinct workers rarely failed to make the difference on election day. Named for an Indian chief, Tammany adapted tribal lore to its own needs, as in the dedication of the pictured "wigwam," its second home, on 14th Street east of Irving Place, at the National Democratic Convention on July 4, 1868.

provided by the James Ingersoll Company came to more than $5,600,000, a sum, according to Upstate Republican leader Roscoe Conkling, that surpassed the cost of running the Unites States mail service. It is generally agreed that taxpayers were defrauded of at least $8 million.

The extent and manner of the Ring's monumental thievery was attributable in large measure to confidence gained through its success at the polls. And that success was an outgrowth both of Tammany's painstaking cultivation of immigrants and its wholesale naturalization of them. This was never more evident than in the 1868 elections, when Hoffman, in his second gubernatorial bid, won election with a huge outpouring of city votes, which in some districts exceeded the registration. With judges such as Barnard, Cardozo, and M'Cunn working overtime, immigrants became citizens (and, most assuredly, voters) at an unprecedented rate. On some days, more than one thousand aliens were naturalized.

Testifying about the election before an investigating committee of the Board of Aldermen in 1878, Tweed stated, "I don't think there is ever a fair or honest election in the City of New York. . . . I think that was the year a great many people were naturalized."

By 1870, with Hoffman in the state capitol and "The Elegant Oakey" in City Hall, Tweed was anxious to end the city's dependence on Albany. He accomplished this by pushing through a new charter for New York City that abolished the state commissions and concentrated power in the office of the mayor. It also created a public works department, which Tweed, of course, headed. The charter gained the surprising support of some Republican senators and assemblymen; *surprising* until it was learned that Tweed had spent from $600,000 (his estimate) to $1 million (the estimate of State Democratic Chairman Samuel J. Tilden) to induce their votes.

With a governor at his disposal, Tweed, himself a senator, had extended his tentacles up the Hudson to grasp the state government as well. The legislators needed no introduction to graft and corruption, but Tweed explained how he helped institutionalize it through the Assembly's "Black Horse Cavalry": "It was understood in the Lower House that there was an organization formed of men of both parties, Republicans and Democrats, called the Black Horse Cavalry, composed of twenty-eight or thirty persons, who would all be controlled by one man, and vote as he directed them. Sometimes they would be paid for not voting against a bill, and sometimes they would not be desired, if their votes were not necessary." Tweed modestly refrained from identifying himself as the man in control.

With Tweed at the acme of his power, civic leaders, businessmen, and partisan newspapers were stumbling over each other to praise him. The *New York World* editorialized that "there is not another municipal government in the world which combines so much character, capacity, experience, and energy as are to be found in the city government of New York under the new charter." When Tweed's daughter got married in May 1871, she received gifts valued at more than $700,000 from New York's elite. There was even a proposal to erect a statue to Tweed in New York Harbor.

Nast and *Harper's Weekly* had been hammering away at the Boss since early 1870, joined by the *New York Times* later that year, without doing any apparent damage. (Although Tweed later confessed: "I don't care what people write, for my people can't read. But they have eyes and can see as well as other folks.") However, in the spring of 1871, Tammany malcontents James (Jimmy the Famous) O'Brien, the sheriff, and Matthew O'Rourke, a new county bookkeeper, turned over startling evidence of corruption in the state comptroller's office to George Jones, the *Times*'s owner. Learning of this, the Ring offered Jones $5 million to refrain from printing anything and offered Nast $500,000 to cease his attacks. The bribes were refused and the *Times*, after an investigation, began publishing an exposé of the Tweed Ring in July 1871 to an angry and vocal public.

Political response to the revelations and, more importantly, to the reaction of the public was prompt and predictable. A Council of Political Reform was organized, then a mass meeting at Cooper Union, which produced a Committee of Seventy to take action. Civic leaders and politicians, who earlier had fawned over Tweed or, at best, maintained a discreet silence, were suddenly astounded by the Ring's activities and demanded justice. It was at this point that Tweed either uttered, or didn't utter, the most memorable statement attributed to him: "Well, what are you going to do about it?" The quotation, which appeared under a Nast cartoon depicting a massive thumb crushing New York, cannot be traced to any specific source, but it no doubt has survived because it seemed so likely to be something he might have said.

State Democratic Chairman Samuel J. Tilden, after ascertaining which way the parade was headed, raced in to lead it. He helped organize the opposition to Tweed, obtained evidence, won election to the Assembly in 1872 as an anti-Tweed candidate, sued to recover stolen money, ran the Ring members out of the Democratic Party, and testified as the principal witness at the Ring trials.

Eventually, justice triumphed; sort of. Of all the stolen millions, the city recovered $876,241. Tweed was reelected to the State Senate in November 1871 but a month later was indicted on one hundred and twenty counts and arrested. Hall was indicted, conducted his own defense, won acquittal through a hung jury, went to Europe, returned, and wound up as city editor of the *New York World*. Sweeny and Connolly fled the country and were never tried. The Ring's judges either resigned or were successfully impeached. Tweed was convicted at his second criminal trial and sentenced to twelve years in prison but was released after twelve months through a Court of Appeals decision. However, he was imprisoned again when he was unable to raise bail after being charged in a civil complaint brought by the state to recover stolen funds. Treated leniently by his jailers, he escaped while being allowed to visit his home and made his way to Spain, where, on the strength of a Nast cartoon, he was recognized by Spanish authorities, arrested, and returned to New York. Tweed went back to jail in late 1876 and, his health failing, sought to gain release by cooperating with investigators. He testified candidly and at length before the committee of the Board of Aldermen in 1877 but died at the Ludlow Street Jail the following year. He was fifty-five and brassy to the end. When asked his occupation on entering prison, he responded: "Statesman."

New York had rid itself of the burden of the Tweed Ring, but the system was still intact and so was Tammany Hall. As Tilden rode the reform wave to the Governor's Mansion (which he, in fact, established) and to the very steps of the White House, the Hall sought to repolish its image under the tutelage of "Honest John" Kelly. A Tammany regular who, like Tweed, had come up through a volunteer fire company to become an alderman and congressman, Kelly had gained his nickname while serving as sheriff, apparently for not getting caught, since he had grown wealthy in the unsalaried post. One of his most impressive credentials seems to have been his presence in Europe throughout the Ring scandals, which left him, through a process of elimination, among the very few untarnished yet trusted Tammany veterans. He also gained a national reputation as the only Catholic in Congress and the vigorous foe of nativist "Know Nothings."

Kelly, in the words of one contemporary, "found it [Tammany] a horde. He left it a political army." He adroitly maneuvered among the many Democratic factions to preserve Tammany's power. His organizational skills and his awareness of the need to present the Hall positively are credited with guiding Tammany through its post-Tweed crisis. Kelly managed to keep the Hall out of trouble while putting it in order, and maintaining Democrats in office. Still, if Kelly never approached Tweed's excesses, his reformational zeal was limited; he continued the timeworn Tammany techniques of ballot-stuffing, "repeaters," bribes, and kickbacks. In the tradition of the Tweed Ring, Kelly himself was appointed city comptroller by William Wickham, whom he had gotten elected mayor in 1874.

Tammany Hall's reputation for corruption and decadence is caricatured in this 1882 Puck *cartoon based on a* New York Times *headline: "Tammany Will Send a Full Delegation to the State Convention."*

The success of immigrant groups in New York has been measurable as much by their political influence as by their wealth or social status. The political arrival of Irish Catholics was apparent by 1871, reflected in such scenes as this one, the "Grand Procession in Honor of the Fenian Exiles" past City Hall in February.

But Boss Kelly's most significant accomplishment may well have been symbolic. He was the first Irish Catholic to run Tammany Hall, thereby initiating a three-quarter-century reign by Irish Catholics that continued into the 1940s. Kelly's installation as head of the nation's most powerful machine thus represented the political arrival of those immigrants who had disembarked in the New World less than four decades earlier. Further, before relinquishing his leadership after thirteen years, Kelly was instrumental in electing New York City's first Catholic mayor, William R. Grace, in 1880, and preparing a protégé, Richard Croker, who would rule Tammany into the twentieth century.

"Dick" Croker (Tammany chiefs, unlike reformers, seemed to relish the implication of unpretentiousness conveyed by nicknames) came from Ireland as a three-year-old during the mass immigration of the 1840s and literally fought his way into politics. A stocky youth who was quick with his hands, Croker ran with the Fourth Avenue Tunnel Gang and served as a volunteer fireman, ward captain, alderman, and coroner before inheriting the Hall's leadership from a dying Kelly. His political career was stalled, but only temporarily, in 1874 when, while coroner, Croker was accused, but exonerated, of the killing of an opposing worker in an election-day brawl.

The new Boss's first test came during the complex, three-cornered 1886 mayoral campaign. Radical Henry George, proponent of antimonopolistic tax reform, was running on the United Labor party ticket, a coalition of socialists, reformers, and trade unionists, and threatened the candidacy of Democrat Abraham Hewitt, a wealthy opponent of Tweed who had been put up by Tammany's bitter intraparty rival, the County Democracy. The Republican nominee was a young legislator named Theodore Roosevelt. Croker demonstrated his political sophistication by backing Hewitt instead of splitting the Democratic vote. This enabled Hewitt to win, thereby keeping the Democrats in control and Tammany in contention.

Croker's tenure encompassed a crucial era, one characterized by the most intense immigration in city history, not of Irish this time but of Jews from Russia and eastern Europe and of Italians. Never before nor since had such a concentrated stream of foreigners arrived in the United States and settled in one location: the Lower East Side. The mass of humanity created a population density unknown in the western world and problems that overwhelmed the city's resources.

If the 1890s were gay for songwriters, they were hardly so for immigrants. Packed into dismal tenements, these impoverished refugees from despotism encountered an enemy no less ruthless: official indifference. Their needs once again

Richard Croker, shown here wearing the bowler hat, whose association with Tammany Hall coincided with the influx of hundreds of thousands of Jews and Italians, put Tammany to work on the immigrants' behalf and won their votes in return.

Right and overleaf:
Union Square, at 14th Street and Park Avenue, has served for more than a century as the city's center for radical demonstrations. Symbolic of alternatives to traditional politics and parties, it serves as another reminder of New York's rich diversity. Radical ideologies and organizations, transported from Europe by immigrants fleeing political persecution, have long played a peripheral role in city politics. As its name suggests, Union Square was labor's territory.

provided a function for Tammany, for it rendered the services that the government withheld and that radicals such as Henry George espoused. Croker keenly recognized the appeal that George's social programs held for the immigrants who were arriving in New York at the rate of 18,000 each month and sought to counter them. "We have thousands of men who are alien born," the Boss warned. "They are alone, ignorant strangers, a prey to all manner of anarchical and wild notions. Tammany looks after them for the sake of their vote, grafts them upon the Republic... and although you may not like our motives or our methods, what other agency is there by which so long a row could have been hoed so quickly or so well?"

But, as usual, Tammany was having it both ways. For while it was aiding the newcomers with handouts and advice, the Hall was simultaneously sustaining crime, vice, and exploitation through police corruption. This was known as "dirty graft" or "dishonest graft" to distinguish it from Tammany's ongoing devotion to "honest graft" or, in today's parlance, "conflict of interest" or "insider trading."

After the Civil War, what is now considered Midtown (roughly, from 14th to 42nd streets, between Fourth and Seventh avenues) seethed with everything illicit. Bordellos, gambling dens, and after-hours saloons, which burgeoned when "Blue Laws" prohibited the sale of liquor on Sundays, flourished, creating vast prospects for shakedowns and making the area choice for police assignment. When Captain Alexander (Clubber) Williams heard that he was to be transferred there, he enthused: "All my life I've never had anything but chuck steak, now I'm going to get me some tenderloin." Thus, was the Tenderloin named; in 1894, the district's commander testified that his graft was worth $8,000 annually.

By looking the other way, Croker not only encouraged widespread corruption (and, of course, opportunity) but increased the likelihood that Tammany underlings would become involved themselves and thus be unable to blow the whistle on him. After his protégé, Hugh Grant, was reelected mayor in 1890, Croker moved into an $80,000 brownstone, which he spent $100,000 in redecorating, and began indulging his interest in horse racing. He purchased a half-interest in a half-million-dollar stock farm upstate, made a similar investment in the Belle Meade stud farm in Tennessee, and bought some expensive thoroughbreds, which he sought to race in England, where he owned three homes, including stables, and an estate at Wantage.

If they knew what was going on, most New Yorkers simply shrugged until Tammany's activities were described from the pulpit of the Madison Square Presbyterian Church in early 1892 by the Rev. Charles H. Parkhurst, head of the Society for the Prevention of Crime. When Parkhurst's sermon portraying Tammany and its hirelings as "a lying, perjured, rum-soaked, libidinous lot" was printed in the *World*, it aroused enough public consternation to engage the interest of a grand jury. The jury, however, not only failed to indict anyone, it criticized Parkhurst for airing unsupported charges. This led the canny minister to hire a private detective named Charles Gardner to conduct him on an incognito tour of the Tenderloin's juiciest bawdy houses, where Parkhurst observed Gardner participating in games with nude prostitutes. When word leaked out, a new ditty made the rounds:

Dr. Parkhurst on the floor
Playing leapfrog with a whore,
Ta-ra-ra-boom-de-ay,
Ta-ra-ra-boom-de-ay.

Despite the ridicule, Parkhurst continued his "crusade" until Republican State Chairman Thomas Platt, the "Easy Boss" who ran the Republican-controlled State Legislature, created an investigatory committee headed by State Senator Clarence

Lexow of Nyack to look into the connection between politics and police corruption in New York City.

The Lexow Committee's hearings, held, ironically, in the Tweed Courthouse, consumed most of 1894, collected more than six thousand pages of testimony, devastatingly revealed Tammany's venality, assured the election of Republican reformer William Strong as mayor, and caused Croker to resign and sail off to his Wantage estate. But before he left, Croker captured the essence of New York City politics in two sentences: "Our people could not stand the rotten police corruption. They'll be back at the next election; they can't stand reform either."

In this instance, however, the Parkhurst-Lexow revelations were to have a more lasting effect. Upstate Republicans, increasingly fearful that New York City's immigrant-fed population growth would soon enable it to dominate the state, concocted a devious scheme to hold the city at bay. At the state Constitutional Convention of 1894, Elihu Root, demonstrating the ingenuity that would later win him fame as a diplomat, devised an amendment that held no two counties divided by a river could have one-half the seats in the State Senate, while each of the sixty-two counties, except Hamilton and Fulton, would have at least one member in the Assembly. The intent was to prevent Democratic New York City (Manhattan and Brooklyn were separated by the East River) from controlling the Senate, while giving a majority in the Assembly to the numerous Republican counties upstate. The delegates, mindful of the overwhelming evidence of urban corruption so recently compiled by the Lexow Committee, readily assented, and as a result, Republicans largely succeeded in holding both houses for the next half-century.

Meanwhile, Strong's reform administration, like its predecessors and successors, soon began making good on Croker's prediction. Germans and Italians were annoyed at the enforcement of Sunday closing laws that prevented them from traditionally enjoying their day off with a few drinks; Jews, struggling to make a living with pushcarts, were irate over demands for peddlers' licenses; the purveyors and participants of such "victimless" crimes as gambling and prostitution resented government intrusion. In a city as culturally diverse as New York, Tammany's sins were mitigated, in the eyes of many voters, by the Hall's laissez-faire approach to morality. And members of the working class surely appreciated the easy access Tammany gave them to the public payroll, which for many was the alternative to charity or starvation. To much of the city's immigrant population, on the other hand, reformers, invariably drawn from the city's well-to-do, native-born segment, seemed insensitive and prone to enforce their own moral values in the quest to stamp out corruption. Moreover, in their zeal to bring about efficiency, reform administrations invariably reduced the budget (and the payroll) as well as instituting civil service reforms that put ethnics at a disadvantage in the competition for city jobs. Under Mayor Strong, these hallmarks of reform were epitomized through the appointment of Theodore Roosevelt as president of a new Board of Police Commissioners.

Roosevelt possessed determination, energy, and, as his subsequent career would testify, a flair for the dramatic. Ever mindful of the benefits of publicity, he would conceal his identity and roam the Tenderloin streets at night to investigate conditions and the behavior of his police force. On one occasion, when he challenged an officer for being too familiar with a prostitute, the cop, failing to recognize Roosevelt, threatened him with a club, whereupon the commissioner identified himself, sending the policeman and prostitute disappearing into the night. While such expeditions found favor with the press, his insistent attempts to enforce the Blue Laws and upgrade civil service did not endear "T. R." nor the Strong administration to the city's substantial immigrant population. Further, Roosevelt's domineering attitude toward his fellow commissioners proved disruptive, and in 1897 he was encouraged to leave the city to become Assistant Secretary of the Navy in the ad-

Charles Francis Murphy, who shunned virtually all activities save politics, is generally regarded as Tammany's most astute operator, no small accomplishment. He ran the Hall for two decades of the twentieth century, nurturing liberal candidates and promoting progressive legislation. Murphy's bland, laconic image was vivified by his habit of practicing politics alongside a lamppost outside his Second Avenue saloon.

ministration of President William McKinley. His association with New York City public service ended, Roosevelt began his swift rise to the Presidency the following year.

The year of 1897 was one of the most significant in the city's history, important enough to bring Croker back from England. At stake was not only the mayoralty (and, as Croker had prophesied, it looked like a "Tammany year") but the mayoralty of a Greater New York, an enlarged city that, beginning January 1, 1898, would combine Brooklyn, the Bronx, Queens, and Staten Island with Manhattan to boast a total population of more than three million.

The consolidation statutes finally had been approved by an apprehensive Republican State Legislature at the urging of "Easy Boss" Platt, who anticipated, incorrectly, that Greater New York would be controlled by the Republicans through state-appointed commissions. Tammany, as might be suspected, had at least one eye on the bountiful patronage opportunities and, after initial reservations, came out solidly behind the plan. The only serious objections arose in Brooklyn, where the Democratic machine of Hugh McLaughlin justifiably foresaw a Tammany takeover, and many Anglo-American Protestants feared subjugation by "a large population of recent immigrants, and into which the political sewage of Europe is being dumped every week," as one observer put it.

As the crucial 1897 election approached, Croker, shrewdly recognizing that his influence would be a major issue, stayed in the background. But he manipulated the selection of an obscure, uncontroversial judge named Robert Van Wyck as the Democratic nominee (after the judge agreed to let Croker dispense the city's 40,000 patronage jobs). Van Wyck's opponents were Fusion candidate Seth Low, the colorless president of Columbia University and a former Brooklyn mayor, and Henry George, the labor champion who would drop dead shortly before Election Day. Tammany, with its finger on the public pulse, campaigned under the no-nonsense slogan, "To Hell with Reform!" and, after the returns poured in, was able to chant: "Well! Well! Well! Reform has gone to Hell!"

Tammany had won; but in the blind rush to reclaim power, it overplayed its hand. Rampant corruption under Van Wyck's unseeing administration evoked newspaper exposés and brought forth another investigation from Albany. This one was headed by Assemblyman Robert Mazet, whose committee report in 1900 accused the American Ice Company, a monopoly created by the city and subsequently called the "Tammany Ice Trust," of artificially inflating the price of ice to the benefit of shareholders, including Croker, Van Wyck, and Docks Commissioner Charles Francis Murphy.

The reaction to the scandal was greatest among those Tammany needed most, the countless poor, for this time they clearly were the victims of the Hall's greed. The election of 1901 held little hope for the Democrats. Croker, with McLaughlin's help, reached out for a Brooklyn lawyer named Edward Shepard who, having uncovered some election frauds in that borough, might at least claim respectability. But the choice could not have been easy for Croker. In the previous mayoralty election, Shepard had not only backed reformer Low against the Boss's Van Wyck but charged that "the most burning and disgraceful blot upon the municipal history of this country is Tammany Hall."

The Republicans and reformers reunited behind Low and this time were rewarded with an easy winner. "It would appear that Shepard is beaten," Croker told reporters as soon as he saw the early returns. "A change is a good thing sometimes. But Tammany Hall will be here when we are all gone." Shortly after, Croker, as if to confirm his pronouncement, gave up politics and left for England. While Tammany stewed under another reform administration, Croker retired to an Irish castle at Glencairn and wintered in West Palm Beach. In 1907, one of his goals was fulfilled when his horse, Orby, won the Epsom Derby.

In New York, however, the reformers, having elected the mayor, discovered they had outwitted themselves by cutting his term in half. In the wake of the Mazet revelations, thinking to harness Tammany, they had succeeded in pushing through an electoral change to limit mayoral terms to two years instead of four. As a result, the Hall was returned to power twice as fast.

The instrument for its return was Representative George McClellan, Jr., the handsome, refined, and politically experienced son of the Civil War general who had lost the presidency to Abraham Lincoln. But the strategy was the work of "Silent Charlie" Murphy, the Hall's new Boss, who would rule Tammany for twenty-two years and earn a reputation as the most brilliant and effective leader in its history. Murphy, whose only salaried public office was as docks commissioner during the "Tammany Ice Trust" scandal, preferred to be called "Commissioner" or "Mister," and was. He generally got what he wanted.

Shrewd, devout, ascetic, and laconic, Murphy was know as a unique politician who kept his options open and his mouth shut. "Most of the troubles of the world could be avoided," he once told a youthful state senator named James J. Walker, "if men opened their minds instead of their mouths." This made him anathema to newspapermen looking for quotes. To a reporter who asked his explanation for losing an election, he replied: "We didn't get enough votes." And when an aide was questioned as to why Murphy had failed to join in singing the "Star-Spangled Banner" at a Fourth of July function, the knowing response was: "Perhaps he didn't want to commit himself."

But when he wanted to, Murphy could make himself understood. William Sulzer learned this the hard way. When Sulzer, whom Murphy had gotten elected governor in 1912, refused to appoint a Tammany hack as state highway commissioner, Murphy successfully impeached him through two other political protégés: Senate Majority Leader Robert F. Wagner, Sr., and Assembly Speaker Alfred E. Smith.

Yet for all the backroom chicanery that enabled Murphy to survive Tammany's infighting for more than two decades, he led the Hall into the twentieth century figuratively as well as literally, developing quality candidates and supporting liberal, humanistic programs. Franklin D. Roosevelt eulogized him as "a genius who kept harmony, and at the same time recognized that the world moves on. It is well to remember that he had helped to accomplish much in the way of progressive legislation and social welfare in our state."

Murphy's enlightened stewardship was surely a product of the times, for this was the Progressive Era, a brief but inspired period marked by demands for new social and economic policies to curb the immense power of trusts and monopolies and to ease the lot of the immigrant masses. From the turn of the century through World War I, a spirit of change swept across the nation, fanned by settlement workers, such as Jane Addams of Chicago's Hull House and her protégé, Frances Perkins; journalists, such as Lincoln Steffens, Ida Tarbell, and Upton Sinclair; and intellectuals, such as John Dewey, William James, Thorstein Veblen, and Charles A. Beard. Linked philosophically to similar movements in England and Germany, Progressivism ignited creative and compassionate impulses in thousands of young college graduates who had ventured into such new academic fields as psychology, sociology, economics, and political science and were eager to put their ideas into practice. For them, the slums and ghettos of New York and Chicago were living laboratories where results could be seen and even measured.

One of the most influential officials to emerge from this era was Frances Perkins, who began her long career in public service at Hull House and, as President Franklin Roosevelt's Secretary of Labor, became the first woman cabinet officer. As a young social worker, she was instrumental in putting politicians in touch with the problems afflicting the poor and powerless and in proposing remedial legislation. In her book, *The Roosevelt I Knew*, she described her first encounter with Murphy.

While improving Tammany's fortunes, Richard Croker did not neglect his own and twice fled the country in the wake of investigations into corruption. From retirement in a castle in his native Ireland, Croker continued a nonpolitical relationship with his adopted land by wintering in Palm Beach, Florida. There, in 1909, he somehow managed to catch a 250-pound shark from a pier and be photographed doing so.

Certainly there was nothing social minded about the head of Tammany Hall, Charles Murphy, whom I went to see when legislation on factory buildings was before the state legislature. I went to enlist his support for this legislation. I climbed up the stairs of old Tammany Hall on 14th Street in a good deal of trepidation. Tammany Hall had a sinister reputation in New York, and I hardly knew how I would be greeted, but, as I later learned, a lady was invariably treated with respect and gallantry and a poor old woman with infinite kindness and courtesy. Mr. Murphy, solemn dignity itself, received me in a reserved but courteous way. He listened to my story and arguments. Then, leaning forward in his chair, he said quietly, "You are the young lady, aren't you, who managed to get the fifty-four-hour bill passed?"

I admitted I was.

"Well, young lady, I was opposed to that bill."

"Yes, I so gathered, Mr. Murphy."

"It is my observation," he went on, "that that bill made us many votes. I will tell the boys to give all the help they can to this new bill. Good-bye."

As I went out of the door, saying "Thank you," he said. "Are you one of these women suffragists?"

Torn between a fear of being faithless to my convictions and losing the so recently gained support of a political boss, I stammered, "Yes, I am."

"Well, I am not," he replied, "but if anybody ever gives them the vote, I hope you will remember that you would make a good Democrat."

Although Murphy's views on Progressivism are unknown, his implementation of its goals was evident. As Bronx Democratic boss Edward Flynn later observed, "You have to remember that none of the progressive legislation in Albany could have been passed unless...[Murphy] urged it and permitted it to be passed." Thus, for probably the first time in city history, reform and political power resided under the same roof. Muckraking journalist Steffens had made the point "that the leading grafters themselves should be the leaders in this 'reform movement'.... Let's give up the good men and try the strong men."

Like some of his Tammany antecedents, Murphy was a saloon owner; like most of them, he lived far beyond any discernible income. For example, when Murphy wanted to play golf, he went to the course he had built at his Long Island estate, a long way, metaphorically, from the Gas House tenement in which he and eight siblings had been reared by their Irish immigrant parents.

But wealth and recreation were secondary interests; Murphy relished politics and developed his capacity for it by listening to complaints and dispensing aid from his sidewalk "office," a lamppost outside his saloon at 20th Street and Second Avenue, the stamping ground of a Tammany local called the Anawanda Club. What set Murphy apart from other Tammany bosses was his restraint and flexibility, qualities that first came to public attention in his masterminding of the successful McClellan campaign in 1903. As Lincoln Steffens had observed: "Murphy says he will nominate for mayor a man so 'good' that his goodness will astonish New York. I don't fear a bad Tammany mayor; I dread the election of a good one."

Murphy was not afraid to put forward outstanding candidates, even though they might resist his importunings. He was responsible for some of New York's most distinguished officeholders, officials who frequently made a point of asserting their independence from him. State Supreme Court Justice William Jay Gaynor, for example, expressed his appreciation for the mayoral nomination in 1909 in these words: "So this is Tammany Hall. It is the first time I was ever here. I did not even know where it was. I had to telephone before leaving my home to find out exactly how to get here. But if this is Tammany Hall, where is the tiger, that tiger which they say is going to swallow me up? If there happens to be any swallowing up, it is not at all unlikely that I may be on the outside of the tiger."

In that election, Gaynor won in a three-way race that included Murphy's frequent foe and occasional ally, newspaper publisher William Randolph Hearst, who

Opposite and overleaf:
Progress in the development of the city's commitment to public recreation is evident in this photographic sequence of swimming facilities. In 1892, young New Yorkers shared the East River with the Fulton Fish Market. A decade or so later, the Progressive Era enclosed a pool-sized portion of the river with wooden bathhouses. In 1938, under the aegis of Robert Moses, the city unveiled the huge Astoria swimming pool, which, like Moses's Jones Beach, was designed to provide mass recreation.

ran as an independent. The new mayor immediately made his position clear. When reporters asked him what he planned to give Murphy, Gaynor said, "Suppose we give him a few kind words." But after this auspicious start, Gaynor's administration was crippled within the year when the mayor was shot in the neck by an aggrieved former city employee at a bon voyage party. The wound affected Gaynor's speech; he became depressed and irascible. Denied renomination by Murphy in 1913 (the four-year mayoral term had been reinstituted), he ran as an independent but died before the election.

Murphy's arrogant treatment of the popular Gaynor and his vindictiveness toward Sulzer, combined with Tammany's embarrassment by a police scandal that resulted in the blatant slaying of protected gambler Herman Rosenthal, made the 1913 election ripe for a reformer. He appeared in the person of John Purroy Mitchel, a socially connected lawyer and attractive president of the Board of Aldermen, who gained the Fusion nomination and easily defeated the Democratic candidate.

Mitchel wasted no time in declaring war on Tammany. In this he got the ready backing of President Woodrow Wilson, whom Murphy had alienated earlier in an intraparty dispute. The reformer dubbed the "Boy Mayor" because he was only thirty-four when elected, Mitchel did his best to hit Murphy where it hurt most: by firing every Tammany worker he could find on the city payroll. The pressure on the Hall's leadership became so intense that normally uncommunicative Murphy even called a press conference to declare that "I'm going to stay here as long as I live."

He survived, which was more than could be said for Mitchel. Various New Yorkers soon began to tire of his elitist "good government" (demeaned as "goo-goo") policies, his criticism of Catholic church-run institutions (although he was a Catholic), and his enthusiasm for American entry into World War I. By the 1917 election, most voters had gotten their fill of reform and of Mitchel. Germans were offended by his exhortations to war against the Fatherland, Irish were angered by his support for England, and Jews wanted no part of an alliance with Czarist Russia.

The stage was once again set for a Tammany comeback, and Murphy felt he had the candidate in John F. (Red Mike) Hylan, a genial, if uninspired, Brooklyn judge. What was essential, Murphy reasoned, was to oppose a reformer with a nominee who appeared free of boss domination. To this end, he reportedly had his cohorts "ram him [Hylan] down my throat." With the support of Hearst, a good friend, Hylan won the four-man race in a landslide; in fact, Mitchel barely edged out Morris Hillquit, a Socialist. (The Socialists had found significant support during this period, particularly among Jews, sending Meyer London to Congress in 1914 and a legislator to Albany in 1915. In the 1917 elections, in addition to Hillquit's strong showing, Socialists elected ten assemblymen and a judge, largely on the strength of opposition to American entry into World War I and sympathy for the labor movement.)

Mitchel, true to his beliefs, enlisted in the Army Air Corps, although overage, and was killed in 1918 when he fell out of a training plane. Interestingly, although a lifelong public official and politician, he was memorialized for his brief military career through the former Mitchel Air Force Base on Long Island.

Hylan's administration proved that intelligence was not essential to governance. The *New York Times* had described him as possessing "marvelous mental density," while an admiring associate said that "his absence of a brain helped him. It made him more congenial." Yet, Hylan presided over a city of more than five million people with skill, resolve, and atypical honesty. In fact, three different investigations failed to demonstrate mismanagement or corruption during his two four-year terms.

This is not to suggest that Hylan was independent; he was very much a creature of Murphy and a captive of Tammany. But he paid his dues through patronage, and what better way to create jobs than through municipal growth? Education got a tremendous lift with extensive school construction, commerce was benefited by the building of the Bronx Terminal Market and Staten Island piers, and the public interest served by plans for the city subway system.

Such developments were characteristic of the new style Murphy gave to Tammany: an emphasis on doing well by doing good. In pursuing such a course, his attention was turned toward a young parochial school dropout from the sidewalks of New York, a product of the Lower East Side tenements who bore the most common name in America: Smith.

Alfred Emanuel Smith's father was of German and Italian descent, his mother came from Irish stock, and he was Catholic, a fact that later would deny him the Presidency of the United States. But in his youth, his religion and his ethnicity were hardly barriers; in the immigrant-laden Fourth Ward, they were tickets to political progress. Smith's talent for making friends and making sense, combined with a distinctive voice and relentless drive, soon caught Tammany's eye. In 1903, at the age of twenty-nine, he won the first of sixteen elections and became a state assemblyman. Painstakingly learning his craft, Smith gained the respect of fellow legislators and, through his unquestioning loyalty to Tammany, the confidence of Murphy.

This unusual mixture of principle and practicality enabled Smith to become Assembly majority leader in 1911, but it made him suspect to reformers until the disastrous Triangle Shirtwaist Company fire that killed 146 immigrant seamstresses later that year. The tragedy, which exposed the greed and indifference of factory owners, inspired Smith to form an investigating commission that resulted in far-reaching social legislation and gained him a reputation as an effective progressive. As Smith's popularity rose, Murphy steered him through the tangle of city and state politics until in 1918 he was elected to the first of four two-year terms as governor. This victory was a political and sociological landmark: Smith had become the first Catholic, and the first representative of the Lower East Side immigrant culture, to be elected to the state's highest office.

But for Murphy, it was still not enough. He envisioned Smith in the White House. It would be Tammany's ultimate accomplishment, and one on which he focused all his abundant experience and sagacity. Aiming to obtain the Democratic presidential nomination for Smith in 1924, Murphy began his strategy by bringing the party's national convention to New York, where, he knew, Smith's dynamic appeal would be demonstrated every time he stepped out into the city's streets. By the spring, Murphy had made his candidate a strong contender for the summer convention that he perceived would be a divisive showdown between the rural, Prohibitionist, Protestants of the South and Midwest and the urban, "wet," Catholic delegates from the Northeast.

Murphy's vision was correct, but the Tammany chief never saw it realized. On April 25, two months before the convention was to open, he died unexpectedly at the age of sixty-five. Murphy's death stunned the city; 6,000 mourners filled St. Patrick's Cathedral and 50,000 jammed the city's sidewalks as his funeral cortege proceeded to Calvary Cemetery, where, as another of his protégés, James J. Walker, observed at graveside, "The brains of Tammany Hall lie. . . ."

But perhaps no one missed Murphy more than Smith. Despite a stirring nominating speech in which Franklin D. Roosevelt described him as the "Happy Warrior," the governor, handicapped by the loss of his mentor, watched in frustration and disappointment as a deadlock developed between him and William McAdoo, a conservative from California. Finally, with no end in sight, both allowed the delegates to nominate a compromise candidate, John W. Davis, on an unprecedented 103rd ballot. Four years later, Smith, having built an unassailable record in Alba-

Opposite and above:
In and among its scandals, Tammany Hall produced some major accomplishments for the city, the state, and the nation. Ranking high on any list would be Alfred Emanuel Smith, the Lower East Sider who, were it not for his Catholicism, might well have been president. Smith, a protégé of Charles Francis Murphy, was a natural politician endowed with crowd-pleasing boldness, vigor, and earthiness. A rare combination of idealist and pragmatist, Smith promoted humanitarian causes throughout a distinguished career as a state assemblyman, majority leader, and governor, while remaining a loyal Tammanyite who posed between Tammany leader James J. Dooling (wearing fedora) and grand sachem Thomas J. Darlington on being inducted as one of thirteen sachems. The first Catholic to be nominated for the presidency, he lost to Republican Herbert Hoover in 1928 and spent his later years attacking the New Deal programs of his erstwhile supporters.

ny, easily won the nomination and became the first Catholic to head a national ticket. However, following a bitter, bigoted campaign, he was crushed by Republican Herbert Hoover, and it would take another thirty-two years for the nation to elect a Catholic President.

It was not yet apparent, but the loss of Murphy marked the beginning of the end for Tammany Hall. There would be successors, almost beyond count, but no replacement. And even if Murphy had lived, it is doubtful that Tammany could have survived, for it was not only leadership but purpose that was to vanish. Ironically, it was Murphy's pioneering of progressive legislation and his espousal of remarkable candidates, such as Smith, Wagner, and Walker, that contributed to Tammany's demise, since it was the very success of these programs that led to their inclusion in Franklin D. Roosevelt's New Deal. And, to a significant degree, it was the New Deal's economic and social reforms that made Tammany's largesse obsolete. Moreover, Tammany's base was evaporating: Manhattan's population, more than one-half the city's in 1900, would drop to one-quarter by 1930.

But that was all in the future. Even before Roosevelt was elected president, Tammany suffered two major blows: the Seabury investigations that resurrected the Hall's affinity for arrogant corruption, shenanigans no longer tolerable to New Yorkers afflicted by the Great Depression, and the imposition of immigration quotas, which sharply depleted its supply of fresh and needy voters.

The probes, conducted by former Court of Appeals Judge Samuel Seabury, were inevitable, no doubt, given the irresponsible and irrepressible behavior of Mayor James J. Walker. Born in Greenwich Village, he was named James John by his politically active father, but everyone knew him as Jimmy, or Gentleman Jim, or Beau James. He dressed like a dandy, sometimes changing his pinch-waisted suits, spats, and derbies three times daily; he lived like a libertine, shipping his wife off to Florida so he could consort openly with his mistress, showgirl Betty (Monk) Compton; he had been a Tin Pan Alley songwriter ("Will You Love Me in December as You Do in May?") and he was quick-witted, charming, and politically shrewd. Had the Roaring Twenties sought personification, Walker would have been it.

He was called in from Albany in 1925, where he was the Democratic leader in the State Senate, when Smith decided to get rid of Hylan, who was seeking a third term. Although he was the governor's third choice, behind Surrogate James Foley and State Supreme Court Justice Robert Wagner, Sr., both of whom declined the primary race, Walker ran extraordinarily well in a nasty campaign to defeat the incumbent. Taking no chances, Walker wrung support from Hylan for the general election by appointing him to Children's Court, so that, he later commented dryly, "Now the children can be tried by their peer." The appointment probably was unnecessary: Walker drubbed the Republican, Frank D. Waterman of fountain pen fame.

It was a buoyant era, and while it lasted, Walker could do no wrong. The public didn't seem to care that he danced all night and got up at noon, giving substance to his contention that no civilized man went to bed the same day he awakened. Nor did it appear to bother them that he poured public funds into the Central Park Casino to create a splendid restaurant for wealthy insiders. After all, wasn't it worth it to be able to read in the tabloids about the antics of Jimmy and Betty or wonder if chorus girls were really whisked over by police escort to "entertain" the Tammany crowd?

Walker may have been a debonair playboy, but he was also resilient and could be tough if necessary. When a representative of Patrick Cardinal Hayes reportedly told Walker, a Catholic, to mend his profligate ways, the mayor is said to have identified two prominent parishioners with immoral reputations. "You go back and tell the Cardinal to take care of his two altar boys," Walker reputedly said, "and I'll take care of myself."

Yet, despite his hedonism, Walker was mindful of the public interest, and his term and one-half reflected such concerns: He established the city's first hospitals and sanitation departments and was responsible for starting the West Side Highway, Triborough Bridge, Queens-Midtown Tunnel, and hundreds of miles of subway track.

But the memory of Walker will ever be tied to the scandals uncovered by three Seabury investigations that began in the magistrate's courts in 1930, went through the district attorney's office, and concluded with a department-by-department scrutiny of Walker's administration. The probes by the anti-Tammany, Democratic jurist ended after the mayor, under threat of removal by then-Governor Franklin Roosevelt, resigned and fled to Europe in the late summer of 1932.

Seabury's findings were reminiscent of the Tweed revelations in their scope and blatancy. For example, James "Peter-to-Paul" McQuade, the Kings County registrar, said that he couldn't remember from whom he claimed to have borrowed a half-million dollars. The question arose when his bank accounts totaled $520,000 over a six-year period in which he had earned less than $50,000. His explanation, from which his nickname was derived, was that he kept borrowing to repay past loans. Also reminiscent of the consequences of past exposés was the fact that McQuade subsequently was nominated, and elected, Brooklyn sheriff.

When it was Walker's turn to testify, the mayor admitted that he had pushed a bus franchise through the Board of Estimate for a company that had no buses, that he shared a joint brokerage account from which he netted almost $250,000 without having contributed anything, and that he had received more than $25,000 in profits from a transaction in which he had risked nothing.

Notwithstanding his witticisms from the stand and his ongoing popularity with much of the public (women tossed roses at him when he left the courthouse), it was clear after the hearings that Walker's tenure was limited. Seabury sent Governor Roosevelt a transcript of the proceedings and recommended that Walker be removed, but while Roosevelt considered the political consequences, the 1932 Democratic National Convention opened in Chicago. The event was extraordinary: both Roosevelt and Smith were leading presidential contenders; Tammany, led by taciturn John Curry, who disliked Roosevelt intensely, backed Smith; other New York Democratic leaders, such as James Farley of Rockland and Edward Flynn of the Bronx, supported Roosevelt; and there was Walker, a Tammany product whose past derived from Smith but whose future rested with Roosevelt.

When the split New York delegation was polled, Walker unhesitatingly voted for Smith, drawing praise from the morally upright former governor who in recent years had become estranged over Walker's life-style. "Good old Jimsie," Smith exalted, "blood is thicker than water." Roosevelt was nominated on the fourth ballot, partially *because* of Tammany's opposition, and, as if to underline his independence, Walker then joined fellow Tammanyites in refusing to make the nomination unanimous. Later that summer, while Roosevelt pondered whether to risk alienating New York's voters by ousting the still-popular Walker or damaging his presidential image by failing to, the mayor quit and, in what had become a Tammany tradition, took off for Europe.

Tammany's stock continued to drop, abetted by Curry's stubbornness in refusing to accept Roosevelt's burgeoning political influence. By the fall of 1932, Smith had sufficiently overcome his differences with Roosevelt to join the governor in backing Lieutenant Governor Herbert H. Lehman for the Democratic gubernatorial nomination. But Curry refused to go along. At the convention, with balloting about to begin, Smith told Curry that if he didn't join in supporting Lehman, Smith would retaliate by running for mayor and dumping the recalcitrant Tammany boss. "On what ticket?" Curry asked defiantly. "Hell," Smith snorted, "on a Chinese laundry ticket."

Few public officials have better reflected their times than James J. Walker, the dapper, devil-may-care, ex-songwriter who nominally occupied City Hall during the rip-roaring Twenties. Known as "Beau James," Walker simultaneously entertained his constituents and showgirl mistress to the apparent satisfaction of both. But the harshness of the Depression made the debonair mayor's excesses unpalatable, and his administration's fiscal capers brought on the Seabury investigations. A host of flunkies preceded the mayor to the witness stand in 1932, unquestionably establishing the transgression probers had charged. While Walker, pictured here during the investigation, appeared nonchalant and retorted wittily under interrogation by former Court of Appeals Judge Samuel Seabury, his guilt was obvious. Seabury, an anti-Tammany Democrat, called on then-Governor Franklin D. Roosevelt to remove the mayor from office, but Walker saved him the trouble by resigning and sailing off to Europe.

The New Deal of President Franklin D. Roosevelt brought significant change to New York City, particularly for the burgeoning poor. Jobs, services, and housing were part of the agenda designed to lift the nation out of the Depression. Among the physical improvements was the replacement of unfit and dangerous tenements with low-income public housing.

The mayoral vacancy was filled temporarily by the head of the Board of Aldermen, Joseph V. "Holy Joe" McKee, a potentially serious reformer who lasted only until Tammany could get rid of him. The first opportunity was the special election called to fill Walker's unexpired term. Curry's man was Surrogate John P. O'Brien, who, with Tammany's backing, beat McKee and wasted no time in establishing his credentials. Asked by reporters who his police commissioner would be, the new mayor replied: "I don't know. They haven't told me yet." Not surprisingly, O'Brien was Curry's choice to succeed himself in 1933, when voters were to elect a mayor for a full, four-year term. O'Brien's performance on the campaign trail provided reporters with plenty of copy and Tammany with plenty of headaches. While seeking Jewish votes in a synagogue talk, he expressed admiration for "that scientist of scientists, Albert Weinstein." His most unintentionally memorable speech may have been made in Harlem, where he proudly declared, "I may be white, but my heart is as black as yours."

But O'Brien's malapropisms were not his only problem in 1933. Anti-Tammany Democrats, led by Farley and Flynn, with, no doubt, the blessing of Roosevelt, created a third party that ran McKee and siphoned sufficient votes from O'Brien to elect a Fusion candidate often described as New York's greatest mayor. In Fiorello H. La Guardia, New Yorkers finally had a reformer of immigrant origins, a leader who was honest, dedicated, progressive, and colorful. Born in Greenwich Village, reared in Arizona and Trieste, he spoke seven languages, was a lawyer, and learned firsthand of immigrant problems as an interpreter at Ellis Island. La Guardia was comprised of so many strains he was a figurative "balanced ticket": His father was Italian, his mother was Jewish, his first wife was an Italian Catholic, his second was a German Lutheran, and he was an Episcopalian.

This image as a man of the people was reinforced by a dozen years in Congress where, as the first representative of Italian descent, he distinguished himself sufficiently in support of liberal causes to alienate fellow Republicans. La Guardia's impact on regular party politics in New York City during his three terms (no other reformer had served more than one) was devastating. Running with both Republican and Independent backing initially, and subsequently with the support of the American Labor and even Communist parties, he avoided obligation to any single political organization and enjoyed the freedom to reward and punish solely in furtherance of his goals. His fierce independence attracted a host of outstanding public servants to his administration, although his egotism and tyrannical demands made such service hazardous. Nevertheless, La Guardia brought a new level of responsibility and expertise to municipal government. This, together with the immense popularity engendered by his compelling personality and spontaneous behavior, dumped the final shovelfuls of dirt on Tammany's coffin.

If Walker personified the Jazz Age, La Guardia was made for the Depression. Determined to revive the city that economic disaster had laid low and that Tammany had ignored, the feisty "Little Flower" cut the payroll, sliced salaries, imposed a sales tax, and lured New Deal funds to raze, rehabilitate, build, and sustain. Washington's assistance was crucial to the city's recovery, and it doubtless was no handicap that Roosevelt saw a way to help bring the city back to life while burying Tammany. Instrumental to La Guardia throughout his tenure was Parks Commissioner Robert Moses, whose dedication and vision matched the mayor's and whose efficiency and thoroughness won the admiration of New Deal administrators and the combination to their vaults.

The relationship between La Guardia and Moses was complex, probably because the two were similar in so many respects: idealistic, autocratic, egocentric, and driven. Both demanded obeisance from subordinates and did not hesitate to extract it through humiliation. And while the mayor would ceremoniously present a bronze bone to commissioners who pulled boners, he was unable to cow Moses and, as a consequence, respected him. Moses, in turn, would use the threat of resigning

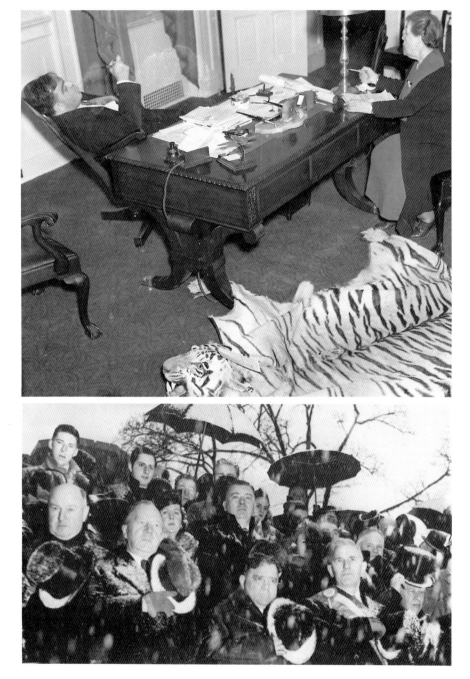

The arrival of the Depression signaled the departure of Tammany, at least as the determinant of New York City elections. The causes were multiple, but a principal factor in the Hall's demise was Fiorello H. La Guardia, a dynamic, progressive Republican who became the city's first reform mayor with immigrant roots. Independent, outgoing, and politically shrewd, he was an extraordinary newsmaker, as demonstrated by his appropriation of a tiger-skin rug to dramatize his second defeat of Tammany in 1937.

All New York mayors are Irish on St. Patrick's Day, assuming they may want to seek reelection, and La Guardia was no exception, his Italian father and Jewish mother notwithstanding. In 1940, he joined in the requisite tribute, together with Postmaster General James A. Farley, bottom left, and former Governor Al Smith, bottom right, shielding his head from the falling snow.

to force reluctant approval from the mayor (a technique La Guardia deflected with ridicule by handing the commissioner a pad of printed resignation forms).

Although working *for* La Guardia might have been painful, *not* working for him hurt even more, as tens of thousands of Irish Tammanyites discovered when they were chopped from the city payroll. The ethnic makeup of the municipal work force was soon altered as the iconoclastic mayor hired Italians and Jews in appreciable numbers. But one substantial segment of New York's population remained unaffected by La Guardia's early budgetary maneuvers. Blacks, long neglected, held an insignificant share of public jobs.

The simmering, immigrant-laden East Harlem ghetto that had produced fiery Fiorello La Guardia replaced him with another unconventional New York politician, Vito Marcantonio. Perhaps the most controversial political figure in recent city history, "Marc" developed an almost worshipful following among his constituents but was maligned and shunned by others as a Communist or Soviet dupe. A committed radical, he infuriated fellow congressmen by uniformly opposing United States foreign policy during the Cold War. When his predominantly Italian-Jewish district became the focal point of Puerto Rican migration, he dutifully met their social and political needs as Tammany had met those of earlier newcomers.

While the flow of immigrants from Europe had been cut to a trickle during the 1920s through federally imposed quotas, New York continued to attract those seeking escape from political persecution and opportunity for economic improvement. These newest arrivals were Americans, blacks from the rural South who migrated North in search of jobs in factories. What they found, more often, was discrimination: in employment, in housing, and in politics. Offered only the most menial jobs, they were shunted into neighborhoods that whites quickly deserted, creating black enclaves that became the vast, overcrowded, untended, and politically ignored ghettoes of Harlem in Manhattan, Bedford-Stuyvesant in Brooklyn, and South Jamaica in Queens.

Franklin Roosevelt's promises of economic and social progress and Eleanor Roosevelt's involvement in programs to help the needy and combat prejudice were pivotal in moving blacks from their traditional Republican affiliation to the Democratic party. Benefited by New Deal housing construction, La Guardia's commitment to civil service reform, and a few high-level mayoral appointments, blacks did experience some gains during the 1930s and '40s.

But there were surely pains. Moses, who was dedicating playgrounds throughout the city at the incredible rate of better than one a week in the mid-1930s, opened only one in central Harlem. And while it is true that not a single school had been constructed in Harlem for a quarter-century preceding La Guardia's election, it took him four years to build the first. Moreover, the deadly Harlem race riots of 1935 and 1943 broke out during La Guardia's administration, although the mayor was credited with intelligence and restraint in handling them.

Associates contend that La Guardia was aware of and sympathetic to the plight of New York's blacks but lacked the resources to deal with the deep-rooted dilemma. He once admitted as much in telling a group of blacks: "I am as helpless in handling a large-scale economic problem as the League of Nations was in preventing the war between Italy and Ethiopia."

Toward the end of the black migration, another immigrant group came to search for fulfillment and to challenge the city's capacity to cope with change. Puerto Ricans began arriving in New York in substantial numbers during the La Guardia years, moved into Italian-Jewish East Harlem, and became the special concern of the mayor's successor in Congress and protégé, Vito Marcantonio.

Among the most controversial politicians in modern city history, "Marc" was worshiped by his constituents and abhorred by most of the Establishment, including the press. Reared in the ghetto that became "Spanish Harlem," he combined a radical left-wing orientation with diligent concern for the bread-and-butter realities of the impoverished district he served for seven congressional terms. His freewheeling style found him perennially gaining and losing organizational support, and at various times he ran as a candidate of the Republican, Democratic, and American Labor parties. But Marcantonio's adherence to positions advocated by the American Communist Party made him a broad target, as demonstrated in 1950 when, after he attacked President Harry Truman's decision to defend South Korea with American troops, the Republican, Democratic, and Liberal parties united behind a challenger, James Donovan. Even so, Marcantonio lost by only 14,000 votes, receiving more than 41 percent of the total. He died unexpectedly from a heart attack in 1954 while preparing a comeback against Donovan. A lifelong Catholic who was wearing a crucifix when he died, he was denied burial in consecrated ground by the New York Archdiocese, although more than 20,000 mourners paid their last respects.

The political careers of Marcantonio and, to a greater degree, La Guardia indicated that the support of Tammany was no longer necessary for success in New York. But in both cases the triumphs were personal, accomplished without benefit of ongoing organizations and without thought to successors. And so when La Guardia, ailing with cancer and sick at heart over failing to gain either Democratic backing for the United States Senatorial nomination he craved or Republican and Liberal support for a fourth mayoral run, left office in 1945, Tammany was able to rise from the grave.

The vehicle for the Hall's resurrection was crusading Brooklyn District Attorney William "Bill-O" O'Dwyer, the Irish-born former hod carrier and cop who had gotten a national reputation breaking up Murder, Inc. O'Dwyer's tenure proved a mixed bag of substance and scandal. His notable achievements, such as locating the United Nations headquarters in Manhattan, building public schools and public housing, and creating the city's first traffic department, were besmirched during his second term by revelations of extensive graft that were tied closely to City Hall. With investigators seemingly on his trail, O'Dwyer wangled an ambassadorship to Mexico from President Truman in 1950. The following year the still-popular former mayor returned to his beloved New York, but it was, sadly, to testify before the Kefauver Committee investigating links between politics and organized crime.

O'Dwyer's departure left the city in the questionable hands of Vincent Impellitteri, who as City Council president became acting mayor. Given "Impy's" political inexperience and passive manner, the title was not inappropriate. (When an aide suggested that Impellitteri call the five borough presidents to a meeting, he wondered aloud, "You think they'll come?") But with the help of a youthful speechwriter named Sydney S. Baron, Impy defeated Tammany Boss Carmine DeSapio's candidate, State Supreme Court Justice Ferdinand Pecora, in a special mayoral election a few months later. Baron, cleverly using scare tactics that meshed Tammany's underworld connections during the O'Dwyer years with reports that crime boss Frank Costello was currently calling the shots there, cast the Hall in its old corrupt image, with Impy as a straight-shooting challenger. ("If Pecora is elected," said one campaign slogan, "Frank Costello will be your mayor.") In November 1950, Impellitteri made New York history by becoming the first Independent to be elected mayor.

But while Impy got elected, Robert Moses became mayor. Moses, who had agreed to endorse Impellitteri if he were given full control of city construction, soon expanded his authority in all directions, dictating policies, determining projects, and even making top-level appointments. That the decisions proved highly unpopular became evident three years later when Robert F. Wagner, Jr., a DeSapio choice, crushed incumbent Impellitteri in the Democratic primary and easily won the 1953 general election.

Tammany, miraculously, was still alive. And with the recent death of veteran Bronx boss Ed Flynn, DeSapio, the first Italian-American to head the Hall, moved quickly to assert leadership throughout New York State. A year after electing Wagner mayor, he put Averell Harriman in the Governor's Mansion and was lauded as the nation's new kingmaker. Despite owing his job to Costello, and notwithstanding the ethnic stereotyping and dark glasses that made sinister connections easily imaginable, DeSapio emerged as far more of a reformer than any of his predecessors save Murphy. Intelligent and far sighted, he sought to combat his—and Tammany's—shadow image by becoming very public. "I am the leader of Tammany Hall," he proudly declared in a Harvard Law School lecture. "I bear this title with gratitude and pride. I am proud of the tradition, the heritage, the record of Tammany Hall." He adopted modern strategies and techniques to enhance the tradition-bound organization's effectiveness, and, like Murphy, he recognized the desirability of running worthwhile candidates who would prove to be able administrators. To this end, he had selected Wagner, and on his election, encouraged and assisted the new mayor in making first-rate appointments.

Wagner had literally grown up learning politics. His father, Robert F. Wagner, Sr., had been instrumental as a United States Senator in bringing about New Deal

The closest thing to a family dynasty in recent city politics has been the Wagners. Robert F. Wagner, Sr., a German immigrant, served as a distinguished United States senator during the New Deal era. His son, Mayor Robert F. Wagner, Jr., shown leaving a polling booth in 1961 when he won a third term, defeated opponents by running against Tammany Hall, which, in fact, had gotten him elected. His son, also known as Robert F. Wagner, Jr., has served as deputy mayor and president of the Board of Education during the administration of Mayor Edward I. Koch.

Republican mayors emerge in New York City perhaps once in a generation, and for the turbulent 1960s, it was John V. Lindsay, a liberal, silk-stocking district congressman who twice captured City Hall. Probably his proudest accomplishment was preventing widespread rioting during the tumultuous summer of 1967, when he toured minority neighborhoods urging calm. Lindsay, second from left, is seen here in Harlem, with Bronx Borough President Herman Badillo, second from right, and two other popular Puerto Ricans, lightweight boxing champion Carlos Ortiz, left, and former light heavyweight champ Jose Torres.

Above right:
The political strength of the city's Puerto Rican community has grown with its population but has been confined largely to areas such as East (Spanish) Harlem and the South Bronx. Although blacks and Latinos constitute a near majority of New York's residents, the inability of the two groups to cooperate politically has limited their power. Attempts to organize at the grass roots, through political clubs such as the one pictured in the early 1960s, have produced some results.

reforms in housing and labor, and young Wagner was there, absorbing the lessons and retaining a social awareness. Although he was bland and indecisive, his administration provided the city with much needed middle-income housing and dealt effectively with problems in education, health, traffic, and civil rights. He modernized civil service, increased the police force, and created the office of city administrator. Running for reelection in 1957, he overwhelmed his Republican opponent.

But as his second term ran down, Wagner sensed problems from a growing reform movement that opposed Tammany and wanted DeSapio's scalp. With incredible gall, instead of running against his Democratic opponent, Arthur Levitt, Wagner ran *against* his mentor, DeSapio, *against* his organization, Tammany Hall, and *against* his own record as mayor. And he won. Perhaps even more important, DeSapio lost. Ironically, because of reforms DeSapio had introduced, he forfeited his district leadership, his twelve-year reign as Tammany chief, his place on the Democratic National Committee, and even his run-of-the-mill membership on the county committee.

Wagner had driven a stake through Tammany's heart. DeSapio's enlightened direction had given a fresh life and look to the old Hall, but without him, the tiger was indeed toothless. The old formulas no longer applied. Turkeys at Christmas had been supplanted by federal welfare programs, patronage jobs had been erased by civil service, disoriented immigrants no longer stood in confusion on the docks, and Tammany had never really reached out to the newest New Yorkers, migrant blacks and Puerto Ricans.

If Tammany now had a function, it was a negative one: Wagner's success provided tangible evidence of the benefits of running *against* Tammany. And so while New York continued to be an overwhelmingly Democratic city, a new strategy evolved: Political hopefuls, including Democrats, stuffed and mounted the defanged Tammany tiger and portrayed the harmless creature as a fearsome alternative.

With Tammany essentially a phantom, the New York political scene took on a somewhat surrealistic appearance. Without the structure provided by the Hall, nothing was quite what it seemed to be. For example, everybody claimed to be running against the "bosses," but who were they? One boss who emerged to run an antiboss campaign was Alex Rose, head of the millinery union and a founder of the Liberal party. (The Liberal party had been formed in 1944 by anti-Communist garment union leaders who had felt uncomfortable in the American Labor party, which by then had fallen under Communist control. The American Labor party had been created in 1936 by garment union leaders to enable New York Socialists and left-wing unionists to vote for Franklin D. Roosevelt without pulling the Democratic lever and simultaneously benefiting the hated Tammany organization.)

Rose helped Wagner endure the loss of DeSapio (which of course Wagner himself had engineered) by becoming Wagner's principal political adviser during the mayor's third term. And Rose had learned to enjoy the role. When Wagner decided he had had enough of City Hall after twelve years and looked hopefully toward Albany in 1965, Rose forged an alliance with the Republicans to sponsor John V. Lindsay, a charismatic, liberal Republican congressman with a loyal constituency that had sent him to Washington for four terms.

As city voters tried to absorb the new alignments, the picture became further distorted when the three-year-old Conservative party entered the 1965 mayoralty campaign in the person of political journalist William F. Buckley. It was Buckley's intention to defeat Lindsay by siphoning off Republican votes, but postelection analysts concluded he actually had helped Lindsay win a slim victory over Democrat Abraham Beame by drawing more from Democrats than Republicans.

Lindsay, a striking contrast to the phlegmatic Wagner, gave the mayoralty a new look as, in a style eminently suited to television, he involved himself actively in the mainstream of city life. Lindsay's most memorable achievement for many came when he walked the festering streets of Harlem to urge calmness while other Northern ghettos were exploding with violence.

But during a period of tense racial relations, the mayor's attitudes gained him harsh critics as well as strong supporters. What some regarded as compassion and concern, others derided as capitulation and surrender. It was thus not surprising when, in his 1969 bid for reelection, Lindsay had to run as a Liberal-Independent after being defeated in the Republican primary by John Marchi, a conservative state senator from Staten Island. What was surprising, however, in a city where three out of four voters were Democrats, was his victory over Democrat Mario Procaccino.

In his second term, Lindsay found himself grappling with a Pandora's box of urban ills: police corruption, fare boosts, rioting, school conflicts, poverty, and fiscal problems. Perhaps as much to get away as to get ahead, the mayor increasingly turned his attention toward national politics. Confirming what many critics had long contended, Lindsay joined the Democratic party in the summer of 1971 to make a run at the presidency via the state primaries. But it was not to be. After defeats in Florida and Wisconsin, he shelved that dream and, edging ever further from the political wars, declined to seek reelection in 1973. His last hurrah, at least to date, came in 1980 when he lost the Republican Senate primary.

While Lindsay was gazing beyond City Hall, the city's top-ranking Democrat, Comptroller Abraham Beame, had his eye on the mayor's office. An accountant and politician, Beame had first combined these two interests in 1946, when Mayor O'Dwyer named him assistant budget director, and went on to keep the city's books for Impellitteri and Wagner. A loser to Lindsay in 1965, Beame went private for four years as a financial consultant before winning the comptroller's post in 1969, in the same election that saw Lindsay returned as mayor. Short, soft-spoken, and sedate, Beame brought one unquestionable qualification to the 1973 campaign: fiscal competence. And it took him to City Hall as New York's first Jewish mayor. It

Old-style politics of the kind that enabled Tammany Hall to run New York City for a century is still being practiced by James McManus at the McManus Democratic Club on West 48th Street. In a room decorated with political memorabilia, including a testimonial to his grandfather, Thomas, who founded the club in 1891, Democratic district leader McManus helps his frustrated constituents through the bureaucratic maze, much as his forebears did with the immigrant New Yorkers of earlier generations.

Edward I. Koch, New York's second Jewish mayor (the first was his predecessor, Abraham Beame) achieved significant popularity despite strong opposition from leaders of minority groups, corruption among appointees, and an irascible personality. He won admiration for his efforts to end the city's fiscal crisis, his down-to-earth manner, and his willingness to confront critics.

was consequently somewhat startling for New Yorkers to discover Mayor Beame presiding over the worst fiscal crisis in the city's history.

The 1975 fiscal crisis had its roots in the post-World War II era when more than one million blacks and Puerto Ricans came to New York City in search of opportunity and found poverty instead: The manufacturing jobs that had sustained prior immigrants had vanished. So they turned to public assistance. During the same era, almost one million middle-class taxpayers had moved to the suburbs, reducing the city's ability to bear these new costs. So the city had to borrow.

Blame for the final crunch has been assigned to a variety of officials and institutions: to Lindsay's spending, to Beame's creative bookkeeping, to the cost of public employees' contracts and municipal services, and to the bankers and businessmen who loaned money to the city for years and then turned off the tap. But if the responsibility was ambiguous, the severity was quite clear. With about $6 billion in debts coming due in early 1975, the public credit markets refused to provide New York with any more loans. And loans were the only means for the city to pay its bills. In all but a strict legal sense, the largest city in the richest nation was bankrupt.

The rescue operation was organized by Governor Hugh Carey, who, together with the financial community, in June 1975 created the Municipal Assistance Corporation (MAC), which sold bonds to raise money on the city's behalf. In September, Carey and the State Legislature formed the state Emergency Financial Control Board to oversee the city's fiscal policies. Austerity measures were then imposed throughout the city: municipal unions agreed to a wage freeze, a 20 percent reduction in their labor force, and investment of their pension funds in MAC bonds; free tuition was ended at the City University of New York; hospital facilities were reduced; day-care centers were closed; free dental care for children was eliminated; construction on thirteen schools was frozen; welfare expenditures were cut below minimal levels; and bridges and roads were allowed to deteriorate.

Despite these measures, by the end of Beame's term in 1977 the city was still in

Tammany Hall's decline was precipitated by a growing bureaucracy that replaced personal relationships and support by political bosses and wardheelers with anonymous municipal employees.

such critical condition that six Democrats rushed in to challenge him in the primary. The winner, who went on to victory in November, was five-term Manhattan congressman Edward I. Koch, a Jewish liberal who was rated "100 percent" by Americans for Democratic Action and who had twice defeated DeSapio for the leadership of a Greenwich Village district. A former member of the House Banking and Currency Committee and the House Appropriations Committee and a congressional observer on the Emergency Financial Control Board, Koch succeeded in wringing more than $1 billion in federal loan guarantees from Congress and Democratic President Jimmy Carter. By 1981, the city adopted a balanced budget, although Koch was accused of accomplishing this feat on the backs of the poor. And by 1986, with the controversial but popular mayor serving his third term, the fiscal crisis appeared over as the Emergency Financial Control Board relinquished much of the power it held over the city's affairs.

Brash, outspoken, and feisty have been some of the adjectives used to describe the mayor, who seemed never at a loss for words, unless, said his critics, they were, "I was wrong." A folksy manner and quick retort carried him through countless challenges, as he deflected criticism about corruption, divisiveness, and insensitivity to the needs of minorities. Yet, without benefit of a Tammany Hall, Koch piled up ever-increasing majorities in a city that is almost half black or Latino. When he asked his favorite question, "How'm I doin'?" it was because he already knew the answer.

New York has surely survived without Tammany; many would contend it has thrived. And, clearly, the need for organizations like it has diminished. But even without nostalgia, it may be possible to lament the passing of an institution that offered advice and encouragement and solace, as well as sustenance; that listened, as well as spoke; that had a heart. For millions of immigrants, a concerned Tammany became the antidote to an indifferent Ellis Island; with all its faults, the embodiment of the real America, a nation that would never quite match the Statue of Liberty's message. For the newest New Yorkers, something is missing.

Like the legendary immigrant who parlays energy, enterprise, and chance into success, New York City's rise to become the commercial capital of the nation, and probably the world, began humbly. For almost all of its first two centuries, it ranked behind Boston and Philadelphia, and, for most of that period, even Charleston, as a trading center for foreign goods. Not until the War of 1812 had ended, fully two hundred years after New York's first recorded commerce, did the city become the nation's leading port, a role that would lead to its overall economic supremacy.

Once established as America's primary seaport, there was no stopping New York. Snatching the initiative in foreign and domestic trade, it took off like a clipper before the wind, never to be challenged seriously. After the Civil War, the new metropolis focused its energies on manufacturing, asserting dominance in that capacity, too, through World War II. Since the 1950s, the city has taken on still another identity—as a purveyor of services: in banking, securities, real estate, law, communications, advertising, publishing, entertainment, data processing.

Each of New York's three economic eras—trade, manufacturing, and services—shaped the destinies of different kinds of New Yorkers. For each manifested different needs, each offered and withheld different opportunities. For immigrants, timing often determined success or failure. Those from Europe, fortunate enough to enter during the city's manufacturing phase, found no shortage of work, although exploitation and hardship surely came with the job. But earlier newcomers, such as the so-called "Famine Irish," encountered unemployment as well as abysmal living conditions. And more recent arrivals, mostly from the rural South or Caribbean, often insufficiently fluent or skilled to compete in a more sophisticated market, have discovered a largely unrewarding and indifferent New York. Yet they and their Asian counterparts still come.

From the outset, immigrants recognized New York's potential. The Dutch, a major sea power during the seventeenth century, were the first outsiders to exploit the area's sterling natural advantages—its location and harbor—as an outlet for their fur trade. In 1664, just about fifty years after the Dutch had created New Amsterdam, the English, their challengers on both land in the New World and sea throughout the whole world, seized the city, renamed it New York, and substituted flour for pelts as the major export. New York did not flourish under British rule. In fact, Boston surpassed it at the beginning of the eighteenth century and Philadelphia did so toward the end. Only by slapping a duty on British goods shipped through Boston did New York manage to meet and eventually beat its New England competition.

New York was severely afflicted by the Revolutionary War. It was devastated by seven years of British occupation while the rival ports of Philadelphia and Boston were held by the enemy for far shorter periods and suffered significantly less destruction. Despite its condition, New York's attributes were not unnoticed. The French statesman Talleyrand wrote to a West Indies trader in 1795 that "the city which appears to me to be the best situated to maintain these constant connections is New York. Its good and convenient harbor, which is never closed by ice, its central position to which large rivers bring the produce of the whole country, appear to me to be decisive advantages. Philadelphia is too buried in the land.... Boston is too much at the extremity of the country...." Such accolades notwithstanding, New York limped through the post-Revolutionary decades. In 1815, however, it was rewarded far beyond its expectations when, at the conclusion of the War of 1812, the British shipped millions of dollars worth of manufactured goods that had been stockpiled during the conflict to the import-starved city, rocketing it ahead of its competitors.

Other developments consolidated this windfall. A vast amount of business was generated in 1818 by the inauguration of regularly scheduled "packet ship" service between New York and Liverpool. But the most significant commercial break-

New York's contemporary self-characterization as a "World Trade Center," a description reinforced by the name of the twin 110-story towers from which this view of the harbor is seen, would have been unimaginable to the city's seventeenth-century and eighteenth-century residents, who saw their city ranked fourth in the country, behind Boston, Philadelphia, and Charleston. But a combination of circumstances after the War of 1812 gave New York a boost as a leading American port, a status that was consolidated with the arrival of the first wave of immigrants in the mid-nineteenth century.

through came in 1825 with the opening of the Erie Canal. This extraordinary project of Governor DeWitt Clinton, eight years in the making, created a water route to the Great Lakes, facilitating easy and cheap access to the burgeoning interior. While it had cost $120 and taken three weeks to ship a $40 ton of wheat from Buffalo to New York overland, the canal reduced the shipping cost to only $6 and the time to eight days. "Clinton's Ditch," by connecting the farmlands of the Midwest with the eastern seaboard and, through it, Europe, established an invaluable conduit that enabled the exchange of agricultural produce and manufactured products.

The growth of New York's waterfront brought other abundant commercial rewards. There was, of course, a need for outfitting and supplying the ships and crews, so a whole range of auxiliary businesses developed: sailmakers, shipwrights, coopers, chandlers, and tailors (whose cheap clothing for sailors was called "slop work"). And other peripheral, although no less substantial, seafaring needs were met by saloons, brothels, and cheap hotels and restaurants, which soon flourished near the docks, along with warehouses and countinghouses.

Shipping involved risks and capital, which generated the need for insurance and credit. This precipitated the creation or expansion of insurance companies and commercial banks. The import and export trade in commodities led to speculation in those products and added to the securities transactions that had engaged brokers for years under a buttonwood (sycamore) tree on the north side of Wall Street, between William and Pearl, or at the Tontine Coffee House. But by 1817, transactions had become brisk enough to organize the New York Stock and Exchange Board, forerunner of the world's most influential trading center for securities.

While the city's financial institutions, and particularly the New York Stock Exchange, often have been characterized as exclusively Anglo-Saxon Protestant preserves, in fact, immigrants and New Yorkers of foreign extraction have played key roles there throughout history. The value of overseas contacts, which immigrants frequently possessed, and the relative ease of entering the stock market in the nineteenth century made Wall Street attractive to many foreign-born New Yorkers. For example, five of the twenty-four signatories of the 1792 "Buttonwood Agreement" setting guidelines for the sale of stocks were Sephardic Jews. And although Anglo-Saxons have dominated the New York Stock Exchange, Irish Catholics and German Jews were active in forming brokerage firms before the Civil War and have maintained a significant presence on Wall Street throughout the twentieth century.

During the colonial and Revolutionary periods, immigration to America came primarily from the British Isles, Holland, and Germany, although a considerable number of black slaves were brought in chains from Africa beginning in 1626, initially by the Dutch and subsequently by the English. The principal occupation in those early days was farming, but as the city's seaport developed, word spread to New England, where entrepreneurs and white-collar workers—merchants, businessmen, clerks, and bookkeepers—scented business, migrated to New York, and readily found it. Foreigners were less fortunate. When the first substantial wave of immigrants arrived in the mid-nineteenth century, it was less because they were needed than because they were fleeing either political oppression or economic dislocation, in the case of the Germans, or starvation, in the case of the Irish.

On their arrival, without plans, funds, friends, or skills, the Irish refugees from the potato famines of the 1840s took what work they could find, which frequently was unskilled and usually unfamiliar. Most of them had grown up in rural areas and were as totally unprepared for urban life as they had been for the terrible voyage that brought them to America. The "Famine Irish" were compelled to subsist on the lowest economic level: the men as laborers, the women as domestic ser-

Shipping was the chief economic activity until the Civil War period, and it stimulated a variety of other businesses, including, naturally, shipbuilding.

vants. It was Irishmen who laid track, dug canals, unloaded cargo, waited on tables, and built roads. And it was Irish women who cleaned houses, washed dishes, scrubbed floors, sewed clothing, and, when necessity demanded, submitted to even greater exploitation as prostitutes.

The status of the Irish in New York was evident to such observers as Mark Beaufoy, a visiting Englishman, who pointed out in 1820 that "the lowest stations of the hard-working classes are generally filled by Irishmen, who are as much vilified here, whether justly or not I cannot tell, as in England or Scotland."

In his travels around North America, Beaufoy noted, "It is a remark made in every society, and every village of this immense country, that the Scotch, English, Germans, and Dutch, all get on and thrive; but the Irish labourer very rarely attains independence, changing only the nature of his toil, from the hackney coachman to the porter, the paver, or the hired drudge."

Two decades later, Charles Dickens recorded similar impressions of two New York Irishmen in *American Notes:* "You might know them, if they were masked, by their long-tailed blue coats and bright buttons, and their drab trousers, which they wear like men well used to working dresses, who are easy in no others. It would be hard to keep your model republics going without the countrymen and countrywomen of those two laborers. For who else would dig, and delve, and drudge, and do domestic work, and make canals and roads, and execute great lines of Internal Improvement!"

Derogation of the Irish was not confined to words. Thomas Nast, the corrosive *Harper's Weekly* cartoonist who later focused public awareness on the corruption of Tammany boss William Marcy Tweed, expressed his nativist feelings by routinely portraying Irishmen as apelike drunkards, helping to create and maintain an atmosphere of bigotry and discrimination.

The relegation of the Irish to the bottom rung of New York's economic ladder is documented by mid-nineteenth century census figures showing that fully seven-eighths of the city's laborers and three-quarters of its servants were Irish. Moreover, other statistics indicated their inability to escape those undesirable jobs: More than half of the city's male Irish workers were day laborers or cartmen and about one-quarter of all Irish females were domestic servants.

As is invariably the case, the workers most oppressed were most vulnerable to victimization. Like contemporary migrant farm workers, Irish railroad laborers were often compelled to buy at company stores, where unscrupulous employers charged exorbitantly or paid them in overpriced whisky or merchandise. When immigrant labor was needed, advertisements were placed in city papers listing attractive jobs in distant places. Irish hopefuls would travel hundreds of miles at their own expense only to discover a surplus of applicants competing to accept reduced wages rather than return empty-handed.

In the winter of 1851, such chicanery was employed by railroad contractors in Upstate New York. A witness reported that "there was no recourse for the unfortunate people; the country presented nothing to the view but a frozen wilderness of ice and snow, and what was to be done? They proposed to work for the reduced wages, and drag out life on it until something better might offer; but a few over half were allowed to stay; the rest were pronounced troublesome, and driven off, with their families, to perish . . . in the midst of a fearful American winter." He added that the Irish were held in such low esteem and such occurrences so common that newspapers barely noted them.

Such frustrations and the tedium of the work often led to drinking and fighting, sometimes through the instigation of conniving bosses. The *Irish American* in 1852 reported, according to a laborer named Michael McQuade, that "a great many of the contractors have themselves confessed to me that they got up those fights on

Driven by hunger, the "Famine Irish," who came to New York beginning in the 1840s, took whatever work was available. For the men, it often meant unskilled labor; for the women, jobs as domestic maids, such as these three photographed in 1890. Within a few decades, the Irish had worked their way into municipal service, particularly on the police force, where they still maintain a significant presence.

Just around the corner from the Fulton Fish Market is Schermerhorn Row, the city's only surviving Federal-style and Greek Revival-style commercial buildings. On Fulton Street, between Front and South streets, the two-story structures were built during the War of 1812 for merchant Peter Schermerhorn as combination warehouses over counting-houses. During the mid-nineteenth century, the Schermerhorn merchants dealt in furs, tea, hemp, and cotton from three continents.

purpose, in order to evade the payment of the men, and said all they had to do coming on pay-day, was to employ some persons to kick up a row, and that they would be sure to get off from paying at all." McQuade said that one contractor told him that "I have no money for the men, so I do not know what else to do. I must have a fight and that will settle all." The fight took place, McQuade said, and only 30 of 150 workers had to be paid. The rest had scattered.

The prospects and experiences of Irish women were equally desolate. Constantly reminded of the contempt in which they were held through such advertisements as those seeking houseworkers of "any country or color except Irish," women who succeeded in being hired as servants often found themselves patronized, ridiculed, and maligned. The intimacy inherent in such work allowed mistresses to supervise the lives of domestics, even to dictating their companions.

The work itself was long and hard; eighteen-hour days were not uncommon and the relatively primitive conditions of the time, even in New York, demanded considerable strength and endurance. According to one memoir of that period: "Oil lamps required trimming and filling; candlesticks, the fronts of grate-fenders, and frequently the shovel and tongs of brass, were to be cleaned; wood and coal to be brought from the cellar to all the fires, and the absence of hall-stoves rendered fires necessary in all sitting rooms. All water required for the kitchen, or bedrooms, or for baths, was drawn from the nearest street pump, and all refuse water and slops were carried out to the street and emptied into the gutter."

As the city developed economically and gave rise to a larger middle class, distinctions between mistresses and "help" grew apace. To make certain that servants were kept "in their place," their quarters were usually located in the least convenient portion of the house, the top floor. Their rooms were poorly ventilated and heated, and even after indoor plumbing became generally available, servants were denied access to toilets and tubs and compelled to continue using backyard privies and chamber pots and to bathe in the kitchen.

Further, as Christine Stansell points out in *City of Women*, "Serving girls were 'universally complained of' and 'generally and unhesitatingly denounced, even in

The city's future seems increasingly tied to such service-oriented fields as finance, banks, and communications. The New York Stock Exchange, on Broad Street between Exchange Place and Wall Street, continues to accentuate New York's role as the securities trading center of the world. At the present site since 1865, the exchange has been housed in its present building since 1903.

their very presence, as pests and curses.' In one sense the servant problem was an element of class-consciousness: One could not really *be* a lady if one did not have a problem with servants. For ladies who were not entirely confident of their own class identity, asserting judgment over the immigrant poor affirmed their position and status." The impact of such relationships on the Irish domestics was heightened substantially by their unfamiliarity with their new surroundings; their crude rural backgrounds provided little preparation for the Victorian pretentiousness of their employers.

Exploitation of women was combatted in the late nineteenth century by such organizations as the Working Woman's Protective Union, where prospective clients are shown waiting for assistance in this 1881 drawing from Frank Leslie's Illustrated Newspaper.

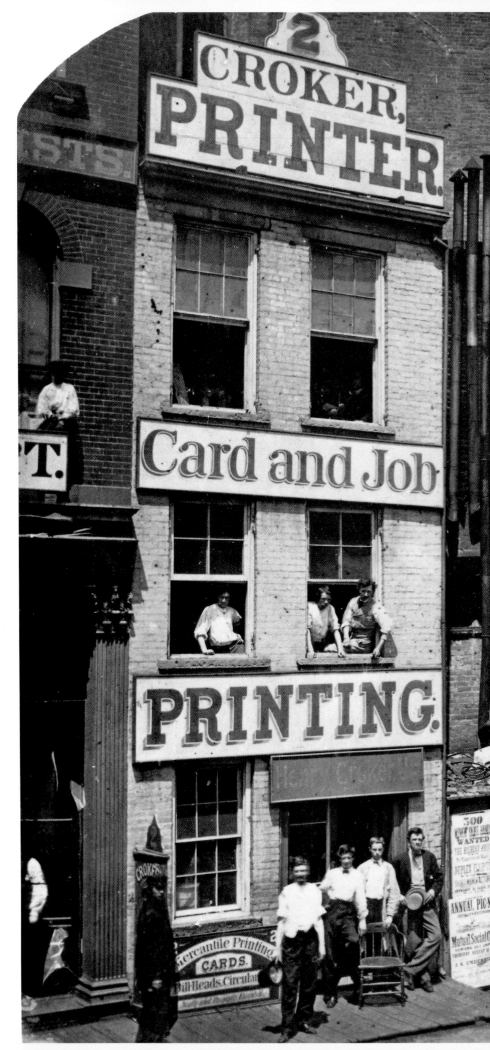

Within a few blocks of the harbor, carpentry, printing, painting, and oilskin merchants flourished.

Overleaf:
The Fulton Fish Market, a New York institution for centuries (albeit in different structures and locations), comes to life when the rest of the city goes to sleep. Successive waves of immigrants found jobs in and around the docks, which have been a major source of employment throughout the city's history. Italians have dominated the market, which also has involved Korean, Japanese, and Jewish merchants. In recent years, sales have dropped, largely because of competition from air distribution.

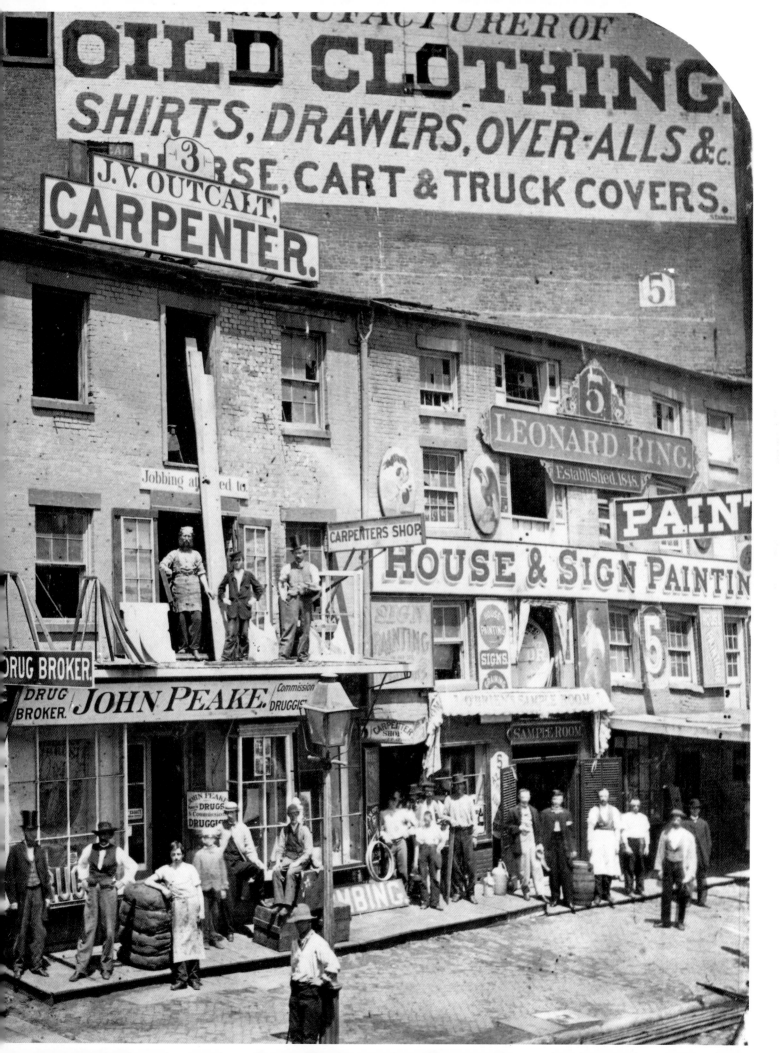

In addition to unpleasant dealings with their mistresses, servant girls had to be concerned about involvements of a different sort with their masters. Alone, dependent, and unprotected, they not infrequently found themselves the objects of sexual harassment. The melodramas that depicted young women as targets of lecherous employers were not based on fantasy alone.

Seduction was one prelude to prostitution but hardly the only instigation. For many early nineteenth century women, the specter of destitution constantly hovered nearby, and to them, prostitution seemed more an economic alternative than a moral descent. The low status and poverty-level wages of unattached females, particularly immigrants, made "selling oneself for a shilling" the equivalent of earning in an hour what would otherwise take a day, without any significant loss of social standing. And in a society where women were regarded largely as male appendages, prostitution represented one of the few opportunities of dealing with men on something resembling equal terms.

The involvement of immigrant domestic servants in prostitution was documented in 1858 through an extensive survey conducted by Dr. William Sanger, resident physician for the venereal disease hospital on Blackwell's Island. Interviews with some two thousand prostitutes elicited a wealth of information, including the finding that almost half the subjects were domestics and that more than a third were Irish. There was also evidence that the tedium of servant life contributed to the lure of the "profession": A substantial proportion of domestics said they had been motivated by the desire for "a change."

Before Sanger's research, New Yorkers had to rely on more flowery and moralistic descriptions of the activities of prostitutes and their customers. When police raided a brothel in 1838, for example, the *Herald* reported: "Clerks of respectable mercantile houses were found in this pious place in the embraces of the most depraved and abandoned denizens of the notorious spot. They were compelled to give their names and the names of their employers. They were then suffered to go home, covered with shame and mortification."

Apparently, however, the passage of time enabled New Yorkers to overcome their shame. Two decades later, Sanger warned that "unlike the vice of a few years since, it no longer confines itself to secrecy and darkness, but boldly strikes through our most thronged and elegant thoroughfares.... It is in your squares, and in your suburban retreats and summer resorts; it is in your theatres, your opera, your hotels; nay, it is even intruding itself into the private circles, and slowly but steadily extending the poison."

However severe the plight of the "Famine Irish," they at least shared a racial affinity with their more successful countrymen, a benefit denied blacks, their primary competitors for low-level jobs as laborers, waiters, and domestics. While not officially emancipated in New York State until 1827, most black slaves in the city had been liberated by the beginning of the nineteenth century and drifted into the unskilled work subsequently sought by the immigrants. Given a choice between Irish and blacks, most white employers readily hired the former, particularly when whites already on the job might refuse to work alongside the latter.

Racism was rampant, especially among the Irish, according to James D. Burn, a visiting English hatter who spent three years with American workers. "I have met with a few well-conditioned men who look upon the blacks as rational beings," he reported, "but the strongly expressed opinion of the majority was that they are a soulless race, and I am satisfied that some of these people would shoot a black man with as little regard to moral consequences as they would a wild hog."

Rivalry between the Irish and blacks often led to violence and occasionally, on the docks and in railroad yards, to rioting. The riots sometimes were precipitated by the hiring of blacks, who invariably were denied membership in unions, as strikebreakers during labor disputes involving unionized Irish workers. Generally, the immigrant Irish pushed the blacks out of tenuously held jobs; this was especially the case in domestic service, where many former slaves had been retained by their owners.

Compared to the Irish and blacks, German immigrants found a more receptive market for their labor. This was largely a consequence of bringing skills that were more adaptable to an urban environment. The Germans were butchers, bakers, brewers, tailors, and furniture makers, cabinetmakers, watchmakers, and shoemakers.

Unlike the Irish, however, Germans faced a language barrier. An inability to communicate in English restricted their employment and life-style. Necessity forced them to work and live with their compatriots, limiting their mobility and delaying their assimilation. Those involved in the building trades, for example, had to find jobs with German builders, the only employers able to direct them.

Americans who dealt with the German immigrants were likely to be impressed by their diligence and work habits, as the *Tribune* noted in an article about shoemakers from an 1846 series on labor in New York: "There is not perhaps a more industrious working class in our city than the Germans. They rise early and retire late, and though when arriving on our shores they do not *drive business*, as is a distinguishing characteristic of our native mechanics; yet after they have been some time among us a decided improvement in this respect can be plainly observed.

"The Germans are pretty much found occupying basements and cellars, and pretty much all the capital one requires to start business is a bench and tools, a side of leather, a ball of thread, a little wax, and a glass show-case, stuck out by the door containing a specimen of work. With these, aided by an untiring industry, economical habits and plenty of *elbow room*, he manages to push along through the world."

As the *Tribune* went on to observe, however, shoemaking was not a prospering field. "There is no class of mechanics who average so great an amount of working for so little money as the Journeyman Shoemakers. The number of Journeymen out of employment is also large, and out of all just proportion. There are hundreds of them in the City constantly wandering from shop to shop in search of work, while many of them have families in a state of absolute want."

Even for these skilled and industrious workers, the *Tribune* made clear, the vagaries of the mid-nineteenth-century New York economy could produce devastating effects. After describing the primitive and decrepit cellars in which many of these German shoemakers lived, the newspaper concluded: "Here is the whole of that thing so noble in the abstract, so lofty in the destiny intended for it, so full of every source of joy and gladness. A Family of human beings. Here they work—here they cook, they eat, they sleep, they pray (if to pray they have not forgotten.) They procure a little something to eat by the chance jobs of gentlemen's or children's mending brought in by the rich people above ground in the neighborhood, who are not celebrated for paying a poor cobbler high prices."

The fate of the German shoemakers became increasingly common among the city's artisans and craftsmen as the advent of the Civil War coincided with the replacement of men by machines, heralding the onset of the manufacturing era, the period of New York's greatest growth. And at the core of this growth was the apparel industry.

From its earliest days as a struggling seaport when sailors needed cheap, durable clothing and tailors sold them "slop work," New York was in the garment business. For much of its existence since, the needle trades have functioned on two levels: made-to-order attire fashioned for the well-to-do by skilled tailors and ready-to-wear clothing produced for a mass market by semiskilled machine operators. This was true for both men's and women's apparel, although firms and workers generally specialized in one or the other.

During colonial and Revolutionary times, virtually every nationality was represented among the tailors, but by the early nineteenth century, German and Irish immigrants predominated. Many of the Germans were Jews, who by century's end would provide opportunities for their coreligionists from Poland and Prussia, England, France, and Russia and become identified with all aspects of the garment industry. But by the mid-nineteenth century, the introduction of machinery, combined with the demands of a fast-growing population, made New York a major supplier of the nation's clothing needs and propelled apparel manufacturing into the forefront of the city's industries (in 1850, the largest firms employed as many as five thousand tailors and seamstresses).

This growth was abetted by the westward movement that distanced potential customers from East Coast producers and put a premium on shipping costs out of New York, enhancing the desirability of lightweight products, such as clothing. In addition to supplying the so-called "cheap trade"—Southern farmers, slaves, Western miners, and the urban poor—the mass producers began to compete with the custom tailors by appealing to the middle class and even the wealthy and sophisticated. *Hunt's Merchants Magazine* reported in 1849 that one ready-made firm's clothing was "adapted to all markets and for all classes of men, from the humblest laborer to the fashionable gentleman."

As the demand reached ever-greater heights, manufacturers sought to increase efficiency and reduce costs by introducing assembly-linelike systems. Procedures were separated, simplifying tasks and diminishing the need for skilled workers. As a result, garments could be turned out more cheaply by low-paid, inexperienced labor. Employers also found that they could reduce their overhead and maximize their profits by having work done outside their factories. This "outwork" was accomplished by distributing material to contractors, who turned it over to tailors as piece work. Inevitably, "outwork" became a family affair, epitomized by the cynical assessment that "a tailor is worth nothing without a wife and very often a child." Sewing by hand left its mark on "outworkers," according to writer Virginia Penny, who was able to identify them on the street by their stooped carriage, the result of bending to see while working by dim candlelight. The "outwork" arrangement soon led to exploitation through the introduction of "sweatshops": unsanitary, dangerous, dimly lit basements and garrets where underpaid tailors, seamstresses, and their children labored long hours on their own equipment and even risked withheld payment for alleged "poor quality work."

This was the system that was in place in 1880 when the first shiploads of eastern European Jews began arriving in New York. Poor and unable to communicate in English, they readily gravitated toward the garment industry, where they felt more likely to find employment and acceptance from the already established German Jews. At least, they reasoned, they could converse in Yiddish.

For many, if not most, of the newcomers, that was the extent of the benefits they received from their employers. They were soon caught up in a new exploitive technique called the "task system," imposed by contractors who, to meet competition, had agreed to take work from a manufacturer at a reduced price. According to an Industrial Commission report cited by Irving Howe in *World of Our Fathers:* "When he came home, he would tell his men that there was not much work and he was obliged to take it cheaper, and since he did not want to reduce their wages and pay them less per day, all they would have to do would be to make another coat in the task. That is, if they were accustomed to make 9 coats in the task, they would be required to make 10, and then 11, and so on. The wages were always reduced on the theory that they were not reduced at all but the amount of labor increased. In this way intense speed was developed. The men who had been accustomed to making 9 coats in a task would make 10, and so on, up to 15, 18, and even 20, as is the customary task at the present time [1901]. The hours began to be increased in order to make the task in a day."

Groups with specialized skills fared best
in New York's manufacturing economy of
the late nineteenth and early twentieth
centuries. For many immigrants, such as
this Bohemian cigarmaker, work was
performed at home with the aid of wives
and children.

Usable skills, disciplined work habits,
and urban upbringings gave German
immigrants relatively easy access to the
job market and social acceptance. Among
their major employers was the Steinway
piano factory in Astoria, where
immigrants had opportunities to
demonstrate their craftsmanship.

Among New York's most enduring industries has been the needle trades, which traditionally served Italian, Jewish, Puerto Rican, and Asian immigrants as a means not only of surviving but of succeeding and even prospering. To meet increased demand, work was brought home, and the infamous "outwork" system led impoverished families to put even the youngest children to work, often late into the night with poor lighting and little heat. This was followed by even greater exploitation through the creation of "sweatshops," unsanitary and dangerous workplaces where seamstresses were jammed into basements, attics, and other undesirable spaces that could be rented cheaply by manufacturers. In time, the size of the sweatshops grew, but the poor working conditions remained. By the first decade of the twentieth century, 60 percent of the apparel jobs in the United States were located in New York City; in the peak year of 1947, this meant 350,000 workers. The industry's multiethnic character was reflected in a 1940 International Ladies Garment Workers Union (ILGWU) poster in Yiddish, English, and Spanish.

It was not only men who suffered exploitation. Many of the garment workers were women. The following, from the pages of the weekly *Independent*, in 1902, describes the experience of one:

My name is Sadie Frowne. I work in Allen Street (Manhattan) in what they call a sweatshop. I am new at the work and the foreman scolds me a great deal. I get up at half-past five o'clock every morning and make myself a cup of coffee on the oil stove. I eat a bit of bread and perhaps some fruit and then go to work. Often I get there soon after six o'clock so as to be in good time, though the factory does not open till seven.

At seven o'clock we all sit down to our machines and the boss brings to each one the pile of work that he or she is to finish during the day—what they call in English their "stint." This pile is put down beside the machine and as soon as a garment is done it is laid on the other side of the machine. Sometimes the work is not all finished by six o'clock, and then the one who is behind must work overtime.

The machines go like mad all day because the faster you work the more money you get. Sometimes in my haste I get my finger caught and the needle goes right through it. It goes so quick, though, that it does not hurt much. I bind the finger up with a piece of cotton and go on working. We all have accidents like that.

All the time we are working the boss walks around examining the finished garments and making us do them over again if they are not just right. So we have to be careful as well as swift. But I am getting so good at the work that within a year I will be making $7 a week, and then I can save at least $4.50 a week. I have over $200 saved now.

The machines are all run by foot power, and at the end of the day one feels so weak that there is a great temptation to lie right down and sleep. But you must go out and get air, and have some pleasure. So instead of lying down I go out, generally with Henry.

I am very fond of dancing and, in fact, all sorts of pleasure. I go to the theatre quite often, and like those plays that make you cry a great deal. "The Two Orphans" is good. The last time I saw it I cried all night because of the hard times the children had in the play.

The resignation revealed by such poignant accounts belied a toughness and determination that soon would manifest itself among thousands of Sadie Frownes. On November 22, 1909, an eighteen-year-old seamstress named Clara Lemlich made labor and feminist history at a dramatic meeting in Cooper Union. The meeting had been called to consider a strike against manufacturers of shirtwaists, or blouses, by Local 25 of the International Ladies Garment Workers Union (ILGWU). There were perhaps one hundred members of the local at the time: young immigrant women, mostly Jewish, some Italian, all victimized.

The ILGWU, formed less than a decade earlier, was indecisive; the union's future could be determined by the behavior of these untested girls. Even Samuel Gompers, president of the parent American Federation of Labor, spoke cautiously. "I have never declared a strike in all my life..," he told the overflow crowd. "I ask you to stand together, to have faith in yourselves, to be true to your comrades. If you strike, be cool, calm, collected, and determined. Let your watchword be: Union and progress, and until then no surrender!"

Another important official was about to speak when a woman's voice from somewhere in the hall said, "I wanted to say a few words." It was Clara Lemlich, who although only a teenager was a popular member of the local's executive board. The frail youngster was assisted to the platform and spoke in simple yet passionate Yiddish: "I have listened to all the speakers. I would not have further patience for talk, as I am one of those who feels and suffers from the things pictured. I move that we go on a general strike!"

The auditorium exploded with applause; the motion was endorsed by wild acclamation. The chairman, Benjamin Feigenbaum, rapped for order. "Do you mean faith?" he asked. "Will you take the old Jewish oath?" Thousands of right hands were raised as the audience repeated in Yiddish: "If I turn traitor to the cause I now pledge, may this hand wither from the arm I now raise."

The strike began. There had been little planning; Local 25's treasury held $4.

The ILGWU was formed at the beginning of the twentieth century to provide a united front in improving pay and working conditions. But the union, almost totally composed of young immigrant working girls, limped along for almost a decade until November 22, 1909, when eighteen-year-old Clara Lemlich ignited the membership into calling a strike of shirtwaist workers (opposite). The walkout lasted three months, and while it failed to achieve its specific goals, it succeeded in swelling the ranks of the union and inspiring other needle trades workers to strike if their demands were not met (left).

But the spirit was contagious; support poured in from both predictable and unlikely sources: the Women's Trade Union League, the socialists, Wellesley students, and society women. During the first month, more than 700 girls were arrested and 19 ordered to the workhouse. Declared one sentencing magistrate: "You are on strike against God and Nature, whose firm law is that man shall earn his bread by the sweat of his brow."

Still the young women endured. And their courage and tenacity became legendary, creating a new comprehension of miserable working conditions and the need for reform. The *New York Sun* sent a reporter named McAlister Coleman to the scene, and his experience was unforgettable.

The girls, headed by teen-age Clara Lemlich, described by union organizers as a "pint of trouble for the bosses," began singing Italian and Russian working-class songs as they paced in two before the factory door. Of a sudden, around the corner came a dozen tough-looking customers, for whom the union label "gorillas" seemed well-chosen.

"Stand fast, girls," called Clara, and then the thugs rushed the line, knocking Clara to her knees, striking at the pickets, opening the way for a group of frightened scabs to slip through the broken line. Fancy ladies from the Allen Street red-light district climbed out of cabs to cheer on the gorillas. There was a confused melee of scratching, screaming girls and fist-swinging men and then a patrol wagon arrived. The thugs ran off as the cops pushed Clara and two other badly beaten girls into the wagon.

I followed the rest of the retreating pickets to the union hall, a few blocks away. There a relief station had been set up where one bottle of milk and a loaf of bread were given to strikers with small children in their families. There, for the first time in my comfortably sheltered, upper West Side life, I saw real hunger on the faces of my fellow Americans in the richest city in the world.

The strike lasted three months; the settlement itself did not constitute a glittering victory for labor, but the consequences proved immensely important. The lo-

cal's membership had swelled to 10,000, and the psychological boost to the needle trade's union movement was incalculable.

Within five months, for example, the potent cloakmakers called a general strike that lasted two months and resulted in substantial benefits, including a "preferential union shop" agreement that put members in the first rank of American labor. In *The Women's Garment Workers*, Louis Levine compared the two walkouts: "One was a sudden emotional outburst; the other was carefully planned. In the former, about 20,000 workers were involved. In the latter, the number of strikers was three times as large. As a result of these and other differences, the two strikes came to be thought of as prologue and principal act. The shirtwaist makers' strike was an 'uprising.' The cloakmakers' strike was 'the great revolt.' "

Aside from their impact on the labor movement, the two strikes generated shockwaves throughout New York's insecure Jewish community, which was represented by a majority of both strikers and bosses. A people invariably united against outside persecution found itself torn by internal strife. Fearful that the dispute was damaging their public image, Jewish leaders enlisted the help of a Boston lawyer named Louis D. Brandeis, later a distinguished associate justice of the United States Supreme Court, to negotiate an agreement, which he did.

Although the labor conflicts had focused national attention on working conditions in the garment industry, it would take a tragedy to bring about legislative action. It came on March 25, 1911, at the Triangle Shirtwaist Company factory off Washington Square, where fire took the lives of 146 young Jewish and Italian workers, most of them immigrant women. William G. Shepherd, a United Press reporter, witnessed the conflagration and phoned in a firsthand account from which the following excerpts are taken:

I was walking through Washington Square when a puff of smoke issuing from the factory building caught my eye. I reached the building before the alarm was turned in. I saw every feature of the tragedy visible from outside the building. I learned a new sound—a more horrible sound than description can picture. It was the thud of a speeding, living body on a stone sidewalk.

Thud—dead, thud—dead, thud—dead, thud—dead. Sixty-two thud—deads. I call them that, because the sound and the thought of death came to me each time, at the same instant. There was plenty of chance to watch them as they came down. The height was eighty feet.

The first ten thud—deads shocked me. I looked up—saw that there were scores of girls at the windows. The flames from the floor below were beating in their faces. Somehow I knew that they, too, must come down, and something within me—something that I didn't know was there—steeled me....

As I looked up I saw a love affair in the midst of all the horror. A young man helped a girl to the window sill. Then he held her out, deliberately away from the building and let her drop. He seemed cool and calculating. He held out a second girl the same way and let her drop. Then he held out a third girl who did not resist. I noticed that. They were as unresisting as if he were helping them onto a streetcar instead of into eternity. Undoubtedly he saw that a terrible death awaited them in the flames, and his was only a terrible chivalry.

Then came the love amid the flames. He brought another girl to the window. Those of us who were looking saw her put her arms about him and kiss him. Then he held her out into space and dropped her. But quick as a flash he was on the window sill himself. His coat fluttered upward—the air filled his trouser legs. I could see that he wore tan shoes and hose. His hat remained on his head.

Thud—dead, thud—dead—together they went into eternity. I saw his face before they covered it. You could see in it that he was a real man. He had done his best.

We found out later that, in the room in which he stood, many girls were being burned to death by the flames and were screaming in an inferno of flame and heat. He chose the easiest way and was brave enough to even help the girl he loved to a quicker death, after she had given him a goodbye kiss. He leaped with an energy as if to arrive first in that mysterious land of eternity, but her thud—dead came first....

The floods of water from the firemen's hose that ran into the gutter were actually stained

Opposite and above:
Unionization notwithstanding, it fell to a tragedy to create the outrage required to obtain the legislation necessary for providing minimal safety and health standards in the garment industry. On March 25, 1911, a fire broke out at the Triangle Shirtwaist Company, killing 146 workers, many of whom jumped to their deaths when locked doors prevented their escape down stairwells. The political career of Alfred E. Smith, then Assembly majority leader in the State Legislature, was accelerated tremendously by his investigation of the disaster.

The charred ruins of the Triangle Shirtwaist company.

red with blood. I looked upon the heap of dead bodies and I remembered these girls were the shirtwaist makers. I remembered their great strike of last year in which these same girls had demanded more sanitary conditions and more safety precautions in the shops. These dead bodies were the answer.

The effects of the tragedy far transcended the fate of its victims. Public outrage at the lack of safety precautions—no sprinklers; only two narrow, winding staircases; locked doors—forced government to involve itself more directly in the workplace. It resulted in immediate remedial legislation and long-range reform. Newly elected Assembly Majority Leader Alfred E. Smith was impelled to conduct a legislative investigation that helped elevate him from a glorified ward heeler to a national political figure. And the seeds that culminated in the National Labor Relations Act of 1935 were planted in the fertile mind of its sponsor, Sen. Robert F. Wagner, Sr.

By the time of the Triangle fire, the garment business had become big business: More than 60 percent of the nation's apparel jobs were in New York. Between 1860 and 1910, the number of workers burgeoned from 30,000 to 236,000, while the number of plants rose from fewer than 600 to more than 10,000. The industry soon outgrew the Lower East Side and moved uptown along Seventh Avenue below 41st Street, where it flourished well into the twentieth century and remains a major, if vastly diminished, operation. In the peak year of 1947, the apparel business provided an estimated 350,000 jobs in the New York area.

But shortly after the end of World War II, the garment industry began to change its style not only seasonally, but historically. Along with other manufacturing businesses, it started to leave New York City. Competition from abroad, where overhead costs were significantly lower, forced some apparel makers out of business and sent others scurrying for sites beyond the traditional district to escape skyscraper-high rents and the demands of unions for adequate wages and benefits. Many went South, to a labor market, as well as a climate, they found more congenial. Some left the country for Puerto Rico, where the government-supported "Operation Bootstrap" dangled inducements that included tax incentives and low salaries.

Victims of the Triangle fire at the city morgue.

Some of the companies that remained in New York reappeared with new addresses, such as Chinatown, Brooklyn, Queens, and the Bronx, outside the customary and costly Midtown area. There were changes, too, inside the factories. While the operations of some firms were assumed by the families of founding Jewish and Italian immigrants, many sons eschewed the world of their fathers and instead sought college-educated careers in law, medicine, accountancy, education, and the arts or in totally different types of businesses. A few even became union organizers. And the shops themselves took on a new look and sound as the postwar influx of Puerto Ricans led to alterations in the ethnic makeup of the work force.

As these new Caribbean immigrants appeared behind the sewing machines and the racks in the low-paying jobs that had kept alive an older generation of Europeans, they confronted a shriveling industry bent more on survival than growth. Yet for the Puerto Ricans, many of whom had learned the trade in their homeland, *any* job in New York seemed preferable to no job in San Juan. They had learned painfully that while "Operation Bootstrap" may have uplifted mainland investors and entrepreneurs, industrialization of farmland had also displaced agricultural workers, creating a labor surplus on the island. Alongside blacks, who found their way into the needle trades after migrating up from the rural South, they discovered that the garment industry no longer offered the opportunities it had provided for their predecessors.

Manufacturers, including those making apparel, continued to flee from New York during the next few decades, catching many newly arrived Puerto Ricans and blacks in an economic vise. Blue-collar jobs—the kind their limited education, skills, and, in the case of Puerto Ricans, fluency in English consigned them to— were evaporating. And racial and ethnic discrimination further limited their chances.

Gloria Maldonado, born in New York in 1928 of Puerto Rican parents, recalled the transition in the composition of garment industry employees that occurred in her lifetime. During World War II, when she began embroidering after school as a teenager, most of her coworkers were drawn from the most recent arrivals in New

York: Puerto Ricans, along with some American blacks. By the 1980s, however, they had been replaced by the latest immigrants: Dominicans and Asians. Unlike the Jews and Italians of an earlier era, she said that very few Puerto Ricans became garment business entrepreneurs. "We were always employees, not bosses," said Mrs. Maldonado, who left her machine to become an ILGWU business agent.

Mrs. Maldonado's assessment is confirmed by a 1979 Hunter College study that states: "The garment industry has commonly been thought to be the typical immigrant industry, providing entry jobs for newly-arrived workers and serving them and especially their children as a steppingstone to upward mobility. While this was true for Jewish and Italian women immigrants, who comprised the bulk of female garment workers until the 1950s, Puerto Ricans do not find themselves today in managerial or ownership positions within this or any other industry. What is more, the overwhelming majority of young Puerto Rican men and women, the children and grandchildren of those garment workers, are still located in low-paying jobs as bank tellers, typists, salesclerks, office workers, secretaries, janitors, restaurant, hotel, and hospital workers. Only a small minority are professionals, partly as a consequence of the civil rights and student movements of the 1960s and 70s."

The fickleness of fashion and intense competition have contributed to the instability and exploitation characterizing the apparel industry throughout this century. Unionization has helped protect workers, but "sweetheart contracts" and non-union shops proliferate during lean years. The minimum wage, to say nothing of benefits, is readily waived by poor immigrants desperate for work.

Marginal firms, often undercapitalized and financially insecure, predictably have been among the most miserly employers. And for them, the passage of time has not meant progress. Mrs. Maldonado remembered a boss refusing her request for a 10-cent-an-hour raise in the 1940s. While in a contemporary Williamsburg sweatshop, a Dominican seamstress said, "The women are not allowed to talk to each other. The boss says it slows down the work. But I think he worries that we would talk about how it is to work here."

Meanwhile, agencies responsible for enforcing wage and hour laws, as well as health and safety regulations, acknowledge widespread violations but plead lack of manpower. Employer irresponsibility is further protected by the reluctance of illegal immigrant workers to seek governmental assistance.

The problems of present-day immigrants with limited language and work skills are not far removed from those of an earlier era. Like contemporary Asian and Caribbean émigrés, Italians who journeyed to New York in 1880 invariably wound up at the bottom of the economic ladder, with three out of four employed at manual labor. In this regard they followed the pattern of their Irish predecessors, taking up pick and shovel and baling hook to fill unskilled street, construction, and waterfront jobs.

When immigrants from southern Italy and Sicily began arriving in the late nineteenth century, the docks were controlled by the Irish, who held about 95 percent of the longshore jobs. Yet the Italians were welcomed by shrewd shipping company executives because they recognized that an ethnically divided work force would forestall employee unity and thwart potential strikes. After a major work stoppage in 1887, recruitment of Italians was stepped up, and by World War I they comprised more than one-third of the dock laborers.

While eagerly sought by the shippers, the Italians were despised by the Irish. "It was difficult to make the Irish work harmoniously with the Italians," according to Charles B. Barnes in his notable 1915 study, *The Longshoremen*. "At first it was impossible. Then Italians were put on in separate gangs or to handle coal; but care had to be exercised. If a gang of 'Ginnies,' or 'Dagoes,' as they were called, was put in the hold with the Irish, the latter would quit. Accordingly, sharp foremen played one race against the other. They took advantage of the irascibility of the Irish to

force them out and so gain the advantage of employing Italians. They could then truthfully say that it was impossible to get 'white men' and that they were obliged to take Italians. The result is that the older types of Irish, Germans, and Scandinavians are now being pushed out to employment elsewhere...."

Such management tactics notwithstanding, the Italian immigrants were not highly regarded as dockworkers. Although ethnic hostility may well have interfered with objectivity, Barnes observed that "it is evident that they have less physical strength than the Irish. On some piers it is said that 'one "white man" is as good as two or three Italians'.... In the main, it is the inferior grades of longshore work which fall to the lot of the Italian. They are used as coal shovelers, pier men, and sometimes as hold men, but rarely on the deck. There are many Italian foremen, but only where large numbers of Italian longshoremen are employed."

In their struggle for survival in America, Italians had to overcome nativist prejudices against Catholics, against the foreign-born, and against cheap immigrant labor. The ethnic prejudice that had greeted the Irish workers in the mid-nineteenth century was visited on the Italians fifty years later, and racist theories were concocted to justify discrimination, just as they would later be applied to blacks and Puerto Ricans. "The great line of cleavage between the older and newer type of longshoreman, between the sturdy races of northwestern Europe and more alien immigrants of southern and southeastern Europe," Barnes contended, "is generally admitted to be an important factor in bringing about a deterioration in efficiency among the longshoremen of the port."

One of the reasons for the rapid concentration of Italians on the waterfront no doubt involved the "birds of passage" syndrome; that is, the desire of Italians to see America as a place of temporary employment rather than as a permanent home. This was made feasible by the fact that they had a homeland to return to and by technological advances that made transatlantic travel relatively cheap. Statistically, the pattern is borne out by figures indicating that between 1880 and 1910, about 80 percent of Italian immigrants to the United States were male. Bent on returning to Italy, they came without families, living on pittances, and focused on jobs that did not require training but were steady and paid off in immediate cash.

"The southern and eastern European wage earner is usually single or, if married, has left his wife and children abroad," reported W. Jett Lauck. "He has no permanent interest in the community in which he lives or in the industry in which he is employed. His main purpose is to live as cheaply as he can and save as much as he can...."

This transience was poetically expressed to Italian researcher Deomede Carito by an immigrant who said: "Doctor, we brought to America only our brains and our arms. Our hearts stayed there in the little house in the beautiful fields of our Italy." Eager Italian workers even accepted a "kickback" arrangement under which part of their wages went to "friends" who had obtained the job for them. Frequently, these "friends" were fellow countrymen, *padrones*, who organized work gangs for the shippers. The *padrone* system operated extensively at the turn of the century for all types of unskilled work. One Italian laborer told a government investigator in 1904 that "they said we should have a shovel and pay for. They charged us 75 cents per shovel. Two of my friends didn't need any shovel, but have been charged 75 cents each the same."

Despite such exploitation, the Italians persisted and, through the traditional process of bringing in relatives, quickly gained access to key hiring positions. This brought waterfront power in such short order that by 1919, Robert Foerster could assert in *Italian Emigration* that it constituted "one of the most striking examples of racial displacement in American industry."

Most of the Italian men who weren't employed on the docks worked at unskilled jobs in the streets to fill an urgent need during a period of explosive expansion. In 1890, more than 90 percent of the public works laborers in New York were Italian. More than four thousand excavated Lexington Avenue subway tunnels in 1900; four years later, five thousand helped construct the Bronx aqueduct and thousands more worked on the Grand Central Terminal. In one of those historical coincidences that seem contrived, the earth dug by those immigrants was used as landfill to expand Ellis Island.

Aside from such major projects, Italians, relying on their Old World farm experience, were swinging picks and shovels to repair, replace, and repave; to remove, build, and rebuild. It was not necessarily what they had anticipated in the New World. Terry Coleman captured this succinctly in *Going to America:* "It was an old superstition, sometimes half believed by the simplest emigrants, that the streets of New York were paved with gold. When they got there they learned three things: first, that the streets were not paved with gold; second, that the streets were not paved at all; and third, that they were expected to pave them."

Such was the experience of Vincent Scilipoti, who came to Harlem from Sicily in 1888 after "friends who had returned to Nicosia from America looked prosperous and well-dressed." He told interviewer Marie Lipari that the friends "told tales of prosperity in America....I thought that work was plentiful and I could get a job easily."

He found out differently. Work was very scarce. His first construction job only lasted two weeks; his second, laying pipe, was of similar duration. It, however, taught him the rudiments of immigrant exploitation. He was required to pay the foreman $3 to work and 50¢ for "Red Cross and medical care." Scilipoti recalled that "this boss never kept men longer than two weeks. After he had collected his $3.50, he discharged the workers and hired others, who were again asked to pay $3 in order to get the job." Of course, none of the money was ever returned.

A series of other misfortunes led Scilipoti, according to his interviewer, to conclude, perhaps unfairly, that Italians "had only themselves to blame for such labor conditions...because they were willing to exploit their fellow countrymen. He said that the Italians had taught these practices to the other nationalities."

Exploitation of Italian immigrants was commonplace because they couldn't un-

Opposite and above:
Like the Irish immigrants who preceded them by a half-century, Italians were handicapped in New York by rural backgrounds that gave them little preparation for working or living in an urban environment. Their agricultural experience translated into jobs requiring unskilled or semiskilled labor: on the waterfront, in construction, and, at the turn of the twentieth century, building the city's subway system. Tunneling through Manhattan's rock and beneath the East River was tough, dangerous, and underpaid.

New York's transition from a manufacturing to a service economy during the mid-twentieth century altered the mechanism through which earlier immigrants had achieved economic success and, through it, social acceptance. The growth of services in New York found the city increasingly expanding employment in the public sector, to maintain its extensive transit network, for example. Instead of making machines for private manufacturers, more and more skilled workers were maintaining machines for various city departments.

derstand English and were thus compelled to trust either manipulative "Americans" or their more seasoned compatriots, many of whom practiced the very deceptions that they themselves had fallen victim to. Pietro di Donato, the son of an Italian immigrant and author of *Christ in Concrete*, a largely autobiographical novel about immigrant construction workers in New York, confirmed such deviousness. He told the story of one Sicilian who was met at Ellis Island by another, who offered to get him a job if he turned over his money, which amounted to about $15 or $20. The immigrant agreed and was taken by horse and wagon to some vacant land in Jamaica, Queens. "He put up some stakes and lines," Di Donato said, "gave the greenhorn some old, worn-out shovels, and said, 'Dig a foundation over here. I'll be back tonight.' Of course, he never came back. So the Sicilian was stranded and penniless, too. They learned their lessons fast."

The lure of America for most southern Italians, Di Donato contended, was solely economic. "A few guys would come back to the village in Italy or Sicily and show off their gold teeth, and that would do it. Once here, they were introduced to the blandishments of materialism and that would be all that mattered," he insisted. "It had nothing to do with the Constitution, the Bill of Rights, the Declaration of Independence, democracy, or freedom. That was all a lot of bull. It was all material. If one family bought a Victrola, the next family would go into hock to get one."

Despite disappointments and injustices, Italian immigrants did arrive at an opportune time in the city's history: a period that could utilize their capacity for labor and productivity. The building boom that provided jobs for so many of them was immeasurably assisted by the development of skyscrapers, a nineteenth-century phenomenon largely responsible for the present look, as well as growth, of New York. Skyscrapers made it possible to accomplish vertically what would have required a spaciousness unattainable on Manhattan Island. By concentrating hundreds of thousands of people within a few blocks, New York was able to create an environment that eventually would establish it as the white-collar capital of the world.

Serendipitously, the city had been founded over a bed of rock located at precisely the underground depth needed to support such structures. With nature having done its job eons earlier, human ingenuity asserted itself in the post-Civil War years. "Three technical inventions are basic to the skyscraper," according to architectural historian William Jordy, "the elevator, fireproofing, and the self-supporting metal frame."

The three elements did not appear simultaneously, accounting in part for disputed claims to the title of "first skyscraper." And although elevators were introduced initially for offices in 1870 through the Equitable Life Assurance Building at 120 Broadway, that seven-story structure was only marginally taller than its contemporaries. Loftier buildings were erected during the next decade or so, but none rose higher than eleven stories because of limitations imposed by materials and design. Load-bearing walls, made of stone or brick, had to be so thick, particularly at street level, that interior space and windows were severely restricted. While the Tower Building, completed in 1889 at 50 Broadway, did not exceed eleven stories, it was supported by a steel skeleton. This revolutionary concept caused some public apprehension, and the architect, Bradford L. Gilbert, perhaps to alleviate it, occupied the top floor himself. The design of the Tower represented a major breakthrough and heralded the "age of skyscrapers."

The new technology, combined with New York's growing reputation as a commercial center, led to the proliferation of tall office buildings to house the varied businesses eager to establish themselves there. The result was thousands of construction jobs, requiring all levels of skills, that provided significant opportunities. The more specialized fields, such as carpentry, masonry, and electrical work, soon evolved into family-dominated trades in which work was passed from one genera-

Manhattan's famed skyline got a big boost during the 1920s, although skyscrapers were a nineteenth-century phenomenon. Also getting a boost were Mohawk Indians, who had perfected their high steel techniques building bridges in Canada. Native Americans literally had a hand in much of the construction that has given the city its distinctive identity.

tion to the next. Nowhere is this more apparent than with the Mohawk Indian ironworkers.

"When they talk about the men that built this country," said Orvis Diabo, "one of the men they mean is me." Diabo was among the hundreds of Mohawks from the Caughnawaga Reservation in Canada who formed four-man teams to rivet the columns and beams and girders that make up Manhattan's unseen skyline. By the time writer Joseph Mitchell had chronicled their exploits in a 1949 article in *The New Yorker*, they had helped construct the Empire State Building and Rockefeller Center, the Waldorf-Astoria and Knickerbocker Village, the West Side Highway and Pulaski Skyway, and the George Washington, Triborough, and Bronx-Whitestone bridges.

Time has served only to increase their accomplishments. A Caughnawagan named Louis Deer, 62, an ironworker since he quit high school at the age of sixteen, is surrounded by his work when he walks the city's streets. "I think, 'Goddamit, I worked on that, and there's another one I worked on over there,' " he says. "Sometimes I pass a bridge, and I think, 'I was on that one.' " And no matter where he looks, Deer is probably right. He helped raise the World Trade Center, Lever House, and 666 Fifth Avenue, along with the Verrazano-Narrows Bridge and the second level of the George Washington Bridge.

Barrel-chested with massive arms, Deer comes from a family of ironworkers. His father and two brothers were in high steel; even his two daughters are married to ironworkers. "It's a 'father-and-son' business," he said, explaining that "the Indian people like that work." But Deer rejected the idea that racial factors were involved. "They always put in the papers that we're surefooted, but it's just that we like this kind of work. It's interesting. There's always something new; it ain't like sitting at a desk doing the same thing over and over." He recalled getting a job in a factory after World War II. "I lasted maybe two weeks," he said. "It was too enclosed."

Deer finds the work "challenging"; others would call it hazardous. Changes in the direction and velocity of the wind, as well as equipment failures, create unpredictable dangers, and he has suffered five major accidents. Remembering a 35-foot fall, he said, "I was coming down head first, and I flipped over and landed on my heels. So I smashed both heels." Since the Depression days when his father was paralyzed by a falling beam, working conditions have improved significantly through union pressure, he contended. "The old days were tough," he said. "They really got blood out of you. Today, everything is for the workingman, so he's not working to death on the job. I'm not saying that the union makes it easy, but they fix it so the companies can't kill us."

Deer is a member of Local 40, which he said enjoys an enviable reputation among the several metropolitan area ironworkers unions. Aside from the Mohawks, high steel men are drawn from a few other tribes and many racial and ethnic groups, including Newfoundlanders and Scandinavians. Construction has kept Deer and other Indians steadily employed for generations.

The same, however, cannot be said for blacks. During the post-World War II building boom, while substantial numbers of Italian immigrants and their sons were excavating basements, laying brick, installing doors, and glazing windows, and while Mohawk teams were riveting girders overhead, thousands of newly arrived southern blacks were denied entry to building trades unions and compelled either to work as unskilled laborers or seek menial jobs in other fields.

Gil Banks, who was trained as a diesel mechanic by the Army Air Corps, said that the only construction work he could get in New York in 1954 was breaking concrete. A decade later, after learning surveying at a community college, he couldn't get into the International Union of Operating Engineers. Nor could he or other blacks get work at the Downstate Medical Center or Harlem Hospital, both being built, ironically, in black neighborhoods. Three decades later, in 1987, Gold-

Among those most severely affected by the switch away from manufacturing were the hundreds of thousands of blacks who had come to New York seeking opportunities after World War II. Even where jobs were available, racism by employers and labor unions created near-impenetrable barriers. Blacks have found construction unions particularly slow to integrate them into their ranks, and even when accepted, they frequently have been isolated. As a result, many turned to jobs in the public sector. Clerical careers that once required relatively simple skills, such as typing and filing, now necessitate the mastery of sophisticated electronic equipment.

ston Charles, a black Virgin Islander, had been waiting eleven years for admission to the Wood, Wire and Metal Lathers Union. "Certain jobs you can't get as a black man," he said. "All we get are the hard, backbreaking jobs."

The United States government, which throughout World War II's crusade to save democracy had not seen fit to desegregate its armed forces, finally outlawed race and sex discrimination in employment by enacting the 1964 Civil Rights Act. In the construction industry, violations by both employers and unions were flagrant, but achieving enforcement proved very difficult. Even a federal study confirming the building trades' denial of work to blacks produced little. And a well-intentioned approach, the New York Plan initiated by Mayor John V. Lindsay in 1970 to train eight hundred minority workers, failed to yield jobs and was dropped three years later. A second and more vigorous attempt by the Lindsay administration, opposed by the construction unions because of its goals and timetables, was ruled unconstitutional by a federal court in 1976.

While government efforts to gain employment for minorities in the building trades have failed to significantly integrate that field, government itself has become an important source of jobs. Like previous generations of immigrants, notably the Irish, contemporary blacks have found the public sector more responsive than the private. On the streets, as postal, sanitation, social, hospital, and public safety workers, and beneath them as transit workers and custodians, tens of thousands of blacks work for federal, state, and city agencies in New York. Still, the proportions of minorities decline as responsibilities and salaries increase, despite the promises and claims of mayors and commissioners. During the past decade, Mayor Edward I. Koch, who opposes job quotas and timetables, has been accused of insensitivity by many black leaders, a charge he denies and has sought to offset through the appointment of highly visible officials, such as Police Commissioner Benjamin Ward.

Summing up the case for black frustration and resentment, Herbert Hill, an industrial relations professor at the University of Wisconsin who formerly directed labor relations for the NAACP, charged: "In the New York City area there has been minimal change after thirty years of protest. Many trade unions have made a token adjustment to comply with affirmative action, but the racial patterns remain the same. Once you strip away all the rhetoric, what you have is an expression of the continuing effort of whites to protect the privileged positions that white men have always had in America."

Eventually, Gil Banks was admitted to the Operating Engineers Union. But only, he said, as a "special case" after having played a highly visible role in 1960s' antiunion demonstrations and as a member of Harlem Fight Back, an activist organization that seeks construction jobs for minorities. "You know," he said, "they thought it might cool me down." It didn't, Banks said, pointing out that he had become assistant director of Harlem Fight Back. Progress has been painfully slow; sometimes imperceptible. "Today, in 1987," he said, "it seems to me that instead of the situation reversing itself, it's exacerbating itself."

Besides facing racism in the building trades and many other fields, blacks who came to New York in the decades after World War II encountered a city undergoing a vast economic change. They found themselves trapped in the shift from manufacturing, which had provided blue-collar jobs for a century, to services, where the best positions required education, training, and skills that neither they nor many earlier immigrants possessed. Together with Puerto Ricans, blacks learned that timing can be critical to success in New York, that ambition and desire can burn out in the absence of opportunity. And in a period of increasing automation, they discovered that even menial jobs can evaporate in a service-oriented economy.

The whir of automation also sounded the economic death knell for Chinese laundry workers. In this instance, the automation involved consumer goods—washers,

Ethnic displacement in New York's economy was very evident in the laundry business. Once dominated by Chinese men, who labored long and hard by hand, the industry's work force was reshaped by the introduction of technology.

dryers, and permanent-press fabrics—and those affected had a long-standing stake in the city. Part of the New York scene for more than a century, they became largely superfluous when most of their customers became do-it-yourselfers.

As might be expected, the first Chinese immigrants to arrive in America settled on the West Coast. Drawn to California after 1848 by tales of quick and easy wealth, instead of gold, they discovered prejudice, discrimination, and exploitation. Barred from prospecting and excluded from the skilled trades, they took jobs as laborers building roads, laying track, filling swamps, and constructing wineries. But when transcontinental trains brought work-hungry Irish and other East Coast immigrants westward after 1869, racism drove the Chinese out of even those menial jobs. Anti-Asian hostility reached its height, or depth, in 1882 with passage of the Chinese Exclusion Act forbidding entry to all but merchants and students and subsequent laws prohibiting even the wives of those already here. What little opportunity remained for the resident Chinese involved serving the white majority, and so they became launderers, cooks, and servants.

Discriminatory pressures in the Western states induced many to return to China, but others decided to venture eastward and settled in urban centers such as New York and Boston. This was reflected in census reports showing the Chinese population of what became Manhattan's Chinatown soaring from only eight hundred in 1880 to more than ten thousand a decade later. They formed a tight and singular society: Restrictive immigration policies and job discrimination had the effect of making Chinatown a virtually all-male community of laundry workers.

The work was hard, the hours long, the pay poor, and the pleasures few. David Chin, who arrived in New York in 1927, recalled, during an interview with the New York Chinatown History Project, his seemingly unending days in a hand laundry. "You get up early, you see the people go to work. And you working there, you see the people coming home. And you working there, see the people going out—a movie or enjoyment. Then you see the people coming home: 'Oh, Charlie, you still open? Wait! I get the laundry.' Eleven, twelve, after one o'clock. . . . I said to myself, 'How many hours?' those days. I said, 'If you work like that—any country you work like that—you will survive. You don't have to be over here. . . . And over here, you just have nothing. Worked to death.' "

By the 1930s, there were more than four thousand hand laundries operating in the city, competing against white businesses that maintained an advantage by monopolizing steam-driven machinery. This compelled the Chinese to offer painstaking and unremunerative "personal services," such as replacing buttons and mending tears, that further extended their workdays and reduced their meager profits.

However, after the Depression, by pooling their resources, the Chinese bought secondhand machinery that enabled them to adopt more financially rewarding mechanical techniques and challenge their Caucasian rivals. While the hand laundries had performed each washing, drying, ironing, and folding process manually, the work could now be handled on a mass production basis. Hand laundries still took in soiled clothing. But they gave it to wet washes and shirt press factories, which often provided everything but the finishing touches. These were added by the hand laundries, which then wrapped the cleaned clothing and returned it to their customers.

But technology, in the form of home washing machines, dryers, and advances in washable materials, soon arrived to end the Chinese laundries' short-lived era of relative prosperity. By the mid-1980s, there were fewer than one thousand Chinese laundries in the entire metropolitan area, and former employees were struggling to subsist.

Shifts in the economy, of course, create as well as eliminate jobs. And the beneficiaries of the most recent changes have been another group of Asian immigrants.

Koreans, who began appearing in significant numbers in the city about 1970, have virtually taken over New York's greengrocery business in less than two decades, as well as making substantial inroads into such other retail operations as stationery and liquor stores. In many respects, including overcoming the language barrier, these Asian newcomers have managed to duplicate the success of earlier European immigrants and done so in half the time.

The Korean phenomenon resulted from a variety of factors, including, but hardly limited to, their own drive and ambition. In their case, too, timing proved critical. The bulk of the Koreans began arriving in New York at the very time that the traditional greengrocers, mostly Italian and Jewish immigrants or their children, began retiring or fleeing the inner city. In many cases, the white ethnic shopkeepers, more interested in entering mainstream occupations than in clinging to the family stores, priced their markets affordably. And the Koreans, unlike the blacks and Puerto Ricans, were likely to be middle class and financially able to buy in.

The homeland experience of the Koreans was another salutory factor that prepared them for America. Many of the earliest immigrants to New York had been reared in North Korea and had fled to the south. A resourceful, tough-minded lot, they were determined to find a niche for themselves and their families. A significant proportion of the immigrants were well-educated and worldly, characteristics that made adaptation easier. Many, in fact, held advanced degrees but were unable to practice medicine, law, or engineering because they lacked language skills.

They did not lack business acumen, however. By closely observing New Yorkers' life-styles, they have adapted their shops to the growing number of singles, for example, by maintaining elaborate salad bars and offering fried chicken, ribs, pasta, and other take-home specialties. Nor did they lack energy. "Owning a business," one Korean immigrant said, "is part of being Korean." Like their European prototypes, one of the Koreans' most valuable resources has been family labor. They have been able to compete with supermarkets and chain stores primarily by staying open later and longer, in some cases a full twenty-four hours. This has been accomplished by utilizing family members, who not only can be trusted fully but who don't join unions, do not have to be paid overtime, and need not be provided with costly benefits. Greengroceries were a "natural" for Koreans because they could be operated with both limited start-up capital and a limited knowledge of English. More than one thousand colorful Korean-owned fruit and vegetable shops now decorate every New York neighborhood.

There is little question that America has always been "the land of opportunity." But has it been the land of equal opportunity? Has each immigrant wave found the same chance to succeed? Or has "making it" more often been a consequence of timing, of need, of supply and demand?

The economic history of New York has been largely an immigrant success story. But it also has been the story of changing times; of an economy that depended first on trade, then on manufacture, and now on service; and of an alien work force that hoped to match its talents with the city's wants. In addition to discrimination, what differentiates contemporary blacks and Latinos from earlier European immigrants may lie in what the city, not the newcomer, has to offer.

Teaching how to become an "American" has traditionally been part of the unwritten curriculum of New York City's educational system. It was a compulsory assignment, required by the presence of millions of immigrant families, most of whom spoke no English and all of whom were strangers to the ways of their adopted homeland. An unprecedented challenge, it achieved unimagined success. Yet, the inculcation of "Americanism" has scarred the history of New York's schools, provoking intermittent but bitter struggles for the hearts and minds of the city's youngsters.

While the goal has been to make one out of many, the result often has been not harmony, but controversy and rancor. For attempts to impose unity have instead created discord within families and between generations, and threatened cultural diversity. Repeatedly, mastery of the educational system has prompted a power struggle between old-timers and newcomers, variously pitting nativists against aliens, Protestants against Catholics, Christians against Jews, and whites against blacks. Over time, majorities have become minorities, minorities have become majorities, and control has become elusive.

Although the Establishment viewed education as a tool for taming the immigrants' children—about whom it had both exaggerated fears and limited expectations—these very students frequently were able not only to flourish under the system but to eventually participate in its supervision and even alter its course.

Public education in its present form is a relatively recent development; it was less than one hundred and fifty years ago that, through the Maclay Act of 1842, the state created a school system for New York City headed by an elected board of education. Previously, broadly based education in the city, even when using public funds, was directed by private boards and contained a substantial religious content.

From the colonial era through the Revolutionary War period, education in New York was unorganized but existed in several forms: tutors, apprenticeship programs, and church and charity schools. Children generally learned to read from their parents, although reading was also taught at "dame" schools, by women who instructed in their own homes for pay. The wealthy had opportunities to receive training for elite careers in medicine, law, commerce, the ministry, and the military, while for the less well-to-do, manual skills were developed through apprenticeships.

By the end of the eighteenth century, New York City children whose parents could not afford to pay tutors or "dames" could gain a rudimentary education in charity schools organized by churches. In the absence of any state system, the role played by churches in the early days was dominant. This precedent, while initially accepted without question, was destined to ignite partisan passions that exist to the present. In those times, however, religion was viewed as the best means of imparting moral values, then regarded as a basic function of education. And although New York was constitutionally committed to a separation of church and state, the fact that publicly supported schools freely indulged in Bible reading, prayers, and hymn singing, and readily used materials from religious sources, was not seen as violating that separation.

The first significant attempt at broadly based education came in 1805 with the formation of the nondenominational, but clearly Protestant, Free School Society, later renamed the Public School Society. Headed by DeWitt Clinton, then mayor and later governor, it was organized principally by Quakers to provide for the increasing number of poor children who were not being taught in New York's church schools. The Society rapidly gained students and adherents through introduction of a new teaching technique, the "Lancasterian system," which was conceived by an English Quaker named Joseph Lancaster who prized efficiency and originated the phrase: "A place for everything and everything in its place." By relying heavily on

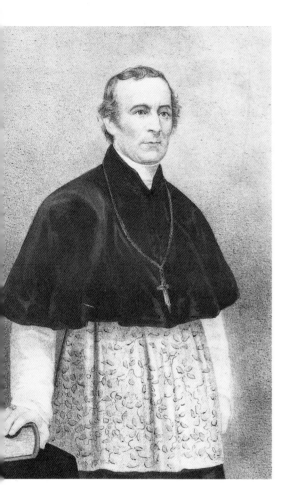

John Hughes, in an 1834 Currier and Ives print.

rote and memorization, utilizing rewards and punishments, and training student monitors as overseers, the method was able to "educate" vast numbers of children with a very small staff at a minimal cost.

The seemingly phenomenal results achieved by the Lancasterian technique by the mid-1820s enabled the Society to propose a publicly supported system, under its aegis, that would educate all the city's children, rich and poor, on a nondenominational basis. The motive was a mixture of egalitarianism and a desire to cut off the public funding of competing Baptist schools. The Free School Society's effort succeeded, as the New York City Common Council, on the authority of the State Legislature, limited appropriations exclusively to the Society, ending the earlier policy of supporting a variety of church-affiliated schools. This decision, coupled with subsequent legislative action, established nondenominational, albeit Protestant, schools as the cornerstone of a publicly supported educational system.

At that point in its history, New York City was overwhelmingly Protestant, and the principal consideration was not whether religion should be present in the classroom or even which religion. What did matter was that no particular Protestant denomination be preeminent. But this would be the primary concern only so long as New York remained a Protestant city. The nondenominational approach came under fire as soon as the city's Catholic population had grown sufficiently to demand recognition. The result was a clash of religious interests that led to political and, even, armed conflict and constituted the first of what has been described as the city's "great school wars."

Fed by a flood of Irish and, to a lesser degree, German, immigrants in the early decades of the nineteenth century, the Catholic church did not hesitate to seek, as a matter of doctrine, to provide its own form of education for its youth. This was normally done through parochial schools, which combined secular education with Catholic religious instruction. But in New York, where its parishioners were impoverished, a lack of funds prevented the church from establishing enough schools to handle the burgeoning population, and young Catholics were confronted with the dilemma of attending the Protestant-oriented, publicly supported schools or foregoing schooling, which in the 1830s was still not compulsory.

The threat to the primacy of Protestantism was heightened by the presence of Catholic Bishop John Hughes, an articulate, outspoken prelate who had no illusions about the church's predicament nor any reservations about the tactics required to deal with it. Hughes, whose sharp tongue and aggressiveness earned him the nickname "Dagger John," recognized that the best solution for the parochial system lay in obtaining public funding. And his strongest argument was provided by the existing state-supported system's open use of materials, such as the King James version of the Bible, which were anathema to Catholics. To buttress his case, Hughes had little difficulty in finding examples of slurring references to Catholics and the Irish in textbooks, such as the contention that immigration would make America the "common sewer of Ireland." He characterized the materials as leading pupils to the assumption that "Catholics are necessarily, morally, intellectually, infallibly, a stupid race."

Such nativist prejudice was common during this first major Anglo-Saxon Protestant confrontation with Irish Catholics, with foreigners who seemed so different in their speech and manner and held such mysterious and dangerous religious beliefs. But to the Protestant majority, who now feared the dilution of their culture and the loss of their power, education represented salvation. As *Putnam's Monthly* put it: "Our readers will agree with us that for the effectual defecation of the stream of life in a great city, there is but one rectifying agent—one infallible filter—the SCHOOL." Through the schools, *their* schools, they would overcome the subversive influences of a foreign culture and teach these alien children to become Americans.

The Catholic cause found influential and unanticipated allies in New York Governor William Henry Seward and his wily political strategist, Thurlow Weed. By

1840, New York City's growing Irish population had been successfully wooed by Democratic Tammany Hall, an affiliation that Weed, as a rival Whig leader, was bent on undoing. In Seward, Weed not only had a cohort who might benefit politically from such a move but one who actually was sympathetic philosophically to the need of Catholic youths for better schooling.

Thus, Seward, a Protestant and nominal head of the anti-immigrant Whig party, split with his supporters to urge the creation of publicly supported Catholic schools. In his 1840 message to the State Legislature, the governor, through a proposal remarkable for its boldness and candor, said, "The children of foreigners, found in great numbers in our populous cities and towns, and in the vicinity of our public works, are too often deprived of the advantages of our system of public education, in consequence of prejudices arising from difference of language or religion.... I do not hesitate, therefore, to recommend the establishment of schools in which they may be instructed by teachers speaking the same language with themselves and professing the same faith."

Encouraged by this invitation, Catholic leaders sought public funds from the New York City Common Council, which turned them down on the grounds that doing so would violate the separation of church and state. Undaunted, Hughes stepped up his campaign and, at a mass meeting in Carroll Hall prior to the 1841 legislative elections, gambled on Catholic political influence by unveiling a ticket that endorsed ten sympathetic Democrats for the Assembly but nominated three independent Catholics for remaining seats. This "Carroll Hall ticket," as it became known, achieved its objectives when the ten Democrats were elected along with three Whigs, making it evident that Catholics held the balance of power in city politics.

While Catholics were publicly flexing their developing political muscle in New York City, an event of equal importance to their cause was unfolding behind the scenes in Albany. There, in response to Catholic appeals, Secretary of State John Spencer, a Seward appointee, was formulating an innovative blueprint for New York City that, while not fully satisfying Catholics, would enable them to coexist educationally with Protestants for the next half-century.

Spencer's plan, which finally gained passage in 1842 through legislation submitted by Democratic New York Assemblyman William B. Maclay, simply gave each

Ward schools, such as this one at 87th Street near 4th Avenue, were introduced in 1842 through the Maclay Act, which gave control of education to the city's wards, generally reflecting ethnic enclaves. This measure was contrived to enable Catholics, who had become increasingly populous through Irish immigration, to instruct Catholic children, rather than having them subjected to the anti-Catholic prejudices of the Free School Society's Protestant teachers.

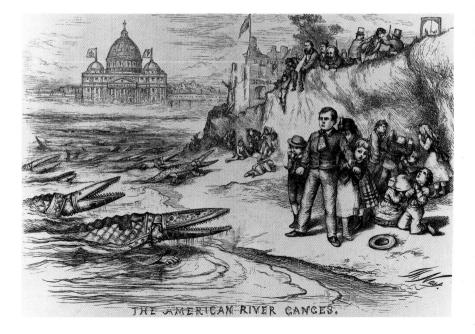

THE AMERICAN RIVER GANGES.

Resentment against Catholic attempts to operate parochial schools in collusion with Tammany Hall was expressed in this bitter 1871 Harper's Weekly *cartoon by Thomas Nast, depicting priests as child-devouring crocodiles.*

At the turn of the twentieth century, few city schools provided a pleasant educational environment. In the 1890s, before it was condemned, the Essex Market School was a warren of dark and crowded classrooms.

of the city's wards control of education within its boundaries. Since the wards generally reflected distinctive ethnic and religious identities, the practical effect was to allow both Catholics and Protestants to run their own schools, even though an amendment barred public funds to city schools where "any religious sectarian doctrine or tenet shall be taught, inculcated, or practiced."

Although a long-term consequence of the compromise Maclay Act was to relieve religious tension for several decades, its immediate impact was just the opposite. Supporters of the Public School Society and many Whigs were outraged at what they saw as a capitulation to Catholic political pressure; Whig leaders and newspapers in New York City denounced the legislation. On election day in 1842, less than a week after Seward had signed the bill into law, nativist mobs ran wild in the Irish Sixth Ward, attacking Hughes's residence and threatening several Catholic churches, including the former St. Patrick's Cathedral.

The Maclay Act affected Catholic educational goals both positively and negatively. By loosening the Protestant grip, it enabled most Catholic children to attend school without being exposed to what they regarded as repugnant religious material. However, it did nothing to further the Catholic hierarchy's aim of providing Catholic teaching; to the contrary, the prohibition against teaching sectarian doctrine underscored to the leadership the necessity of developing a parochial system. Accordingly, Hughes gave this top priority, and, indeed, parochial school enrollment did grow after the ward school system began. However, statistics indicate that in 1865, a smaller percentage of all pupils were attending parochial schools than had done so in 1840. Since the proportion of Catholics in New York City increased substantially during that period, it is clear that despite Hughes's efforts, a significant majority of Catholic children were attending public, not parochial, schools. Apparently, in the Catholic wards the presence of Catholic teachers under the supervision of Catholic trustees, coupled with such permissible elements as the use of the church-approved Douay edition of the Bible, was sufficient to convince most parents that their children were receiving an appropriately religious education.

So far as the Public School Society was concerned, the ward system proved fatal. In 1853, after more than a decade of subservience to the elected Board of Education, the once-independent and powerful Society merged with the Board and went out of existence.

The effectiveness of the ward school system was difficult to assess. There is evidence that many of the trustees, however unprofessional or even uneducated, took their responsibilities seriously and were devoted to the children and the task of providing them with a decent education. There is also evidence that the system led to various forms of corruption, as well as payroll-padding, patronage, and favoritism.

If these transgressions have a familiar ring, it is no doubt because the ward school arrangement coincided with the growth of Tammany Hall's power under infamous William Marcy (Boss) Tweed. The fledgling educational system apparently represented a plum too enticing to ignore, for Tweed, retired from Congress out of boredom and defeated in a city race for alderman, got himself on the Board of Education in 1855.

In succeeding decades, as Tammany abandoned its earlier nativist stance to court the Irish and German immigrants who were crowding New York's tenements, streets, and schools, Tweed did not lack ingenuity in seeking to benefit the Catholic cause. In 1869, as a state senator, he introduced a bill permitting any city or county board of supervisors to subsidize "any free school or schools, in which not less than two hundred children have been or are taught or educated gratuitously." The effect would have been to aid Catholic parochial schools in New York City, a fact discovered by the Senate's Republican majority in time to defeat the measure.

Thus thwarted, Tweed concealed a provision for aiding parochial schools in a routine budget appropriation that was passed without scrutiny in the rush for adjournment. Uncovered by the *New York Times* subsequent to its becoming law, the notorious "Section 10" was repealed following a furor but only after providing two years of subsidies to the city's Catholic schools.

Tweed, whose instinct for chicanery was probably unparalleled in municipal history, quickly sized up the opportunities present in the educational system, as evidenced by his service on the Committee on School Furniture. And it was, of course, his stationery firm that filled the schools' needs for pens, ink, and paper. Nor was he reluctant to exercise power vengefully. Harper Brothers, whose *Harper's Weekly* had skewered Tweed through the cartoons of Thomas Nast, soon found that its textbooks had been thrown out of the schools.

Revelations of the scandalous depredations of the likes of Tweed and his cronies in the late nineteenth century were seized by a group of avid reformers whose aim was to get rid of the ward schools and replace them with a centralized system. Their declared motive was not primarily to eliminate corruption, although they contended that centralization would do just that, but rather to eliminate politics and promote professionalism. But there were strong suspicions that they were propelled by an antiforeigner, anti-Catholic bias that sought to reinstate the Anglo-Saxon Protestant elite in the positions of power they had occupied before the mass immigration movement. And as the twentieth century approached, immigrants from southern and eastern Europe, essentially Italians and Jews, began arriving in numbers sufficiently large to further exacerbate the fears and hostilities of the once-dominant Protestant minority.

Thus, the campaign for centralization soon took on the appearance of the religious and ethnic conflicts that have characterized so much of the city's history. The reformers—wealthy, well-educated, socially prominent, and politically conservative—believed themselves not only superior to the penniless, untutored, alien masses but responsible for shaping them in their own well-formed image. The State Legislature rang with condescending demands that slum children be brought "under the influence of educated, refined, intelligent men and women, so they will be elevated and lifted out of the swamp into which they were born and brought up."

Such blatant snobbery and ethnocentrism offended the ward trustees and teachers as much as it did the immigrants; a majority of the teachers were either immigrants or children of immigrants themselves. And they felt that the demands for change were not based on experience or even reality. "The trustees are gentlemen," one teacher testified, "and devote every spare minute and even sleeping time to the care of the schools. The present attempt to abolish the trustees is all wrong and has not been brought about by those who know our public schools."

But the reform movement was influential in the halls of power. Leadership was taken over by a young Columbia University professor named Nicholas Murray Butler, who was informed, articulate, persuasive, and driven. He was convinced of the need for revision of the system and worked tirelessly to achieve it. Still, the resistance was formidable. The reformers' calls for "professionalism" and "efficiency" not only struck the teachers and administrators as undemocratic but clearly threatening to their careers. They organized and campaigned against centralization, collecting 100,000 signatures and joining as many as four thousand colleagues and supporters at mass meetings.

The city's educational controversy wound up on the state's political agenda as centralization found favor in Albany (where Upstate Republicans saw it as a blow against Tammany), and the Legislature easily passed a measure that required only the approval of reform Mayor William Strong and the signature of Republican Governor Levi P. Morton. While the motivations of both sides were complex, "Americanization" was a dominant issue. The argument for keeping the ward sys-

The influx of immigrants in the late nineteenth century gave schools the burden of not only teaching reading, writing, and arithmetic but "Americanism," as well. More than developing allegiance and patriotism, the schools tried to instill respect for "the American way of life," sometimes by demeaning the cultures from which the pupils' parents had come. This instruction in saluting the flag took place in 1889 at the Mott Street Industrial School.

The struggle for survival that permeated the immigrant experience made learning job skills a critical part of education. Manual training classes developed carpentry expertise, while for some boys and girls, the Industrial School on West 52nd Street presaged a future in the trades.

Above and left:
The importance of outdoor activity and fresh air to inhabitants of dark, stifling tenements was not ignored by city educators. Youngsters took noon naps bundled up on beach chairs in a fresh air class or, in milder weather, worked off energy in school playgrounds, such as this one in the Bronx.

Settlement houses such as the Educational Alliance involved themselves deeply in the lives of immigrant families. In the first decade of the twentieth century, they concerned themselves with physical and social well-being, along with learning. This is a rooftop milk station at the Baron de Hirsch School, named for a Jewish philanthropist.

Preschool children got an opportunity to learn about music at the Harlem River Houses' day care program in 1938.

More than forty years ago, New York City's cultural and ethnic diversity was evident in this classroom at Brooklyn's P.S. 5.

tem that had recognized the immigrants' distinctiveness was expressed by Robert Maclay, president of the Board of Education: "New York is a peculiar city. It is a cosmopolitan city. If you do away with the trustee system, you do away with the people's schools. The trustees are in touch with the schools, and none others are or can be but those who live in the locality of the schools. We have a peculiar population, made up of all nationalities. They are people whose children we want to get in our public schools. There is a fear on the part of these people that we are going to interfere with their religion. If we have ward trustees representing all classes, confidence will be maintained."

The reformers' contention was contained in a mayoral staff member's view that it was not "a good thing in a city like this so largely impregnated with foreign influences, languages and ideas that the schools should be controlled locally, for in many localities the influences that would control would be unquestionably un-American. In some districts there are vast throngs of foreigners where one scarcely hears a word of English spoken; where the mode of living is repugnant to every American idea. The best interests of the city demand that the children of such population be brought under American influences and instruction."

The reform bill became law in 1896. It ended neighborhood involvement in the schools and placed control entirely under a central Board of Education, assisted by a professionally trained Board of Superintendents. The new plan had some far-reaching effects: It provided an educational model for the rest of the nation, and it set a precedent within New York for the dismantling of other neighborhood offices outside the school system and their reorganization into citywide agencies. But it did not accomplish what presumably was its goal: to improve the education of the pupils. It failed, for example, to reduce class size or to replace incompetent teachers or their immediate supervisors.

The original centralization legislation principally affected only what is now Manhattan. Even after 1898, when Greater New York City was formed, the other boroughs retained considerable autonomy over education and continued to do so until 1901, when they joined the central system.

While the new arrangement may have had limited academic impact, the experience of attending public school at the turn of the century, with its heavy emphasis on "Americanization," proved difficult and often wrenching for many children of immigrants. Recollections of the sons and daughters of Italian and Jewish newcomers are replete with anecdotes reflecting the generational tensions that were triggered by the pressure to assimilate.

Leonard Covello, an educator and author of *The Heart Is the Teacher*, remembered what happened when he brought home his first report card. "What is this? Leonard Covello!" asked his father. "What happened to the *i* in Coviello?... From Leonardo to Leonard I can follow... a perfectly natural process. In America anything can happen and does happen. But you don't change a family name."

When the young student explained that both his teacher and he found Covello easier to pronounce, his mother joined in protest, drawing the response, "Mama, you don't understand."

"Will you stop saying that!" she cried. "I don't understand. I don't understand. What is there to understand? Now that you have become Americanized, you understand everything and I understand nothing."

Although many teachers were unaware of the effect that their instruction was having on their pupils' family relationships, the noted educator Julia Richman recognized the problem. Americanizing the child, she said, means weaning the child "away from the standards and traditions of its home. The parents remain foreign; the children become American. There is thus created an almost unbridgeable gulf between the two."

English homework was often a multi-generational activity, as immigrants and their children struggled to master the intricacies of reading and writing the new language.

The inner conflicts of Italian-American pupils often were heightened by a cultural tradition that distrusted formal education. As Richard Gambino pointed out in *Blood of My Blood*, "To do well in school was equivalent in emotional terms to a betrayal of the family. The guilt of such a position was unbearable."

The reasons for this attitude are complex and steeped in the timeworn traditions of southern Italy, the impoverished, illiterate, agricultural region that overwhelmingly accounted for Italian immigration to America. Formal schooling, as opposed to *learning*, was regarded by southern Italians as a threat to the family orientation that for countless generations had been pivotal in their lives. When a law providing for three years of free compulsory education was enacted in Italy in 1877 by northern Italians seeking to modernize and reshape the nation, it was resisted so broadly and vigorously in the south that efforts to enforce it were abandoned.

Such attitudes accompanied the southern Italians to New York, where, Gambino wrote, "Second-generation children were forcefully impressed in public schools with the doctrine of assimilation in American ways, a program that made them feel odd and guilty about everything in their own identities from their mannerisms, clothes, and food to their operatic, vowel-filled names. Little wonder that the immigrants perceived the schools as a new form of an old immorality and adopted a mocking attitude toward their efforts. Any manner, idea, or value the second-generation child carried home from the school was slapped down with the perjorative 'American.' "

Because of their rural background, many Italian immigrants experienced considerable difficulty in adapting to urban ways. Deprived of farm work, they took to manual labor, often winding up with pickax and shovel in poorly paid construction gangs. Able-bodied sons and daughters were needed to contribute to the families' survival, and it was difficult to reconcile such pressing demands with what was being taught in the schools. One Italian immigrant who clearly demonstrated his native bias against schooling was quoted by Covello in his dissertation entitled, *The Social Background of the Italo-American Schoolchild:* "My two boys went to school against my will. And what do I see now? By having forced them to learn things they do not need, their health is gone, and they are just two stupid donkeys who cannot take care of themselves; [they] have no use for what they learned and even forgot long ago whatever they did learn in school. In Italy they would have been healthy young men, with a sense of dignity; responsible men. Men, I say, because this school made them children."

Gambino also explained how even well into the twentieth century, Italian-American youngsters formed groups or gangs that represented a compromise and served as a refuge from both the Old World traditions of their families and the contemporary attitudes of their American schoolmates. "The values of these street corner gangs took precedence over the demands of the public school, and the things we valued did not include high achievement in school. In fact any child who achieved high grades was suspect, a fact that tormented me in my earliest years in school because I did well in studies without much effort. I even tried to play down my ability to excel in classroom exercises. I finally was accepted by my peers despite my successes on the report card."

Among Jews, the other major immigrant group to arrive in New York around 1900, the generational gap was similarly aggravated by the Americanization program. Suspicion of the schools and their personnel played a significant role. William Henry Maxwell, New York's first superintendent of education, described a near riot at a Lower East Side school in 1907 that was precipitated by the fears of thousands of Jewish parents that their children's throats were being cut. In fact, a surgeon had been brought in by the principal to remove pupils' enlarged adenoids.

Becoming an American created an aching ambivalence in many Jewish children. Alfred Kazin, in his *A Walker in the City*, expressed the anguish in these terms:

I worked on a hairline between triumph and catastrophe. Why the odds should always have felt so narrow I understood only when I realized how little my parents thought of their own lives. It was not for myself alone that I was expected to shine, but for them—to redeem the constant anxiety of their existence. I was the first American child, their offering to the strange new God; I was to be the monument of their liberation from the shame of being—what they were. And that there was shame in this was a fact that everyone seemed to believe as a matter of course. It was in the gleeful discounting of themselves—what do we know?—with which our parents greeted every fresh victory in our savage competition for "high averages," for prizes, for a few condescending words of official praise from the principal at assembly. It was in the sickening invocation of "Americanism"—the word itself accusing us of everything we apparently were not. Our families and teachers seemed tacitly agreed that we were somehow to be a little ashamed of what we were. Yet it was always hard to say why this should be so.

The conflict within the family prompted by the schools' drive for Americanization no doubt took its heaviest toll on the immigrant parents. As Julius Drachsler observed, "The fear of...losing the children haunts the older generation. It is not merely the natural desire of parent to retain influence over child. Nor is it simply the dread that the wayward offspring will mar the good name of the immigrant group by abuse of his newly-found freedom. It is a vague uneasiness that a delicate network of precious traditions is being ruthlessly torn asunder, that a whole world of ideals is crashing into ruins; and amidst this desolation the fathers and mothers picture themselves wandering about lonely in vain search of their lost children."

A similar thought was expressed by writer Norman Podhoretz in his autobiography, *Making It*, when he pointed out that "my mother wanted nothing so much as for me to be a success, to be respected and admired. But she did not imagine, I think, that she would only purchase the realization of her ambition at the price of my progressive estrangement from her and her ways."

Whether they were Jewish or Italian, few children of immigrants were exposed to English at home or even in their neighborhoods. Consequently, the difficulty of the educational experience was compounded by a lack of familiarity with the language. A young Jewish man named Gregory Weinstein, who had struggled to attend and then had gone on to teach night school, recalled the confusion many encountered: "The principal once dropped into my classroom with a cheery 'Good evening, gentlemen.' All arose and responded, 'Good evening, Mister Principal.' He then asked the pupils, 'Are you making any headway?' Almost with one accord they answer, 'No, sir.' The principal looked at me quizzically, and wrote the question on the blackboard. 'Now,' he asked, 'translate the word headway.' '*Kopfweh*' (headache), they answered. The principal smilingly said, 'I now understand why you are making no headway.' "

Unfortunately, learning English was more often a serious affair, and many teachers lacked Weinstein's patience and good nature. Irving Howe called attention to the arduous task of adult immigrants through Edward Steiner's comment that "if our teacher had met us as men and not as children, if into that weary hour he had thrown a grain of humor to relax us, if someone would have sung a simple tune in English, more might have remained after a week than fourteen out of a class...ten times that number."

In *World of Our Fathers*, Howe reported the grim description of night school portrayed by Samuel Strook: "The immigrants will be pushed into school benches intended for eight-year-old children, their knees reaching to the very desks. They will be uncomfortable and sorely puzzled. And then a teacher, in all probability tired from a day's hard work, will undertake the task of teaching them English. For a few days perhaps he will have patience with pupils who are exhausted after their ten-hour day. He will treat them gently, sympathetically. But after a while his own fatigue will show its effect, and he will become capricious and unduly exacting. The students will lose heart.... One by one they will cease to come until barely a third of

City College of New York (CCNY) played a critical role in New York's social and political development, as well as in its educational history. The tuition-free institution enabled thousands of Lower East Side youths to get otherwise unattainable college educations. While the North Campus of CCNY on Convent Avenue had the look of serenity and scholarly contemplation, its alcoves and classrooms exploded with political and social ferment.

the original number is left. Then there will be talk in a different tone—censure, this time of the laziness of the foreigner, of his unwillingness to make sacrifices to learn English."

Despite such painful adjustments among the older generation, there is a substantial body of literature devoted to the accomplishments of Jewish pupils, their affection for education, and their superiority to other immigrant students. In 1901, for example, a government report stated that "the poorest among them will make all possible sacrifices to keep his children in school; and one of the most striking social phenomena in New York City today is the way in which the Jews have taken possession of the public schools, in the highest as well as the lowest grades....In the lower schools, Jewish children are the delight of their teachers for their cleverness...obedience and general good conduct, and the vacation schools, night schools, social settlements, libraries, bathing places, parks and playgrounds of the East Side are fairly besieged with Jewish children eager to take advantage of the opportunities they offer."

Frequently, such paeans to the Jewish children are accompanied by speculation that historic respect for learning, European discrimination that deprived Jews of land and forced them to absorb an urban experience, and a fierce determination not only to remain in America but to flourish are among the reasons for their achievements.

There are, however, some dissents, such as the contention of Irving Howe, in *World of Our Fathers*, that "the bulk of Jewish children...were not very different in their capacities or performance from the bulk of pupils from most other ethnic groups....To read the reports of the school superintendents is to grow impatient with later sentimentalists who would have us suppose that all or most Jewish children burned with zeal for the life of the mind."

And Julia Richman, as school district superintendent, found that many Jewish children encountered serious classroom difficulties because of such generally undiscussed problems as parental neglect and abuse, delinquency, child labor, disease, malnutrition, and even sexual abuse by roomers who shared their homes.

On the other hand, there is significant evidence that Jewish students were distinguished by their pursuit of higher education. Sherry Gorelick pointed out that by the end of World War I, Jews, although comprising only 25 percent of the city's

Above and opposite:
In the 1920s, '30s, and '40s, the significance of higher education in achieving intellectual and material rewards led many immigrants' children to aspire to New York's public colleges, such as Hunter College, where women unraveled the mysteries of chemistry in well-equipped laboratories and did calisthenics in middie blouses.

population, constituted almost 40 percent of the students in the nine colleges and universities serving the New York metropolitan area, including almost 80 percent of the students at the City College of New York (CCNY).

However, the writer went on to explain that "this increasing proportion of Jews among college students has nourished the widespread belief in the miraculous rise of the Jews through education. What is forgotten is that although more and more students were *Jews*, very few Jews were *students*. (In 1913, for example, the entire graduating class of CCNY had only 209 students.)"

Because it charged no tuition, CCNY had great appeal for poverty-ridden Jewish immigrants and their children. And it was attractive as well because its reputation for free-wheeling inquiry and tolerance of radical political ideologies would complement the socialist leanings they had acquired in Europe. Morris Raphael Cohen, a revered CCNY professor who had been a turn-of-the-century student there, ruminated about this in *A Dreamer's Journey:* "In my undergraduate years, and even more in later decades, an increasing proportion of the students was Jewish, many of them foreign-born, and very many of the others children of foreign-born parents. Many of us, therefore, were familiar with what are today provincially called 'un-American' ideas. Certainly, a large part of the student body of the College has always been particularly open-minded and critical towards the accepted commonplaces of the complacent. These students came prepared to weigh and consider new, as well as old, ideas, and their intellectual eagerness was encouraged rather than restrained by home conditions."

While some CCNY graduates discovered painfully that their collegiate political activities of the 1920s, '30s, and '40s would be considered subversive in the 1950s,

many remembered them with sad fondness as a time of extraordinary intellectual stimulation. In *A Margin of Hope*, Irving Howe recalled the period from 1936 to 1940:

> The real center of life at City College was in our Alcove 1, dark-stained, murky, shaped like a squat horseshoe, one of perhaps ten along the edge of the lunchroom. Alcove 1 was the home of heresy, left sectarianism, independent thought, and—to be honest—a share of fanaticism and intolerance. Here gathered Trotskyist, Socialist, Lovestonite students with their books, pamphlets, ragged overcoats, and cheese sandwiches. Also, one or two deviants from deviancy who were sharp enough to criticize our view that things had started going bad in the Soviet Union mostly with Stalin's usurpation of power. Nearby, in Alcove 2, gathered the far more numerous and powerful Stalinists. The Young Communist League must then have had about four hundred members at City College, while the quarrelsome anti-Stalinist Left, all groups together, had perhaps fifty. The YCL controlled the student paper, using it to print editorials defending Moscow trials. Closely knit, the YCL had a major advantage in possessing secret allies within the faculty—perhaps a dozen party members.
>
> You could walk into the thick brown darkness of Alcove 1 at almost any time of day or evening and find a convenient argument about the Popular Front in France, the New Deal in America, the civil war in Spain, the Five-Year Plan in Russia, the theory of permanent revolution, and "what Marx really meant." Anyone could join in an argument, there was no external snobbism: but whoever joined did so at his own risk, fools and ignoramuses not being suffered gladly....
>
> I can remember getting into an argument at ten in the morning, going off to some classes, and then returning at two in the afternoon to find the argument still going on, but with an entirely fresh cast of characters. The more versatile among us prided themselves on being able to carry on more than one argument at a time, like chess players before two boards....

New York's monumental task of educating adult immigrants, as well as their children, was borne largely by settlement houses, private institutions dedicated to uplift and progress. Originated in England in the mid-nineteenth century, settlement houses proved effective in teaching English and useful skills. Here are shown an English class for adults at the Educational Alliance before World War I (above right) and one at the University Settlement House in 1987 (above left). Learning to become an "American" was also part of the curriculum at the Henry Street Settlement (above). The settlement houses, surely well-intentioned, affronted some immigrants through their condescension.

The fact that first-generation and second-generation Americans were graduating from colleges such as CCNY by the 1930s was indeed remarkable considering the handicaps they had faced only a few decades earlier. The problems of language and custom had initially appeared overwhelming, so much so that new institutions called settlement houses had emerged to respond to those needs. Conceived in England in the mid-nineteenth century as "a colony of learning and fellowship in the industrial slums," settlement houses came to the Lower East Side in the 1880s when the University Settlement was organized as the Lily Pleasure Club by an earnest social reformer from Ohio named Stanton Coit.

The movement, ignited by the zeal of the Progressive Era and the abominable conditions of the city's slums, grew rapidly, spawning such institutions as the Educational Alliance, Henry Street Settlement, Grand Street Settlement, Christadora House, Hudson Guild, and Stuyvesant Neighborhood House. For the most part, the organizers were middle-class Anglo-Saxons; the objects of their well-intentioned but often condescending aid were working-class immigrants. Among Jews, the benefactors were drawn largely from established uptown Germans; their beneficiaries were recent arrivals from Russia and Poland. This missionary concept was evident in the constitution of the University Settlement Society, which stressed its belief that "good results can be accomplished by bringing men and women of education into closer relation with the laboring classes."

The settlement house provided a wide variety of services, including kindergartens, libraries, gymnasiums, loan societies, legal aid, concerts, dances, baths, and an extensive range of classes where one learned how to cook and sew, as well as how to become an American. The effect of the Americanization attempts was clearly diverse. Irving Howe noted differing responses in writing about the Educational Alliance in *World of Our Fathers:*

Parochial schools have played an important part in New York's educational picture since the arrival of the "Famine Irish" in the 1840s, although the ward system made them less vital from the Catholic standpoint. In 1910, St. Rita's in the Mott Haven section of the Bronx had enough ballplayers to fill every position, enough resources to afford uniforms for them, and enough influence to gain the support of the police department.

The memories of Eugene Lyons were bitter:

"We were 'Americanized' about as gently as horses are broken in. In the whole crude process, we sensed a disrespect for the alien traditions in our homes and came unconsciously to resent and despise those traditions, good and bad alike, because they seemed insuperable barriers between ourselves and our adopted land."

The memories of Morris Raphael Cohen were warm:

"It was at the Alliance that my father and mother went regularly to hear the Rev. Masliansky preach...in Yiddish. It was there that I drew books from the Aguilar Free Library and began to read English....It was there that I first met Thomas Davidson who became the light of my life and of my intellectual development...."

Interestingly, even as these efforts at acculturation were going on, another type of organization operated to sustain the immigrants' Old World traditions. Called *landsmanshaftn*, these Jewish mutual aid societies flourished on the Lower East Side during the height of the immigration tide from eastern Europe. The intent was to enable the newcomers to meet earlier immigrants from the same geographic areas to share new experiences and old memories, to cushion the transition, and to provide practical assistance, such as unemployment insurance, medical care, and burial plots. The *landsmanshaftn* have been described as "a personal, friendly Ellis Island."

While most Jewish immigrant families had been able to reconcile the pursuit of a secular education in New York City's public schools with obtaining a religious education in private Hebrew schools, their Catholic counterparts continued through the nineteenth century to seek state aid for parochial schools. This, of course, put them on an intermittent collision course with Protestants, although their clashes never reached the levels of violence and bitterness that surrounded the Maclay Act in 1842. As Catholic immigrants, mostly from Ireland and Germany, swelled New York City's population and, through involvement with Tammany Hall, gained increased influence, they were able to pursue their goals through the political process. The parochial school issue was resolved at the New York State Constitutional Convention of 1894 through a compromise that prohibited the expenditure of public funds for religious schools but permitted such aid to religious charities. With a few exceptions, the prohibition—known as the Blaine

Amendment because it was similar to legislation proposed by presidential hopeful James G. Blaine of Maine—still stands.

In 1935, supporters of aid to parochial schools were encouraged when the State Legislature passed a bill exempting busing from the prohibition. Herbert H. Lehman, New York's first Jewish governor, vetoed the bill and was criticized by Catholics, although the following year he signed a modified version that called for local referenda on the issue. In 1938, the Court of Appeals invalidated the law, but the state constitution was amended to permit public financing of busing for private and parochial students, and in 1939 Lehman authorized such assistance.

Periodically, proponents of aid to parochial schools, primarily the Catholic hierarchy, joined by Lutheran and Orthodox Jewish educators, have sought to repeal or, at least, chip away at the barrier, frequently relying on an economic argument. They hold both that it is unfair for Catholics (and Lutherans and Jews who educate their children solely in religious schools) to support two educational systems—public and parochial—and that the taxes of everyone else would soar if the parochial system collapsed and its pupils entered the public schools. The response, primarily from civil libertarians, and Protestants and Jews, has been philosophic; that is, that the constitutional separation of church and state clearly bars such aid, and that a parochial education is a choice, not a public obligation.

Repeal of the Blaine Amendment became a major issue at the state's 1967 constitutional convention, and although both sides lobbied vigorously, and while the subject clearly sparked religious hostility, antipathies were channeled into such nonviolent arenas as the press and legislative chambers. Despite the rhetoric, attempts to end the prohibition against state aid were unsuccessful. In recent years, opponents of the Blaine Amendment have chosen more indirect strategies, such as seeking tax credits for parents of parochial school pupils.

Conflicts involving religious differences, or the role of religion in education, surfaced during the twentieth century on issues other than public funding. Under pressure from parochial school advocates, "release time" programs permitting pupils to leave public schools in order to receive religious instruction were initiated in the 1920s on an experimental basis and enacted into state law in 1940. Efforts to prevent such programs in New York City failed, and they became effective there the following year.

School prayer was the focus of intense controversy for more than a decade in New York City after a recommendation by the State Board of Regents in 1951 that the school day open with one. Two years later, the city's Board of Education engineered a compromise by ordering pupils to sing the fourth verse of "America" as an alternative. This issue, together with "release time" and the busing of parochial pupils, later moved into the judicial arena, where, in 1962, the United States Supreme Court held the Regents' prayer unconstitutional but has upheld "release time" and parochial student busing.

While these issues often promoted acrimonious debate during the second quarter of the twentieth century, that period was notable chiefly for the reputation the New York City school system had acquired for innovation, progressivism, leadership, and general excellence. Federal laws restricting immigration in the mid-1920s enabled the strained system to turn its attention away from the task of educating recurrent waves of immigrants' children, while pioneers such as John Dewey had transfused it with new insights gained from psychology and sociology. Further, the teaching ranks had become invigorated by the energies of the children of earlier immigrant generations who found the field of education a stimulating and respectable ladder out of the ghetto. And even adversity proved useful, as the Great Depression of the early 1930s induced many New Yorkers to seek the sanctuary of teaching rather than risking the economic vagaries of other professions.

Essentially, the development that most distinguished the "new education" was a focus on the individual needs of the pupils rather than on the efficiency of the system. Armed with achievement and intelligence tests and aided by psychologists and social workers, progressive educators began to separate students according to their perceived potentials and then seek to fulfill them. For those who scored high, the rewards were plentiful: enriched programs, academic tracks, and, most highly prized, access to the city's elite high schools.

While there is some dissent over just how deserving New York was of its fame, there is no question about its glowing national image. Ironically, it was this very reputation that would soon become a factor leading to the most divisive conflict in the city's educational history. For although the school system was reputedly one of America's best, by the mid-1960s, black and Puerto Rican pupils, who now constituted a majority, complained that the system was failing them miserably.

How non-Caucasians came to occupy more than half the seats in the city's schools was the consequence of a post-World War II migration from the rural South and Caribbean, a phenomenon rivaling earlier immigration in the nineteenth and twentieth centuries. This time, however, although the newcomers were Americans, albeit of a different race, language, or culture, they faced hostility and neglect at least as formidable as that which confronted the aliens who preceded them.

This movement to New York in search of greater economic opportunities and, in the case of blacks, escape from a legally segregated society was no more likely to achieve immediate success than had the prior attempts of Irish, German, Jewish, and Italian immigrants. In fact, the odds were considerably greater, since the arrival of blacks and Puerto Ricans did not coincide with the need for labor that had greeted their predecessors and enabled them to catapult out of poverty within a generation. And for blacks in particular, the ability to blend into the life of the city was far more difficult. Obviously identifiable, their chances to assimilate depended upon the entrenched white majority's willingness to look beyond color.

That New Yorkers failed to do so became evident in the housing patterns that quickly developed in Manhattan, the outer boroughs, and the suburbs. Discrimination in accommodations and employment relegated both groups to the city's least desirable neighborhoods: blacks to Harlem, Bedford-Stuyvesant in Brooklyn, and South Jamaica in Queens; Puerto Ricans to East Harlem, the South Bronx, and that traditional compound for newcomers, the Lower East Side. And as their numbers swelled, the classrooms reflected their presence. The response of many whites was to remove their children from the public schools, either by enrolling them in private or parochial institutions or by fleeing themselves to enclaves in the city or beyond, where they could live—and educate their children—among members of their own race and class.

Such reaction was widespread: As about one million blacks and Puerto Ricans moved into New York, nearly one million whites moved out. There were many reasons for the exodus, but those who left, whether by intention or inadvertence, sharply reduced the possibility for meaningful integration. As a result, New York's racial minorities became majorities in the educational system, and, increasingly, schools became segregated.

This occurred despite the proclaimed opposition of the city's Board of Education, which, following the United States Supreme Court's 1954 landmark ruling that outlawed *de jure* segregation, announced: "We recognize it as a decision which applies not only to those cases in litigation, but also as a challenge to Boards throughout the nation, in Northern as well as Southern communities, to re-examine the racial composition of the schools within their respective systems in order to determine whether they conform to the standards stated clearly by that Court. The Supreme Court of the United States reminds us that modern psychological knowledge indicates clearly that segregated, racially homogeneous schools damage the personality of minority group children. These schools decrease their motivation and thus impair their ability to learn. White children are also damaged.... We will seek a solution to these problems and take action with dispatch...."

But the city's educators soon found that while good intentions coupled with any of several innovative school grouping plans might be sufficient to achieve integration in some suburban areas, the size, traffic, and housing patterns of New York defied such solutions. They were left with busing, a means generally unappealing to parents and one that contravened the notion of the "neighborhood school," a hallowed concept that immediately gained added popularity. Arguments against busing were raised by both races: Whites were reluctant to educate their children in ghetto schools, which they regarded as inferior and dangerous, while blacks were fearful of the abuse their youngsters would suffer in hostile white neighborhoods and the considerable time and distance involved.

Among whites who actually opposed integration by any means but were uncomfortable saying so, busing became a convenient target. The opposition was effective; racial mixing in the schools was frustrated. But the dilemma continued, and the distinguished black City College professor, Kenneth Clark, posed hard questions not only for ardent racists who believed blacks were intellectually inferior but also for liberals who believed blacks were victims of cultural deprivation. In his book *Dark Ghetto*, Clark pointed out:

> The central questions that lie behind the entire network of problems are these: Are Negroes such—in terms of innate incapacity *or* environmental deprivation—that their children are less capable of learning than are whites, so that any school that is permitted to become integrated necessarily declines in quality? Or has inferior education been systematically imposed on Negroes in the nation's ghettos in such a way as to compel poor performance from Negro children—a performance that could be reversed with quality education? The answer to these questions is of fundamental importance because the flight of whites from the urban public school system in many American cities is based on the belief that the first is true and the second false. If the first is false and the second true—and the centers of power in the white community can be convinced of that fact—one of the basic injustices in American life could be corrected.

It was Clark's contention that "a child who is expected by the school to learn does so; the child of whom little is expected produces little. Stimulation and teaching based upon positive expectation seem to play an even more important role in a child's performance in school than does the community environment from which he comes." Then he added a moderately worded premise: "A key component of the deprivation which afflicts ghetto children is that generally their teachers do not expect them to learn." Because of black rage, frustration, and political impotence, the essence of that sentence would serve as a rallying cry for community control of ghetto schools and provoke a bitter confrontation between ghetto leaders and the United Federation of Teachers (UFT). And because a significant majority of those teachers were Jewish, the ensuing clash would expose buried resentments between the city's blacks and Jews and help shatter a generation-long national political alliance between two aggrieved American minorities.

For blacks, whose hopes and expectations had been raised by the Supreme Court decision and a decade of civil rights activism, the failure to integrate New York's schools seemed further proof of the intransigence of the "white power structure." Their struggle to improve the quality of their children's education through their admission to the more effective "white" schools had met with fierce resistance. The fact that white parents had organized citywide "Parents and Taxpayers" groups to picket, rally, and sue to prevent integration made clear to them its dim prospects and the hypocrisy of official promises.

With the dream of integration faded, by 1966 blacks reversed direction: If inferior education could not be improved through having their children attend white

Like New York's immigrants of earlier generations, Puerto Rican newcomers in the mid-1950s were taught to be "American." And like their predecessors, they generally found themselves learning in dilapidated classrooms, such as this one in East Harlem. The race, religion, and ethnicity of immigrants have changed, but their treatment remains sadly similar.

schools, they would bring quality education to the schools their children did attend. And they would do this by taking control of the ghetto schools themselves. Surprisingly, perhaps, this concept of "community control" won broad support from both white segregationists and white radicals; segregationists saw it as reinforcing racial separatism, radicals as a step toward political independence. Among those less supportive or actually opposed were the liberals who believed in integration and the UFT, which perceived a threat to their hard-won contractual rights.

Under the sympathetic administration of Mayor John V. Lindsay and with the support of the Ford Foundation, black leaders and parents campaigned for a variety of proposals from 1966 through 1969. What they got ranged from a modest decentralization of the Board of Education's power to limited community control over local schools. Most provocative was an experimental plan announced by the Board of Education in April 1967 establishing three demonstration districts where a degree of neighborhood control could be exercised over education: Intermediate School 201 in East Harlem, Ocean Hill-Brownsville in Brooklyn, and Two Bridges on Manhattan's Lower East Side. All three districts were in impoverished areas where income, housing, and education levels were below average.

In September of that year, the schools opened to a fourteen-day strike by the UFT over a number of bread-and-butter issues, as well as the right to expel "disruptive" pupils from class. This latter provision was seen as racially motivated by black parents, who challenged the strike, exacerbating animosities between them and the predominantly Jewish teachers union. When the UFT won its demands and ended the walkout, attention focused on the demonstration districts' power to name their own teachers and administrators. With the rise in racial tension, teachers assigned to the demonstration districts were afraid that they would be tyrannized by vindictive black community school boards; the boards wanted to get rid of teachers they felt were inadequately educating black children.

In May, 1968, the Ocean Hill-Brownsville board ordered the involuntary transfer of nineteen teachers and administrators, charging that some of them were undermining the district's community control experiment. Their fears realized, teachers argued that the transfers were in fact illegal firings, instituted without hearings and other forms of due process protected by their contract. To back up their argument, 350 of them in the demonstration district walked off their jobs.

Court examinations failed to settle the issue conclusively over the summer, and in September 1968, the UFT, joined by the Council of Supervisory Associations (principals and other administrators), which normally opposed them, went on strike throughout the city. Most of the more than nine hundred schools in New York were shut down, but the demonstration districts remained open through a harsh two-month strike marked by extreme hostility that included overt acts of racism and anti-Semitism. Despite mediation and brief reopenings, it was not until mid-November that a negotiated agreement satisfactory to the union finally ended the walkout.

The strike was over: The city's sixty thousand teachers and almost one million pupils were back in their classrooms. But outside the classrooms, the situation was not normal. Like the educational battles of the 1840s and 1890s that heightened religious and ethnic antagonisms, the antipathies and the venom that characterized this conflict exposed the enmity of Jewish-black relations in New York.

In *Confrontation at Ocean Hill-Brownsville*, Maurice R. Berube and Marilyn Gittell write of a "unique social phenomenon" in which "a large Jewish community, fearful of undercurrents of black anti-Semitism, was hesitant to ally itself with the black cause; for many Jews already weary of the black struggle, a convenient escape hatch was placed before them." Further, they held that the controversy reflected a crucial misapprehension by an important faction in the nation's political structure. "What is most distressing is the failure of many American liberals to perceive the nature of the struggle. Instead of recognizing the community control movement as part of the same fight for respect, dignity, and democratic rights as the civil rights struggle in the South was in the early 1960s, many northern liberals condemn school activists as extremists."

In analyzing the conflict, they criticize the teachers union for fighting social progress in order to defend self-serving rules. "Whereas the protection of workers was a major social priority in the 1930s," the authors argue, "the right to hold public groups—even labor unions—accountable to an urban alienated poor emerges as the prime social priority of the 1960s. The unions, however, are still operating on a 1930s program."

From their vantage point, the teachers, many of whom had been in the forefront of the struggle to establish their union only a few years earlier, saw themselves as lower-middle-class workers who needed the contractual protection they were being asked to forfeit. Moreover, they felt that they were being called upon to make sacrifices by upper-middle-class liberals and intellectuals who had positioned themselves out of the firing line. Assessing the confrontation for the typical UFT member, one teacher wrote, "He does not feel that he is the singular perpetrator of education crimes committed against black and Puerto Rican children, and he therefore does not feel that he should be made the scapegoat to assuage the guilt felt by much more affluent whites over their much larger role in committing these crimes."

Similar attitudes, it should be noted, were also widely expressed by many white working-class parents in Queens and Brooklyn over proposals to bus their children to ghetto schools during the search for integration. They were particularly critical of Establishment figures who extolled the virtues of integrated public education while sending their children to private schools.

The community control issue was laid to rest, at least for the time being, in 1969 when the State Legislature, reacting to the furor surrounding Ocean Hill-Brownsville and responding to pressure from the UFT, passed a tepid decentralization law that effectively killed the three demonstration districts by absorbing them into larger entities. It allowed the central Board of Education to retain authority, while dividing the city into thirty-one districts (one more was created in 1973). Ironically, this number was the *minimum* that had earlier been proposed in the innovative Bundy plan, a far-reaching decentralization formula developed in 1967 by a Lindsay-appointed panel under the leadership of Ford Foundation President McGeorge Bundy. That plan would have reorganized public schools into a federation of largely autonomous districts and a central education agency. The districts, to be governed by parents and professionals, would be responsible for all elementary and secondary education within their boundaries and for adhering to state standards.

The new law was roundly damned by proponents of community control, including Gittell and some of her colleagues who had prepared the Bundy plan. In *Community Control and the Urban School*, they asserted: "Summing up, we can say that the legislation rolled back even those few gains the demonstration districts were able to make in their short lifetime, to say nothing of rejecting all the major reforms proposed by the Bundy plan and even compromise adaptations of the plan. The text of the legislation need hardly have stated, as it does in several sections, that the new local districts are not to be considered local educational agencies but, rather, subdivisions of the central agency. The 'decentralization' bill was a mockery of its own title."

Other than to stifle the vociferous black and Puerto Rican demands for neighborhood control, the 1969 law was seen by many educational experts as having had little effect on the city school system. Of greater impact, they said, were the budget cuts imposed during the fiscal crisis of the 1970s.

A major concern of the 1980s, which recalls recurrent educational problems over the past hundred and fifty years, once again involves an influx of new pupils whose needs are not shared by the majority. This time the issue is bilingual education, and those primarily involved are Latinos, although the number of Asians is growing. By 1988, fully one of nine pupils in the city's school system had been identified as Limited-English-Proficient, including 40 percent of those entering kindergarten. But about half of these language-deficient students were receiving instruction only in English.

Aside from being handicapped by a lack of funds, particularly from the federal government, the bilingual program, which seeks to teach some subjects in a pupil's native tongue, is threatened by a growing movement to enthrone English as the "official" American language. Nonetheless, there appears to be a recognition of the need to keep immigrant children learning in the language they know best while simultaneously easing their transition into English.

Seen within the context of New York City's conflict-ridden educational history, the problems and the opposition faced by the most recent newcomers, whether they be blacks, Latinos, or Asians, seem sadly familiar. The demand for conformity that provoked Irish Catholics in the 1840s and beset Jews and Italians at the turn of the century has not been eradicated. Although there are programs and techniques that reflect a new sensitivity to minorities, there is evidence as well that the nativist sentiments that denigrated immigrant children of previous generations are still afflicting those who look or sound different.

From Greenwich Village to Radio City, from Tin Pan Alley to 52nd Street, from blackface to the Great White Way, New York's long-standing prominence as a source and promoter of popular culture has drawn deeply on its rich and contentious ethnic mix. English actors, Irish tenors, Italian conductors, Jewish comedians, and black blues singers who entertained America for more than a century made their debuts in the city's vaudeville and burlesque houses, music and dance halls, minstrel shows, cabarets, and nightclubs.

During vaudeville's heyday in the early twentieth century, New Yorkers could have watched and heard George M. Cohan give his regards to Broadway, tearfully shared Sophie Tucker's "Yiddishe Mama," emoted with Enrico Caruso's Canio in "I Pagliacci," and tapped their toes at the legendary Palace Theatre to the ragtime piano of Eubie Blake, the son of former slaves.

These performers provided far more than entertainment. "Their background make an important point," wrote urban historian Robert W. Snyder. "Vaudeville and the twentieth-century mass culture derived from it—expressed in movies, Tin Pan Alley, radio and their successors—were not simply imposed on ethnics. Instead, vaudeville and mass culture were often created by people from immigrant backgrounds who supplied both their creative talent and audiences."

Yet while individual ethnics saw their (frequently anglicized) names up in lights, fellow countrymen were subjected regularly to the sight of unflattering stereotypes parading before the footlights to evoke laughter. For ethnic and racial caricaturing, long a staple of American entertainers, received respectability and broad currency on the New York stage, often performed by members of the very group being ridiculed. As usual, blacks came off worst: Not only mocked and derogated, they were compelled to watch themselves—sometimes from segregated seats—portrayed by whites with burnt-cork-blackened faces.

During much of New York's history, its immigrants were thus simultaneously benefited and maligned by the city's popular culture. They benefited directly through employment: onstage, backstage, in the orchestra pit, on the dance floor, behind the bar, and, more than is generally suspected, behind red lights. As actors and musicians, singers and dancers, songwriters and stagehands, hostesses and waiters, pimps and prostitutes, significant numbers of New York's ethnics have made their livings through show business and entertainment over the past three centuries. Indirectly, immigrants derived some value from the exposure (and, hence, understanding) their particular culture received from the songs, dances, skits, and plays that drew large and diverse audiences. Such material often gave New Yorkers their first "inside" glimpse of the aliens' life-style. For this, however, the immigrants paid a price, which varied depending upon their race or ethnicity, through the misinformation, exaggeration, and denigration that frequently accompanied these characterizations.

There is little doubt that New York always has been a lively town; apparently even before it was New York. In November 1653, Nicasius de Sille wrote to a friend in the Netherlands that in New Amsterdam, as it was then called, "they all drink here, from the moment they are able to lick a spoon. The women of the neighborhood entertain each other with a pipe and a brazier; young and old, they all smoke."

The late eighteenth century found New Yorkers' tastes and appetites presumably well met. There was one tavern for every dozen adult males, a similar ratio of prostitutes, and a playhouse (the John Street Theatre), where everything from Shakespeare on down was performed. The distractions, in fact, were sufficient to provoke the annoyance of Bostonian John Adams, who spent a month in Manhattan in 1774 on his way to the Continental Congress and grumbled about the extent of "breakfasting, dining, drinking coffee, &c., about the city." The future president may also have started the rumor that New Yorkers are rude. "With all the opulence and splendor of this city," he fretted, "there is very little good breeding to be found.

Opposite:
"The Crossroads of the World" was what the Times Square intersection of Broadway and 42nd Street was called in its glory days. The lights, crowds, and excitement made every night New Year's Eve in the 1930s (when this photograph was taken) and during a few succeeding decades.

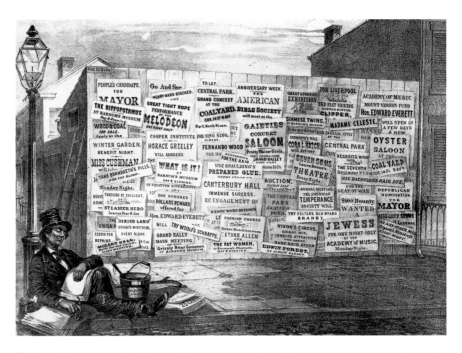

We have been treated with assiduous respect; but I have not seen one real gentleman, one well-bred man, since I came to town. At their entertainments there is no conversation that is agreeable; there is no modesty, no attention to one another. They talk very loud, very fast, and altogether. If they ask you a question, before you can utter three words of your answer, they will break out upon you again, and talk away."

New Yorkers who did not flee the seven-year British occupation during the Revolutionary War enjoyed little entertainment. In the aftermath, however, the Park Theatre was opened with a two-thousand-seat capacity, suggesting that neither the war nor the occupation had diminished the residents' cultural desires. But there was considerable evidence that the concept of democracy, which had helped trigger the revolution, did not apply subsequently to social relations. Visiting Englishman John Lambert noted in 1807 that the city was divided into "three distinct classes" and that the two most prestigious included professionals, the wealthy, merchants, and clerks while the bottom was composed of the "inferior orders of the people."

This social dichotomy, which would affect cultural predilections throughout the city's history, evidently determined not only what New Yorkers did but where they did it. Lambert observed that the Battery and Park, for example, had become "too common" by the turn of the century and were not "much resorted to by the fashionable citizens of New York." Instead, they spent their time "in the Broadway, from eleven to three o'clock, during which time it is as much crowded as the Bondstreet of London."

As ill-mannered and teeming as the city may have appeared to visitors even then, New York, at the beginning of the nineteenth century, also possessed a tempo that made it distinctive and exciting. Recalling his Manhattan experiences during two decades of touring America, British actor-playwright John Bernard wrote of the merchants: "At four they went home to dress for dinner; at seven, to the play; at eleven, to supper, with a crew of lusty Bachanals who would smoke cigars, gulp down brandy, and sing, roar, and shout in the thickening clouds they created, like so many merry devils, till three in the morning. At eight, up again, to scribble, run and roll hogsheads. What a day's work this would have been for a Carolinian! Thus the New-Yorker enjoyed his span of being to the full stretch of the tether, his violent exertions during the day counteracting the effects of his nocturnal relaxations, besides giving him a relish to return to them. Certainly few men throughout the Union worked harder for enjoyment."

Although New York was clearly developing a personality, it was equally clear that its personality was split. While the elite took to Broadway, the working classes made the Bowery their playground. And it had a style all its own. "The Bowery," rhapsodized journalist George C. Foster in 1849, "is celebrated for its drinking and gambling houses, its poultry-raffling shops, and its 'crack' ice cream saloons. It is the grand parade ground of the 'b'hoys' and the 'g'hals,' the arena where 'high-life below stairs' makes its grandest demonstrations; and to a philosopher a walk through the Bowery would furnish abundant food for thought and contemplation."

By the 1840s, the "b'hoys" and "g'hals," later characterized on the stage as "Mose" and "Lize," were instantly recognizable by their appearance and behavior. Charles Haswell observed in *Reminiscences of an Octogenarian* that "the Bowery boy of that period was so distinctive a class in dress and conversation that a description of him is well worthy of notice. He was not an idler and corner lounger, but mostly an apprentice, generally to a butcher.... In the evenings, other than Saturdays (when the markets remained open all day and evening) and on Sundays and holidays he appeared in *propria persona*, a very different character; his dress, a high beaver hat, with the nap divided and brushed in opposite directions, the hair on the back of the head clipped close, while in front the temple locks were curled and greased (hence, the well-known term of 'soap-locks' to the wearer of them), a smooth face, a gaudy silk neck cloth, black frock coat, full pantaloons, turned up at the bottom over heavy boots designed for service in slaughter houses and at fires."

In the unlikely event that "Mose" failed to attract attention, he could surely count on "Lize," who, according to Foster, was "gotten together in utter defiance of...conventional laws of harmony and taste." They were most likely to be seen together on Sunday, "the great day for the b'hoy." Foster reported that "in the warm spring and summer seasons it is to Hoboken, to Harlem, to Staten Island or Coney Island that he steers with his red cheeked and red ribboned gal, blooming like a garden of poppies, sunflowers and daffydown-dillies, hanging lovely upon his arm, and his own brilliant soap-locks fresh plastered and burnished for the occasion." With zoologistic style, Foster noted that "at these times the b'hoy is a perfectly interesting animal, perfectly docile except when irritated; but you had better be careful not to encroach in any possible manner upon his comfort or his dignity. Incidents that he might during weekdays be disposed to pass over with a grunt and a growl, now that Lize is by his side would be instantaneously resented upon the spot...."

The Bowery's denizens inhabited a bazaarlike neighborhood of cheap shops, slaughterhouses, dance halls, gambling dens, concert halls, saloons, oyster houses, bordellos, and, after 1827, the Bowery Theatre, which Foster described as "the largest and most permanently popular place of public amusement in the city." Allowing that "we are accustomed to connect with the name of this establishment, peanuts, red woollen-shirts, tobacco chewing, and rowdyism, with its trousers tucked into its boots," he maintained, "in point of fact, the Bowery stage would compare favorably as to the strength and talent of its performers with any other theatrical establishment in the country."

Despite the area's plebian character, the Bowery Theatre attracted a relatively diverse audience. The dress circle would be occupied, according to Foster, "by the more quiet and respectable families and children of the east end of the city, and with the exception of the flaming conspicuousness of the dress and accoutrements of the ladies, the prevalence of children of all sorts and sizes, and the circulation of lemonade, candy and oranges, and other refreshments, around the circle between

Nineteenth-century entertainment in New York was unlikely to hold much appeal for playgoers with ethnic sensitivities. The portrayals were heavy-handed caricatures, relying on the most broadly drawn stereotypes for their humor. Ethnic, religious, and racial enmities undoubtedly were fed by characterizations that depicted the Irish as drunk and unruly, Jews as scheming and mercenary, and blacks as simple-minded or pretentious. Among the earliest stock characters was "Mose, the fireboy," a swaggering "Bowery b'hoy" whose popularity lasted for decades.

the acts, you would not know but that you were in ever so fashionable an establishment."

Other sections, however, catered to a different clientele. "The upper tiers and galleries are a bad and dreadful region," Foster warned. "They are filled with rowdies, fancy men, working girls of doubtful reputation, and, last of all, the lower species of public prostitutes, accompanied by their 'lovers,' or such victims as they have been able to pick up. The central point of this stratum is the punch room, where a continual flood of poisoned brandy, rum and whisky is poured down the reeking throats of these desperate wretches; until steam being up to the proper point, they take their departure one by one, to the haunts of crime, debauchery and robbery, whence they issued at nightfall like broods of dark ill-omened birds."

An evening at the Bowery Theatre was likely to be as memorable for the audience's behavior as for the actors' renditions. As Foster put it, "Compared with the performances in the audience, the ranting and bellowing and spasmodic galvanism of the actors on the stage are quite tame and commonplace." Poet Walt Whitman, then a journalist, described a Saturday night at the Bowery as "no dainty glove business, but electric force and muscle," with the patrons "as much a part of the show as any."

What transpired onstage by the 1830s was often comedy and melodrama that dealt with the growing complexity and bewildering diversity of urban life. Like caricaturists who succeed by exaggerating deviations from the "norm," entertainers distorted ethnic, racial, and social traits. They thus created characters intended to evoke emotions that ranged from affection and sentimentality to arrogance and superiority. The earliest target was the Yankee, identified as "Jonathan" and characterized by an unlikely combination of naïveté and shrewdness. One moment he might mistakenly wander into a theater and think he was witnessing a quarrel in "the next neighbor's house" and a few minutes later hope a minister would preach on Sunday since "if he does, I can let out my pew for double price, and sell lots of new shoes."

Other objects of regard and derision were Germans, Irish, blacks, and "Mose," the Yankee's urban counterpart. These broad ethnic and racial characterizations would dominate American entertainment for the next century, siring such spiritual descendants as Amos 'n' Andy and Archie Bunker. For the nineteenth century marked the birth and growth of minstrelsy, which historian Robert C. Toll has called "the first uniquely American show business form." At the foundation of the minstrel show—albeit involuntarily—were American blacks, whose culture was being exploited in the antebellum North at the very time that their labor was being exploited in the slavery-ridden South.

Originally self-described as "Ethiopian delineators," white entertainers blackened their faces and claimed to accurately portray the life-styles of Southern blacks, a group few New Yorkers had ever seen. While the showmen may have derived their inspiration from actual blacks, as apparently was the case with Thomas D. (Jim Crow) Rice, their depictions were gross misrepresentations that frequently ridiculed and always diminished the humanity of their subjects. Rice, seeking new material in the late 1820s, put on blackface and ragged clothes to imitate the homely song and dance of a crippled black stableman he had seen. He called his routine "Jumping Jim Crow," and it became an international hit. For more than two decades, Rice performed his act throughout the United States, and even London, to such extensive acclaim that the term "Jim Crow" was adopted to describe the South's elaborate system of racial segregation.

A development that was to have an even greater impact on show business and American political and social attitudes occurred in New York in 1842 when four out-of-work "Ethiopian delineators" combined and, appropriating the name of a

One of the earliest stage acts to become a national craze had its roots in racism compounded by unusual insensitivity. Called "Jumping Jim Crow," it was a dance devised by Thomas D. Rice in 1828 based on the movements of a crippled black stablehand. This 1833 painting captured Rice, who had introduced the routine in Louisville, Kentucky, performing at the Bowery Theatre in New York. "Jim Crow" became so popular, it was used to describe the system of racial segregation in the South.

Southern state and the popularity of a European singing group called the Tyrolese Minstrel Family, put on the world's first minstrel show. Response to the "Virginia Minstrels" was instantaneous and overwhelming. The result was a new kind of entertainment, scores of competitors, and an insatiable demand. Across the country, the minstrel show *was* show business.

It did not take long for minstrelsy to transcend entertainment and become, as well, an effective propaganda technique that utilized racial stereotypes to shape public opinion. In the decades preceding the Civil War, slavery and the status of blacks was a vital national issue. The new nation, although committed ideologically to democracy and equality, relied significantly upon the subjugation of blacks for the functioning of its economy. To reconcile such incongruities it was necessary to perceive blacks as not only unequal but as undeserving of equality. The minstrel show strove to create just that perception.

"Everything about minstrel caricatures of Negroes—their grotesque looks, their silly dialects, their strange behavior, their incredible stupidity and their unusual music and dance—made blacks something to feel superior to and laugh at," Toll contended. "These stereotypes allowed Northern whites to feel superior to Negroes, to justify treating them as inferiors (if they had to treat them at all), and to embrace the myths of the happy plantation, myths that described an undemocratic but benevolent society that kept Negroes in their places as inferiors, not only because it was good for them, allowing them to live happy, fulfilled lives, but because blacks wanted it that way."

As minstrelsy evolved, blacks generally were portrayed in two roles: either as simple-minded loafers who wished to maintain the plantation system (slavery) or as pretentious freedmen who, in the persona of "Jim Dandy," ineptly sought to ape their white superiors. Clearly, in either capacity, they were shown to lack the requisite credentials for full and equal status. Despite the didactic overtones, minstrel shows maintained a joyous, fun-loving approach whose structure, style, and content, appealed to audiences seeking entertainment, not indoctrination.

By the 1850s a standard format had emerged and was described as follows by Toll in *On With the Show: The First Century of Show Business in America:*

To open the three-part show, all the performers entered singing an upbeat song, took their places in a semi-circle, and waited for the command: "Gentlemen Be Seated!" The order came from the interlocutor, the master of ceremonies and onstage director—the ringmaster of the minstrel show—who sat in the center of the semi-circle. On the ends sat the company's leading comedians, Brudder Tambo and Brudder Bones, who were named for their instruments, the tambourine and the rhythm clacker bones. Besides comic repartee between endmen and interlocutor, the first part of the show offered individual and group songs and dances, ranging from sentimental tearjerkers to foolish nonsense songs, from ballroom dances to high-stepping Irish jigs. The first part closed with an upbeat, group musical number. After an intermission, the second part, the variety section or olio, offered a wide range of individual acts including song and dance teams, acrobats, comedians, and novelties like people playing combs, porcupine quills, or water glasses. This part of the program, which ultimately evolved into the variety show, took place in front of a drop curtain with only the performing act on stage, so the stage crew could set up the scenery for the one-act skit that concluded the evening's performance. In early minstrel shows these finales were almost invariably set on plantations. But by the mid-1850s many minstrel troups closed with takeoffs on current events or popular fads.

Minstrelsy's profound impact on Civil War-era America seems ironic, if not absurd, given the fact that its impressions of the Southern way of life were recorded primarily from a New York City vantage point. The Old South's most-prized music, including "Dixie," the veritable anthem of the Confederacy, was churned out by Tin Pan Alley songsmiths. The person most responsible for the romantic image of plantation life below the Mason-Dixon line—Stephen Collins Foster—was both Northern and urban. Born near Pittsburgh in 1826, he wrote hundreds of songs idealizing the South, including such classics as "My Old Kentucky Home," "Old Black Joe," "Oh! Susanna," "Camptown Races," "Massa's in de Cold Ground," and "Old Folks at Home," before dying a penniless alcoholic thirty-eight years later in a Manhattan flophouse.

But audiences were seeking escape, not truth, in minstrel shows, although contemporary concerns did provide much of the material. Anti-intellectualism was a staple of popular culture during this period of Jacksonian democracy, and minstrelsy lampooned pomposity and pretension. One of the most popular routines during the olio portion of the show was the so-called stump speech, which managed to ridicule both "uppity" blacks and verbose intellectuals. Typically, according to Toll, such a speech might begin: "Transcendentalism is dat spiritual conoscence ob psychological irrefragibility, connected wid conscientient ademption ob incolumbient spirituality...."

In addition to feeding white prejudices with the implication that blacks were both ignorant *and* arrogant, this type of act played on the class hostilities that had taken hold in New York and other urban centers. Cleavage between the elite and working classes had widened appreciably during the nineteenth century, and the distance was apparent in many aspects of city life, including tastes in entertainment.

On occasion, these differences erupted in such unlikely places as the Bowery Theatre, where working-class audiences, hardly restrained to begin with, got sufficiently worked up at what they regarded as snobbish English actors to drive them from the stage with barrages of coins and rotten fruit. These anglophobic outbursts, frequent and frenzied enough to be designated as "theater riots," created sufficient damage at the Bowery in 1831 to cause the management to defensively drape the theater in patriotic bunting.

But these confrontations were simply preludes to the rampant violence that transformed Astor Place into a battlefield on May 10, 1849. Prompted by the long,

Ethnic conflicts and popular culture collided in New York in 1849 with the violent Astor Place Riot, a melee triggered by nativism and animosities between, of all things, fans of two prominent Shakespearean actors, the American Edwin Forrest and the British William Macready. The outbreak, which resulted in twenty-two deaths and scores of injuries, came after Forrest's supporters threw debris at the theater during a Macready performance. Troops, called to preserve order, fired on the crowd, causing the deaths.

bitter rivalry between two popular Shakespearean actors, the emotive American Edwin Forrest and the cool British William Macready, its complex social origins involved hatreds between the poor and rich, between American nationalists and anglophiles, and between Bowery street toughs and Astor Place aristocrats.

Macready, closing out a tour of the United States with a performance of *Macbeth* at the elite Astor Place Opera House, was assailed on opening night by a variety of missiles, including four chairs, that were hurled from the gallery by Forrest partisans. The incident led Macready to consider an early return to Europe, but yielding to the entreaties of many prominent New Yorkers, including Washington Irving and Herman Melville, he stuck it out, agreeing to perform two nights later. During the interim, tension was exacerbated by nativist and working-class agitators, who made speeches and posted placards throughout the city urging action, although disdaining violence.

On the night of the riot, thousands of workers of diverse ethnicities and political sentiments gathered outside the theater. "Anglophobia," wrote historian Peter George Buckley, "was one of the few feelings in which both native born and Irish—therefore the majority of the city's working population—could share. The imminent (sic) tragedian [Macready] and the passive aristocracy served as an extremely wide target of dissent."

Despite some minor disturbances and arrests inside the theater, the show went on. Outside, however, the scene grew forbidding. The crowd of more than five thousand rapidly turned into a mob that threw itself on the building, hurling stones that pierced the boarded windows, broke the chandelier, and rained on the audience. The police, overwhelmed, called for the militia. When a troop of horse and infantry arrived, the demonstrators became inflamed. Although the police chief warned that the soldiers would use force, only those nearby heard. Some of the rioters, aware of the traditional tolerance for such behavior, taunted: "Fire, fire, you damned sons of bitches! You durst not fire! You durst not fire!" But the troops *did* fire. First, into the air; then into the mob. More volleys followed as the militiamen drove the crowd from Astor Place and the adjacent streets. Eighteen people were killed outright; four more died from their wounds within a week.

The next day, angry protests filled City Hall Park, and all manner of reactions filled the editorial pages of the city's divergent press. A crowd gathered and again moved toward the opera house, but further disturbances had been anticipated, and the police were able to maintain order. Reaction was widespread. And the *Philadelphia Public Ledger* expressed a profound national anxiety in stating that "there is now in our country, in New York City, what every good patriot has hitherto considered it his duty to deny—a *high* class and a *low* class."

It is not unlikely that the Astor Place Riot's manifestation of class warfare was on the mind of Frederick Law Olmsted when, just four years later, he expressed in a letter to a friend the fragment of a philosophy that later would transfigure New York City through the creation of the nation's first major public park: "... to force into contact the good & bad, the gentlemanly and the rowdy." For Olmsted, who, with Calvert Vaux, designed Central Park, envisaged it not only as a place of relaxation and recreation but as a representation of the democratic ideal, a place where people of all backgrounds could mingle, share, and learn from one another. As historian Thomas Bender points out in *Toward an Urban Vision:* "Olmsted urged the development of large urban parks and suburban neighborhoods. Parks and suburbs historically have served the needs of the middle classes more than the poor, but Olmsted's intention was to provide all classes with relief from the less happy aspects of urban life. Parks, especially, should bring various classes into familiar contact, into a community. The city park, for Olmsted, symbolized the possibilities of democratic urban life."

Despite its seeming naturalness, Central Park, Olmsted's and Vaux's winning entry in an 1857 competition, was totally man-made, "sculpted out of a ragged northern fringe of New York City, a mostly barren, long and too-narrow rectangle inhabited by squatters and goats, littered with refuse, studded with jagged outcrops of Manhattan schist and miry with low-lying swamps." It took sixteen years and $14 million to create the 843 acres that currently cater to more than three million people annually who, surveys find, almost precisely mirror the city's demographics.

This social mix would undoubtedly please but hardly surprise Olmsted, who in 1870 was able to report that "you may ... often see vast numbers of persons brought closely together, poor and rich, young and old, Jew and Gentile. I have seen a hundred thousand thus congregated." In the same year, with the park clearly a success despite being unfinished, its designer maintained with satisfaction that "no one who has closely observed the conduct of the people who visit the Park, can doubt that it exercises a distinctly harmonizing and refining influence upon the most unfortunate and lawless classes of the city—an influence favorable to courtesy, self-control, and temperance."

Courtesy, self-control, and temperance had a special meaning in that Victorian era when elitists sought to domesticate the immigrant working class and eliminate what they regarded as its immoral and wasteful habits. While Olmsted was content merely to provide a salubrious environment, reformers intently sought to uplift the "underprivileged" by imposing lofty, puritanical moral values and work-oriented goals. Their efforts to affect the city's recreational, cultural, and social institutions even extended to Central Park, where sports facilities and programmed activities were added to Olmsted's unstructured milieu. The immigrants, most of whom experienced few joys outside of traditional family or religious celebrations and visits to neighborhood taverns, variety theaters, and dance halls, were understandably resistant to Victorian restraints. It is unsurprising then that the urban masses yearned for opportunities to pursue pleasure in their own fashion, to break out of the rigidities conceived for them.

Since the early nineteenth century, wealthy New Yorkers had enjoyed the seashore at Coney Island, a minimally developed retreat appreciated because it was accessible by steamboat yet out of the mainstream. After the Civil War, however, its reputation had suffered through the notoriety of Norton's Point, a section at the

Central Park, the most obvious presence of nature in New York City, is actually man-made or, at least, man-designed. Once a barren, hilly, rutted area of ramshackle huts and rooting swine, and now one of the most desirable pieces of real estate in the world, the park was the creation of Frederick Law Olmsted and Calvert Vaux. Even more than a haven of serenity and recreation, Central Park was conceived by Olmsted as a sort of grand, al fresco meeting place where social democracy could be achieved through the mingling of all the city's classes. Despite its after-dark notoriety, the park largely has filled that role, as nannies steer costly baby carriages among inner-city roller skaters and suburban day-trippers.

western extremity known as a hangout for prostitutes, gamblers, pickpockets, and hoodlums. As New York became increasingly crowded and trolley and railroad lines were extended into the environs, developers recognized the potential of Coney Island as a popular summer resort and began erecting large, stylish hotels on the beach. Their success encouraged other investors to broaden the appeal by providing restaurants, dance halls, bathhouses, and game facilities. Before long, more exotic entertainment was introduced, including the 300-foot-high Iron Tower observation deck from the Philadelphia Centennial Exposition of 1876 and the incredible Elephant Hotel, built in 1882 as a tin-covered wooden structure resembling that animal and containing an observatory, shopping mall, cigar store, and guest rooms. "Seeing the Elephant" became such a common phrase it was used as a code to mean indulging in illicit pleasures.

And Coney soon had many of these to offer. By the 1890s, it had reestablished itself as a successor to Norton's Point and was frequently referred to as "Sodom by the Sea." However, that era in its colorful history was ended when fires destroyed the entertainment facilities in 1893 and again two years later.

But Coney Island's possibilities were too promising to lie dormant, particularly with the number of potential customers increasing exponentially as hundreds of thousands of immigrants from Italy, Russia, and Poland arrived in New York to join earlier waves of Irish and Germans. And so within a decade at the turn of the century, not only the area but the concept of popular culture were transformed with the opening of three imaginative, elaborate amusement grounds called Steeplechase Park, Luna Park, and Dreamland.

When George C. Tilyou opened Steeplechase in 1897, it quickly overshadowed Coney's first fenced-in amusement center, Sea Lion Park, which had begun business two years earlier with forty trained seals and a water slide called Shoot-the-Chutes. Tilyou, a philosophic entrepreneur, believed that "we Americans want either to be thrilled or amused, and we are ready to pay well for either sensation." Accordingly, he loaded Steeplechase with mechanical thrill-makers and made their victims provide amusement for others. Among his specialties, for example, was the "Blowhole Theater," where jets of compressed air lifted skirts to the approbation of an audience viewing from a darkened auditorium. Similarly, a parachute ride called the Dew Drop allowed onlookers to watch skirts rise while their wearers descended.

Besides offering such harmless titillation, Tilyou challenged Victorian propriety by enabling men and women to come into unexpected physical contact in the "Barrel of Fun," a large, revolving cylinder that upended patrons as they attempted to walk through it. Even the gravity-operated hobbyhorse race, from which the park derived its name, was outfitted with seats that placed riders in touch with their companions.

Symbolically, Coney Island was doing for New York what the Mardi Gras did for New Orleans. "By creating its own version of carnival," wrote John F. Kasson in *Amusing the Million*, "Coney Island tested and transformed accustomed social roles and values. It attracted people because of the way in which it mocked the established social order. Coney Island in effect declared a moral holiday for all who entered its gates. Against the values of thrift, sobriety, industry, and ambition, it encouraged extravagance, gaiety, abandon, revelry. Coney Island signaled the rise of a new mass culture no longer deferential to genteel tastes and values, which demanded a democratic resort of its own. It served as a Feast of Fools for an urban-industrial society."

This opportunity to fantasize openly, to act out one's dreams, was elevated to new heights with Luna Park, which drew an opening night crowd of 45,000 in 1903, and Dreamland, which opened across the street within the year. Luna, the brainchild of two Tilyou employees, Frederic Thompson and Skip Dundy, reinterpreted the

No less than Hollywood, Coney Island
sought to make dreams seem real.
Originally a honky-tonk district of saloons
and brothels, it was turned into a
wonderland when George C. Tilyou
opened a fabulous amusement park there
in 1897, bringing the exotica of every
continent to the Brooklyn beach site. The
success of Tilyou's Steeplechase inspired
competition from Luna Park (opposite and
left) and Dreamland, which vied in
imagination and extravagance. A magnet
for all kinds and classes of New Yorkers,
Coney Island's early appeal was directed
toward young couples who could be
together, in those straitlaced days, without
parental presence. The beach scene
(below) was captured by a photographer
who used the famed Parachute Jump
(originally at the 1939 New York World's
Fair) as a vantage point.

world within its fences, permitting middle and working class New Yorkers to walk the streets of a turn-of-the-century magic kingdom. "There were gilded chariots and prancing horses, and trained elephants and dancing girls, regiments of soldiers, and an astonishing number of real Eastern people and animals in gay and stately trappings," reported the *New York Times*. "The magnificence of the scene was such as to make those who witnessed it imagine they were in a genuine Oriental city."

It was like an unending drama of the extravagant and the bizarre. "They boasted the largest herd of show elephants in the world," Kasson wrote, "and delighted in including them in special stunts, such as sliding down a special Shoot-the-Chutes. For the 'Streets of Delhi' they offered a choice of elephants or camels for visitors to ride upon and play the part of rajas. They installed a three-ring circus on raised platforms over the lagoon at the foot of the Shoot-the-Chutes, featuring equestrian acrobatics, a cakewalking pony, trained bears, and of course more elephants. In their effort to provide gripping, thrilling amusement, Luna's managers occasionally appealed to a latent cruelty in the audience in features such as 'King,' the diving horse, who leapt from a high platform into a tub of water, or, much more overtly, in the public and highly publicized execution of an old elephant, 'Topsy,' first by supposedly poisoned carrots, then, with undeniable authenticity, by electrocution."

Electricity, clearly, was not conserved. By night, 250,000 light bulbs converted Luna into a spellbinding wonderland that prompted Albert Bigelow Paine to exclaim in *The New Coney Island:* "Tall towers that had grown dim suddenly broke forth in electric outlines and gay rosettes of color, as the living spark of light traveled hither and thither, until the place was transformed into an enchanted garden, of such a sort as Aladdin never dreamed."

Dreamland was Luna *plus*. Financed through the efforts of politicians, including former State Senator William J. Reynolds, who later sought to make Long Island's Long Beach into the "Venice of America," Dreamland took Luna's creations and enhanced them. Everything about it was more, bigger, better, costlier. But, perhaps, it was too much. Before it was destroyed by fire in 1911, Dreamland never enjoyed the popularity of the rival it tried so excessively to best. One of its investors, George Dobson, claimed Dreamland's problem lay in an overestimation of public taste. "The promoters of Dreamland sought to appeal to a highly developed sense of the artistic," he eulogized, "but it did not take us long to discover that Coney Island was scarcely the place for that sort of thing."

Yet Coney was surely unique and deserving of a prominent niche in the pantheon of popular culture. "For immigrants and especially for their children, notoriously eager to assimilate," Kasson stated, "Coney Island provided a means to participate in mainstream American culture on an equal footing. Far more immediately and successfully than agents of the genteel culture, Coney's amusement parks and other institutions of the new mass culture incorporated immigrants and working-class groups into their forms and values."

Paradoxically, the acculturation and fusion that were occurring spontaneously at Coney Island through involvement with fanciful spectacles were being accomplished on the New York stage through a deliberate absorption with realism. The person responsible was a playwright named Edward Harrigan, who with his partners, songwriter Dave Braham and actor Tony Hart, dominated the city's footlights from the 1870s through the '90s. Harrigan, the son of immigrant Irish parents, diverted popular theater from the gross exaggerations of minstrelsy by introducing entertaining, colorful, and humanistic portrayals of urban life. His influence was profound enough to warrant, in his 1911 obituary in the *New York Times*, the accolade that "America has produced nothing more national, more distinctly its own, than these plays of the Irish in New York."

Harrigan's commitment to authenticity and his skills in reproducing it onstage

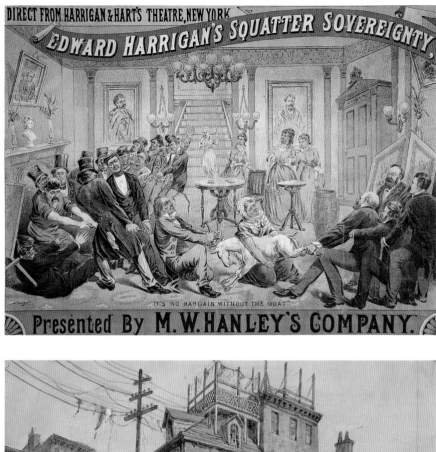

By the late nineteenth century, musical comedy as created by Edward Harrigan and Tony Hart, although it relied heavily on slapstick, offered New Yorkers a more realistic view of immigrant life. "Harrigan and Hart" set a national standard for entertainment, and posters advertising these productions drew patrons into theaters across the country (left). The producer-playwright-performers' dramatizations of the everyday life and behavior of Irish newcomers, albeit highly exaggerated, often provided New Yorkers and other Americans with their first intimate look at the immigrant experience. Even the sets were authentic (below left).

were quickly recognized by the foremost critics of the day. William Dean Howells wrote in *Harper's* in 1886 that Harrigan "accurately realized in his scenes what he realizes in his persons; that is, the actual life of this city . . . Irish-American phases in their rich and amusing variety, and some of its African and Teutonic phases. It is what we call low life, though whether it is essentially lower than fashionable life is another question. . . . In his own province we think he cannot be surpassed."

Harrigan's characterizations created that flash of recognition that is the hall-mark of superior dramaturgy. One notable example was the creation of a "hoodlum

girl" named Kitty Lynch, who was portrayed by a seventeen-year-old actress named Ada Lewis. Kitty and Ada became instant hits. As Richard Moody pointed out in *Ned Harrigan: From Corlear's Hook to Herald Square:* "Kitty's sensation was not accidental. Harrigan had studied the tough girl in her native habitat: She lives in a tenement close to the dump; her parents are foreigners—Italians, Irish, or Hebrews. She has learned her speech from them, and like them has great difficulty with past tenses: 'He brung it and when he bringed it I was sorry dat he brang it.' Her peculiar 'tough-girl gesture' gave the audience 'an immediate flashlight picture of the entire characterization.' "

But Harrigan's popularity no doubt was most tied to the "Mulligan Guard," an outrageous satirization of what Moody described as "the ridiculous pseudomilitary target companies that were manned by the immigrants who were excluded from the regular militia. With more than a hundred groups in the city, every loyal, patriotic, able-bodied man who loved to march, shoot, and carouse could join the Cleveland Light Guards, Lafayette Battery, Oregon Blues, First War Magnetizers, Mustache Fusileers, or Washington Market Chowder Guard."

With his partners, Braham and Hart, Harrigan turned out a series of "Mulligan Guard" productions; first, short sketches and, after these caught on, full-length plays. Filled with slapstick as well as wit, the material poked fun not only at the manners and mores of the Irish but—by bringing in Germans and blacks—of the ethnic and racial conflicts that were so much a part of nineteenth-century New York life. Wrote journalist Richard Harding Davis, "As a historian of the war of the races, Mr. Harrigan makes no mistakes."

Typical, according to Moody, was *The Mulligan Guard Ball*, which was "loaded with Harrigan hilarity on every page, in every minute on the stage. He climaxed his previous exploits in slambang, melee, and general melee when the Negro Skidmore Guard plunged through the ceiling of De Harp and Shamrock and crashed on the Irish Mulligan Guard dancing in the ballroom below. The pileup of arms and legs, smothered in plaster and entwined with the chandelier, created an astonishing spectacle—and a dreaded nightmare for the stage mechanics. There were also milder melees: Dan Mulligan's exploding cigar, Lochmuller's butchers flailing the air with cleavers, a suckling pig jumping from the table to escape its fate, a stray rat tormenting the ladies, Briget and Cordelia mopping the floor with their husbands before tackling each other. Harrigan actors had a bruising evening."

Harrigan and Hart not only conveyed a detailed sense of the culture of their times for succeeding generations, they opened a window on immigrant life for their contemporaries in an era when clannishness was widespread. An evening with Harrigan and Hart was the cultural equivalent of a safe guided tour through New York's tight-knit ethnic neighborhoods. And the success of these productions emboldened others to seek larger markets by broadening their appeal. A result was vaudeville.

In reaching out for a wider audience, vaudeville endeavored to provide "something for everyone." This was evident in the format, the material, and the ambience. Vaudeville's format, a series of eight unrelated acts—singers, dancers, comedians, jugglers, and even animals—was organized so that few, if any, potential customers would find *nothing* of interest to them. The material was designed to cut across ethnic lines by presenting entertainers from different backgrounds who learned to tailor their acts to a pluralistic audience. And the ultramale ambience that offered liquor along with raw jokes was sanitized to encourage the patronage of women and children, too.

In aiming at universality, vaudeville did not abandon ethnic humor, it simply modified it. Urban historian Robert W. Snyder analyzes the various interpretations present in the following brief exchange between Irish Pat Rooney and Marion Bent:

Rooney: *What's your favorite stone?*
Bent: *Turquoise.*
Rooney: *Mine's a brick.*

"Audiences could easily derive different meanings from this," Snyder wrote. "A working-class Irishman could see it as a confirmation of life in the building trades. Others could see it as the difference between a hard-working laborer and an acquisitive woman. Non-Irishmen could see it as a humorous look at the immigrant working class."

Among the richest forms of ethnic culture to reverberate across the New York stage was the Yiddish theater. Conveyed from eastern Europe by Jewish immigrants toward the end of the nineteenth century, it was initially European in content but soon adapted to the new milieu by utilizing American expressions and Lower East Side scenarios. Relying on what Irving Howe in *World of Our Fathers* called "vivid trash and raw talent," the fare was highly eclectic, ranging from Ibsen in Yiddish to lachrymose melodrama, and generally produced highly audible reactions. The ambience can be best appreciated, perhaps, through the comments in the following letter that appeared in *The Day*, a Yiddish newspaper, in 1915:

> …I went to the English theater. The play is passable, but the theater! It is not like our Jewish theater. First of all I found it so quiet there…that I could not hear a sound! There were no cries of "Sha!" "Shut up!" or "Order!" and no babies cried—as if there was no theater at all!…
> And then, there is a total lack of apples, candy, or soda, just like in a desert.
> There are some Gentile girls who go around among the audience handing out glasses of water, but this I can get at home, too.

At the height of the institution's popularity in 1918, thirty-six years after the first Yiddish playhouse opened on East Fourth Street, there were twenty theaters in operation, drawing audiences from throughout the metropolitan area, including fascinated American critics, producers, directors, and actors. Meanwhile, the Yiddish theater was producing its own stars, who became cultural heroes to their immigrant admirers. Jacob Adler, Boris Thomashefski, Bertha Kalish, Maurice Schwartz, Sholem Asch, Menashe Skulnik, and Molly Picon attracted enthusiastic crowds when they dined or shopped or strolled in the neighborhood.

In the 1930s, the Yiddish theater's aura began to fade. Audiences dwindled along with the proportion of Yiddish-speaking New Yorkers, and performers, such as Paul Muni, were lured by the money and glamor of Hollywood and Broadway.

The performers who most successfully made the transition from purely ethnic theater to broader-based vaudeville were those who were able to adjust and revise their acts to fit a new kind of audience. Sophie Tucker, who fled the Hartford, Connecticut, home of her immigrant Russian-Jewish parents as a teenaged mother to seek independence and a career in New York show business, clearly understood the difference. As she recalled in her autobiography, *Some of These Days:*

> I introduced it ("My Yiddishe Mama") at the Palace Theatre in New York in 1925 and after that in the key cities of the U.S.A. where there were many Jews. Even though I loved the song, and it was a sensational hit every time I sang it, I was always careful to use it only when I knew the majority of the house would understand the Yiddish. However, I have found whenever I have sung "My Yiddishe Mama" in the U.S.A., or in Europe, Gentiles have loved the song and have called for it. They didn't need to understand the Yiddish words. They knew, by instinct, what I was saying, and their hearts responded just as the hearts of Jews and Gentiles of every nationality responded when John McCormack sang "Mother Machree". You didn't have to have an old mother in Ireland to feel "Mother Machree" and you didn't have to be a Jew to be moved by "My Yiddishe Mama". Mother in any language means the same thing.

What George M. Cohan meant to the Irish, Sophie Tucker signified for the Jews. The daughter of Russian-Jewish immigrants, she transcended the ethnic appeal of "My Yiddishe Mama" to become a "Red Hot Mama," the prototypical American entertainment idol of the Roaring Twenties.

The Yiddish theater, which flourished along Second Avenue and still exists on the Lower East Side, was once a principal source of culture and recreation for Jewish immigrants. Comedies (opposite below) and tragedies shared overacting, to the delight of audiences, if not critics, and the reactions of the playgoers frequently drowned out the declarations of those onstage. Among the most talented and popular performers of the Yiddish Art Theater was Maurice Schwartz, seen here in a 1937 production of "The Brothers Ashkenazi" (opposite above), which he had dramatized from a novel and directed.

A living refutation of the notion that immigrant stock would never contribute to American culture was George M. Cohan, the nation's most popular entertainer during the early twentieth century. His fame as a song-and-dance man, playwright, and producer was derived largely through his emphasis on patriotism and signaled the acceptance of an Irish-American as a molder of national values, the epitome of a Yankee Doodle Dandy.

"My Yiddishe Mama," which Tucker sang in both Yiddish and English, was symbolic of vaudeville's major contributions to American popular culture: providing a vehicle for ethnic performers seeking to move out of their immigrant backgrounds and into the mainstream and enabling audiences of various ethnicities to share enjoyment under the same roof. In some respects, the song resembles the Rooney-Bent routine by overcoming ethnic boundaries. Although dealing with Jewish concerns, its adoration of motherhood is universal. And its story of a Jewish child's love portrayed Jews in a far more positive light than did earlier stereotypes of befuddled immigrants or sharp businessmen.

While vaudeville liberated immigrants from either performing or being depicted through denigrating stereotypes, it did not extend this understanding to blacks. In addition to perpetuating blackface—and, in the case of entertainers such as Al Jolson, expanding its popularity—vaudeville continued to portray blacks negatively, substituting the "uppity" Jim Dandy characterization for that of the traditional "plantation darky."

Racist jokes were commonplace in early twentieth-century vaudeville, which also popularized the "coon" song, whose lyrics demeaned blacks as ostentatiously dressed, razor-wielding thieves who were obsessed with alcohol, gambling, and sex. The enthusiasm for "coon" songs was invigorated by the emerging rebellion against Victorian repression and the projection of white New Yorkers' fantasies upon newly arrived blacks.

Regardless of the reason, there is no doubt of the manner in which blacks were presented or expected to perform. Many black entertainers, including the notable singer, dancer, and comedian Bert Williams, were compelled to wear blackface. While many blacks complied, Eubie Blake, the outstanding ragtime pianist and composer, resisted. With the assistance of a Palace Theatre functionary named Pat Casey, who argued that blackface was unseemly for an artist of Blake's caliber, he was permitted to appear onstage dressed as a serious musician, not in patched overalls and burnt cork. That was, said Blake, always a source of great pride.

Vaudeville's popularity began to fade with the introduction of the movies and radio, but its influence, if anything, was extended by the new media. Its legacy,

however, was a mixed bag, for along with ameliorating some ethnic tensions, it surely reinforced racial stereotypes and passed them along to wider audiences through films and over the airwaves. But there was no question about its positive impact on the lives of its stars. For many of the performers who later achieved national, and even international, fame perfected their skills on the stages of New York's vaudeville houses. Some, such as Al Jolson, Eddie Cantor, and Bill (Bojangles) Robinson, made it in Hollywood; some, such as Sophie Tucker, Eva Tanguay, and Jimmy Durante, moved into the higher-priced cabaret scene; while still others, such as Harry Houdini, Will Rogers, and George M. Cohan, showcased their artistry before theater crowds.

The career of Cohan epitomized the transition from vaudeville to theater and from ethnic to American. Breaking into show business through vaudeville, where with his parents and sister, he sang and danced as one of "The Four Cohans," he became a fixture on Broadway, where he wrote, produced, directed, and starred in more than twenty rousing, fast-paced musicals. Transcending his Irish background, the multitalented trouper was identified as the ultimate American for the irrepressible patriotism he demonstrated through such songs as "Over There," "You're a Grand Old Flag," and "The Yankee Doodle Boy". Cohan's success represented a triumph of the immigrant culture; here was the grandson of aliens defining for the nation what it meant to be American.

Cohan's colleagues, fellow lyricists and composers whose show tunes became many of the country's most enduring popular songs, were themselves products of the immigrant environment. Mostly Jews, such as Jerome Kern, Richard Rodgers, George Gershwin, Irving Berlin, and Harold Arlen, they went beyond operetta to help develop a new genre—American musical theater—whose lyrics reflected their urban backgrounds and whose rhythms were heavily influenced by jazz.

Their contributions during the first third of the twentieth century anchored popular culture in New York and created a new entertainment district centered at Times Square. By 1940, when the following vivid description appeared in a guide compiled by the New Deal's Work Projects Administration Writers' Program, the area savored a worldwide reputation.

For black entertainers, however talented, the price of success during the early decades of the twentieth century was humiliation. Even accomplished artists such as Bert Williams and George Walker (above) were compelled by the white-dominated show business industry to "cork up" (apply blackface) or adopt stereotypical mannerisms. Williams, who began his career with Walker as a partner, later, as a single, was the first black to become a major Broadway attraction. One who rejected the strictures of racism was Eubie Blake, shown here in 1921 with his orchestra (left). Blake, the premier "ragtime" piano player and composer, said his proudest moments involved his refusal to bow to such demands. Ironically, Blake called this musical group the "Shuffle Along Orchestra."

Although jazz musicians traditionally were free-spirited and open-minded, many club owners frowned on racially mixed groups, even after World War II. Billie Holiday, possibly the most memorable American female vocalist ever, was forced to use freight elevators at the New York hotels in which she entertained. Born illegitimate in Baltimore in 1915, a rape victim as a child, a teenaged prostitute, and lifelong drug addict, "Lady Day" expressed her pain and her needs through a distinctive voice and intimate style that broke ground for a generation of singers, both male and female. Her all-too-full and tragic life ended in a New York hospital in 1959, with a drug charge pending and police stationed outside her door. A dominant performer in the 1930s, '40s, and '50s, she is pictured here between tenor saxophonist Ben Webster, left, and Johnny Russell in Harlem in 1935. Ram Ramirez is in the foreground. Guitarist at rear is unidentified.

The glow in the sky when dusk has fallen is the reflection of Times Square, amusement center of the country. At Times Square, Broadway becomes the Great White Way, its night turned into synthetic day by flashing, glittering, multicolored light-pictures advertising the Nation's products. The scene is cheap and tawdry, yet impressive and stimulating. The ebb and flow of the human tide never ceases here. The Times Square district, embraced by 39th and 57th Streets, from Fifth to Eighth Avenues, abounds in theaters, hotels, movie houses, small shops, lofts, spacious automobile showrooms, night clubs, restaurants, and "taxi-dance halls." Tin Pan Alley, workshop of the song-makers, jingles here. To the Metropolitan Opera House, Town Hall, and Carnegie Hall on the rim of the district come the great singers, the great solo performers, the great conductors, from everywhere.

Not all the music being written and performed in New York during the post-World War I era emanated from Times Square. In fact, to hear what many regard as America's most significant cultural creation—jazz—one had to go uptown, to Harlem. There, in settings that ranged from theaters like the Apollo and block-long ballrooms like the Savoy, through elaborate cabarets like the Cotton Club and Connie's Inn, to "Jungle Alley" joints like Pod's & Jerry's and Mexico's, and at Saturday night "rent parties" in almost anyone's apartment, the world's finest jazz musicians and vocalists were putting out sounds. Through the twenties and into the Depression, legendary figures came from New Orleans, Kansas City, and Chicago to make Harlem the jazz capital of the world: W. C. Handy, Fletcher Henderson, James P. Johnson, Ethel Waters, Willie (the Lion) Smith, Louis Armstrong, Coleman Hawkins, Charlie Parker, Eubie Blake, Scott Joplin, Fats Waller, Duke Ellington, Count Basie, Art Tatum, Benny Goodman, Artie Shaw, Bix Beiderbecke, Jimmy Lunceford, Lucky Millinder, Earl Hines, Chick Webb, Bessie Smith, Ella Fitzgerald, and Billie Holiday.

The music was spectacular, but not everyone could hear it. At the white-owned Cotton Club and Connie's Inn, for example, blacks were barred. Handy, called the "father of the blues," was not permitted into the Cotton Club, although from outside the door he could hear his music being played inside. Both clubs were gaudy, featured sexy, *light-skinned* chorus girls, and aimed their entertainment at well-heeled whites. The concept involved portraying Harlem as exotic and libertine. At the Cotton Club, elaborate revues were performed in front of sets designed to represent a romanticized version of black plantation life. Lena Horne, who performed there in the thirties, recalled the atmosphere: "The shows had a primitive naked quality that was supposed to make a civilized audience lose its inhibitions. The music had an intensive, pervasive rhythm—sometimes loud and brassy, often weird and wild. The dances were eloquently provocative; and if they were occasionally stately, that stateliness served only to heighten their abandon."

At Small's Paradise, blacks were permitted if they could afford the tabs. The presence of blacks proved an inducement for many downtown whites, who assumed, perhaps correctly, that this lent greater authenticity to the entertainment, although the fact that the waiters danced the Charleston while delivering food and beverages should have discouraged such notions. Nevertheless, Small's had a reputation for big-band jam sessions, as well as for exciting floor shows.

Musicians were more likely to hang out at places like Mexico's, where, after hours, they would match talents in what were called "cutting contests." Milton (Mezz) Mezzrow, a white musician who played Harlem clubs with blacks at a time when bands were rarely integrated downtown, recalled the scene at such sessions in *Really the Blues:*

> The contests generally happened in the early morning, after the musicians came uptown from their various jobs. There was always some small private club or speakeasy that had a piano in it, and when some new musician came to town he was obliged to come up with his instrument and get off for the other musicians. If he didn't show, that proved he wasn't sure of

The Roaring Twenties were lots of fun in Harlem, especially for whites. For blacks, it was a different story, the old story: segregation spawned by racism. When New Yorkers discovered Harlem as the place to dance, drink, watch, and listen, they clearly drew the line and held it for decades. Perhaps the ultimate indignity was committed against W. C. Handy, who, while barred from the Cotton Club because of his color, could hear the music he had written being played inside. Of course, blacks were allowed inside as performers and musicians. Duke Ellington played at the Hurricane ballroom in 1943 so that white couples could dance (left). But at the Savoy, blacks could dance, and did they ever (below left).

himself in the fast company around Harlem. The one that rated best on his particular instrument was told, "Hey, man, So-and-So's in town and he was looking for you at Such-and-Such's this morning." All the contenders for the title were worked up that way, each being told the others were looking for him because they wanted to cut him down.... Things really got stirred up that way, and before the night was over all the cats were in some smoky room, really blowing up a breeze. If it was a close call—say, for instance, Lester Young and Ben Webster and Don Byas were all blowing their saxes, and the people couldn't come to much decision about who was best—then somebody would sneak out and get Coleman Hawkins, and when he unwrapped his horn it settled all arguments and sent the boys back to practice some more. These contests taught the musicians never to rest on their laurels.

Nightclubs in Harlem, such as Elks Rendezvous, featured light-skinned black chorus lines.

Competition was intense not only among individual musicians but between bands, as well. At the Savoy, big-band battles were a regular weekend feature and leader Chick Webb, a short, scrawny drummer, knew what the dance crowds wanted and was the acknowledged "king" of that ballroom. The Savoy may never have rocked more than when Benny Goodman went uptown to battle Webb before five thousand dancers on the floor and another five thousand in the street. The event was heightened, according to the *New York Age*, because "it was the first time that Harlem would get an opportunity to see the Goodman aggregation which includes two Negroes [Teddy Wilson and Lionel Hampton] as featured musicians in action." The encounter, wrote Samuel Charters and Leonard Kunstadt in *Jazz*, lived up to its advance notices: "Benny came into the Savoy with his greatest band, but the Savoy was jammed with Chick's loyal fans. The Goodman band played at their best, but they couldn't win the crowd away from little Chick. He finished the session with a drum solo, winning a thunderous ovation, while Goodman and his drummer, Gene Krupa, just stood there shaking their heads."

Occasionally, competition in the Harlem music scene took on harsher forms. The Cotton Club, "the aristocrat of Harlem," according to no less an authority than English noblewoman Lady Mountbatten, resented pressure from the Plantation Club, which sought to emulate the Cotton Club's success by copying its style. "The rivalry went too far," wrote Edward Jablonski in his biography of Harold Arlen, "when the management of the Plantation persuaded Cab Calloway to bring his orchestra from the Cotton Club to the Plantation. Calloway was one of the major attractions at the Cotton Club with his famous 'Minnie the Moocher' routine. As he was an irrepressible night-club-floor personality...his leaving the Cotton Club was looked upon as pretty unfair competition. One night 'some of the boys' dropped in on the Plantation Club...all the tables and chairs, reduced to splinters, shattered glasses and bottles, even the bar was deracinated and replanted at the curb.... When the boys finished with the Plantation Club, the street was the healthier place to be. Calloway and band, needless to say, returned to their old stand."

Violence was no stranger to Harlem, particularly during Prohibition when many of the clubs were owned by white bootleggers and gangsters, such as Owney Madden, who ran the Cotton Club. Adding to the excitement of patrons during that era, of course, was the knowledge that racketeers, who had been elevated to celebrity status by the press, were likely to appear at any time. Besides those from the underworld, customers from downtown might be Broadway stars, such as Helen Morgan, Mae West, and Tallulah Bankhead; athletes, such as Jack Dempsey and Gene Tunney; and politicians, such as Mayor James J. Walker and Governor Alfred E. Smith.

Going uptown for fun, "slumming," became routine for Jazz Age thrill-seekers, according to Jervis Anderson in *This Was Harlem:* "In the twenties, *Variety* said, Harlem had 'attained preeminence' as an 'amusement center.' Up there one saw 'as many limousines from Park and upper Fifth Avenue parked outside its sizzling cafes, "speaks," night clubs, and spiritual seances as in any other high-grade white locale' in America." But Harlem's appeal began to dim with the repeal of Prohibition in 1933 and the realities of the Depression. The economic problems of the nation were devastating in the ghettos, giving rise to racial and class tensions that triggered riots in Harlem in 1935 and again in 1943. Even before World War II, the jazz scene had largely moved out of Harlem to a cluster of small, crowded, smoky clubs on West 52nd Street, later called "Swing Street" or simply, "*The* Street."

A new jazz style that came to be known as "be-bop" or just "bop" was being developed in those clubs by Dizzy Gillespie, Charlie Parker, and Thelonious Monk, among others, and musicians as well as aficionados squeezed in to listen. Billy Taylor, the pianist and musicologist, recalled the days in *Hear Me Talkin' To Ya'* by Nat Shapiro and Nat Hentoff: "In 1943, I remember The Deuces, the Downbeat, the Onyx, the Famous Door, Kelly's Stables, and the Hickory House.... The three big draws on The Street then were Art Tatum, Coleman Hawkins, and Billie Holiday. And things were flexible for musicians on The Street. Like Don Byas might have an engagement at the Three Deuces as a leader, and then he'd go next door to the Downbeat as a sideman with Coleman Hawkins. The cutting sessions there were just fantastic. With all of the musicians regularly working on The Street and with all those sitting in, astonishing sessions were inevitable."

Jazz historian Charles Edward Smith noted that "52nd Street was a place where musicians came to relax and sometimes to 'sit in.' Outside of isolated clubs it was the first place where customers paid to sit down to listen to jazz music, without dancing. Musicians, even those who worked for much less than they'd previously earned in 'name' bands, liked its informality and the chance to be themselves."

Although blacks were making 52nd Street jump, their role was pretty much circumscribed: They were welcomed as performers but prohibited as patrons. White jazz impresario John Hammond seized an opportunity to change that.

It is quite true that in the middle thirties and early forties, 52nd Street was a haven for all sorts of jazz combos, big and small. For my part, I did not frequent it as much as I might have, partly because I had more fun in the Harlem spots, but mostly because 52nd Street adhered to the severe Jim Crow patterns of downtown New York City in the 1930s.

My first active participation on 52nd Street was the summer of 1937 when Count Basie's

The Audubon Theater, whose striking entrance features the sculpture of a woman on the prow of a ship, has witnessed more than its share of New York history. Built in 1912 at Broadway and 166th Street by the founder of the Fox (later, 20th Century-Fox) movie chain as a vaudeville house, it became a movie theater, and its upstairs ballroom was the site, in 1965, of the assassination of Black Muslim leader Malcolm X.

band was at The Crossroads. Basie had done reasonably well in Harlem spots but suffered from infrequent exposure on the radio and had not been very successful before white audiences. Willard Alexander, then with MCA and the booker of Count Basie, had an idea to put the fourteen-piece Basie band into New York's Famous Door, a tiny club on 52nd Street which could seat, with difficulty, about sixty people at tables. The Famous Door had that most prized of all possessions, a coast to coast CBS radio wire which Alexander was convinced was necessary for the ultimate acceptance by the American public of Basie's music.

Aside from being small and cramped, the Famous Door was insufferably hot, and the owners, Al Felshin and Jerry Brooks, had no money to invest in such gadgets as air conditioning. This is where I came in. I put up the money for the air conditioning as a loan in return for which I would get preferred treatment at tables any night I wished to go there. And also there would be no questions asked if I brought Negro guests. My investment was an unqualified success. Basie made a sensation with his broadcasts. The place was jammed every night. My loan was repaid. The Jim Crow pattern of the Famous Door was broken, at least for the time of Basie's stay....

By the end of World War II, The Street had begun to fall victim to commercialization, first by sleazy strip joints and ultimately by sleek, soulless office buildings. Critic Leonard Feather remembered that "what was once a healthy meeting place for musicians and fans, a street on which racial barriers were broken down, by 1945 had turned into something that parallels the notorious Barbary Coast of San Francisco." Some of the clubs reopened on Broadway under new names, such as Clique (which became Birdland), Royal Roost, and Bop City, where they survived until the 1950s. Greenwich Village, a traditional home to jazz, has been the center of the revival that erupted in the 1980s. It has also been hospitable to other musical forms, particularly folk and occasionally Latin.

In a city whose popular culture has been enriched and even transformed by immigrants, Latin music has left its distinctive imprint on New York's dance floors. From the pre-World War I introduction by Vernon and Irene Castle of their version of the Argentinian tango to the latest salsa sound, the city has served a vibrant role in an ongoing process of collaboration and cross-fertilization that involves Cuba, South America, and Africa.

The recent past has witnessed a harmonious relationship between jazz and the Latin beat through such musicians as percussionist Tito Puente, Cuban trumpeter Mario Bauza, and jazz innovator Dizzy Gillespie. Puente, known as "El Rey" (The King) of Latin music, absorbed American swing influences while listening to the big bands at the Savoy Ballroom in Harlem. Bauza introduced Gillespie to Latin styles and, in turn, combined jazz with his native Cuban rhythms.

Cuba, with the rumba, mambo, and cha-cha-cha, has been the most significant provider of Latin music, so far as Americans are concerned, although Brazil's samba and bossa nova and the Dominican Republic's merengue also have gotten warm receptions. In New York, Latin music itself has been integrated: Salsa, which embraces many different Latin styles, developed partly through the influence of Puerto Ricans and "Nuyoricans" (New Yorkers of Puerto Rican descent), who added new tempos and played them on electrified instruments.

While political conflict has disrupted the process of musical exchange between the United States and Cuba, the Latin beat, however less resonant, goes on. American music, like other forms of popular culture, has been shaped by a wide variety of ethnic influences. And as with other aspects of New York life, the presence of immigrants has changed not only them but the land they adopted.

In popular culture, this symbiotic relationship between foreigners and the city is particularly evident in prizefighting, whose history reads like a chronicle of ethnic succession. Because professional boxing offers impoverished youths the promise of wealth and fame for enduring pains not unlike those inflicted freely by their daily lives, the sport has traditionally appealed to ghetto dwellers of every race and na-

The post-World War II arrival of Puerto Ricans in New York had a significant impact on the city's—and the nation's—music. Among the many notable Latino musicians who brought their talents to the clubs and dance halls were percussionist Tito Puente (left) and, in the group pictured below, Tito Rodriguez (third from left), Joe Valle (fourth from left), and Cesar Concepcion (far right). Latin night clubs offered such entertainers as Yayo el Indio, singing with the Andino Orchestra (opposite).

tionality. The pattern is clear enough to be depicted, which is what sociologists S. Kirkson Weinberg and Henry Arond did in a 1952 article in the *American Journal of Sociology.* They showed that, with few exceptions, the ethnicity of prominent boxers changed over decades in conjunction with immigration trends. For example, the ring was dominated by Irish fighters in 1909 and 1916, by Jews in 1928, by Italians in 1936, and by blacks in 1948.

There are, to be sure, other factors, for as they pointed out, "The traditions of an ethnic group, as well as its temporary location at the bottom of the scale, may affect the proportion of its boys who become boxers. Many Irish, but few Scandinavians, have become boxers in this country; many Filipinos, but few Japanese and Chinese...." It is important to recognize, too, that for all its potential rewards, boxing is a tough business, not only physically but economically, and that ethnic groups vacate the ring eagerly when they are able to move up into more desirable fields. Thus, an ethnic group's dominance in the ring during any period is, most likely, also a reflection of its adversity.

Boxing's place in the history of New York City rests on far more than enabling some ethnics and minorities to escape poverty; it is based on the sport's significant role in fueling pride and igniting conflict. Its partisans, an intense breed, from the beginning have infused bouts with a significance that far eclipsed the ring itself, fancying them as symbolic of local, regional, national, ethnic, or racial superiority. For example, the bare-knuckled heavyweight championship fight in 1849 between James "Yankee" Sullivan, an Irish immigrant, and Tom Hyer, a native-born American, encapsuled the building conflict between the "Famine Irish" newcomers who were surging into the city and the nativist majority that felt threatened by them. The press, not content with merely feeding ethnic and religious prejudices (the Irish were Catholic, the Americans Protestant), stirred up class hatreds as well. The *New York Herald* identified Sullivan as "the chief and champion of a class of society comprised of persons similar in every respect to himself—not refined." However, they found Hyer "the pet of fashionable society in this city...and in appearance and symmetry of person, almost equals the statue of Apollo." Given the buildup it received, the fight itself was anticlimactic. In an era when bouts sometimes exceeded one hundred rounds, it lasted a measly sixteen, although *American Fistiana* enthused that "never had the American ring shown so much fighting in so little time." Hyer was declared the winner when Sullivan failed to come out for the seventeenth round.

Fervor reached even greater intensity in 1860 for the first international heavyweight contest, "the championship of the world," still bare-knuckled, which matched an American of Irish ancestry, James Camel Heenan, against Tom Sayers, the English titleholder. At a time when the United States was becoming a rival commercial power and the British were belittling the alleged decline of Anglo-Saxon stock with its transplantation in America, both nations viewed the fight, to be held in a Hampshire hamlet, as a test of national preeminence. *Wilkes' Spirit of the Times* even advocated the abandonment of principle in the interest of chauvinism. "The ordinary objections to vulgar pugilism," it insisted, "are waived in the real importance of this first-class struggle, and there is scarcely a mind that is amenable to the influence of national pride, which does not once lay aside its prejudice against fighting, in the hope to see the American champion win."

The outcome was dissatisfying to all concerned. In *A Sporting Time*, Melvin L. Adelman reported that "the fight pitted Heenan's youth and his height and weight advantage against Sayer's experience and savvy. The American broke Sayer's arm early in the fight while the Englishman cut one of Heenan's eyes, yet both fighters continued gamely until the thirty-seventh round when the ropes were mysteriously cut and the police rushed in to break up the fight. Who was winning at the time depended on which side of the Atlantic you lived on. English journalists believed that Sayers would have eventually won; American reporters were even more adamant that Heenan was on the verge of victory.... The fight was declared a draw and each fighter was awarded a championship belt. Then Sayers retired and Heenan emerged as the heavyweight champion, an inadequate solution for most Americans."

However displeased with the decision, New Yorkers were ecstatic over Heenan's performance, and an estimated 50,000 of them were on hand to hail him on his return. The tumultuous reception distressed the *New York Herald*, which sanctimoniously denounced this "glorification of brutality and vice and its exaltation over the noblest sentiments of the human heart." Yet there was little doubt about the tremendous interest of city residents in the event, or of the global significance they attributed to it. "Not until the Joe Louis-Max Schmeling fight in the 1930s," wrote Adelman, "was any boxing match, or quite possibly any international sports contest in which an American was involved, so highly charged with nationalistic sentiments."

In Yankee Stadium on the night of June 22, 1938, 70,000 fight fans witnessed an event whose drama challenged fiction. Nominally for the world heavyweight championship, it had become immeasurably more, involving revenge, racism, jingoism, and ideology. With the possibility of a major war looming in Europe, it virtually became a metaphor for that anticipated conflict. The combatants were the champion, Joe Louis, black son of an Alabama sharecropper, proclaimed as living proof of the opportunity inherent in a democratic system, and the challenger, Max Schmeling, the product of Adolf Hitler's Germany, the personification of the Nazi "master race" theory that denigrated blacks. In addition to these political considerations, there was a critical personal aspect: Two years earlier, before Louis took the title from James J. Braddock, Schmeling had handed him the only defeat in his career.

The return match, heard by millions throughout the world, lasted little more than two minutes. Louis, the twenty-four-year-old underdog who had been fighting professionally for only four years, attacked the powerful and experienced German

Beginning in the 1960s, with champions such as light-heavyweight Jose Torres and lightweight Carlos Ortiz, Latinos made their presence felt in the ring. Puerto Rican fighters maintained close ties through reunions, such as this one at Restaurante Diaz, at Madison Avenue and 110th Street.

with a ferocity that left Schmeling bleeding, whimpering in pain, and unable to rise before the count of ten. The reaction in the stadium was thunderous, but it hardly compared with the scene in Harlem. Traffic was stalled for hours, and celebrants jammed the streets to pay tribute to Louis, whose skills and dignity made him not only a black hero and role model but, in the words of columnist Jimmy Cannon, "a credit to his race—the human race."

The racial pride generated by Louis had its counterpart in such ethnic paragons as Benny Leonard and Barney Ross for Jews, James J. Braddock and Jimmy McLarnin for the Irish, Rocky Marciano and Jake LaMotta for Italians, and Jose Torres for Puerto Ricans. The popularity of these fighters, some of whom promoted their ethnic identification by wearing such insignia as Stars of David or shamrocks on their trunks, not only gave their followers a heightened sense of self-esteem, it sold tickets. Appeals to racial and ethnic pride—and to their baser counterparts, prejudice and hatred—proved to be good business. Declared promoter Tex Rickard: "Give me a Jewish fighter who can be built up into a challenger for the heavyweight championship and I'll show you the man who can bring back the million-dollar gate."

During the '20s and '30s, New York became a figurative ethnic battleground between the Irish and Jews over the exploits of three fighters: McLarnin, Leonard, and Ross. McLarnin, a tough welterweight, added to his box-office luster by knocking out a series of Jewish fighters with apparent ease. He put away Jackie Fields in two rounds, Louis "Kid" Kaplan in eight, Sid Terris in one, and Ruby Goldstein, who would later become a notable referee, in two.

Leonard, who came out of the Lower East Side to win the lightweight title in 1917 and retire undefeated eight years later, had captured the imagination of American Jewry with his success in the ring and admirable behavior outside it. For a people stereotyped as bookish and submissive, Leonard was the aggressive, daring antithesis. *Evening Journal* Editor Arthur Brisbane contended that the stylish boxer "had done more to conquer anti-Semitism than a thousand textbooks have done." After seven years, Leonard emerged from retirement, thirty-six and overweight, to whip a few unknowns and challenge McLarnin. "One of the reasons I want to lick

McLarnin," Leonard told drumbeating sportswriters before the bout, "is that I want to wipe out his successful record against Jewish fighters." All Leonard succeeded in doing, however, was to add to McLarnin's roster of Jewish conquests and diminish his own reputation. McLarnin put the drained and sluggish former champion away in six rounds and sent him back to retirement.

At about the time Leonard was ruefully concluding his career, Jews were discovering a new hero, an exciting lightweight named Barney Ross. Born Rasovsky on the Lower East Side, Ross made his reputation in Chicago, where his family had moved and his father had been killed by hold-up men. True to the ghetto tradition, Ross entered the ring to help support his widowed mother and five siblings. In 1933, he won the lightweight title from Tony Canzoneri on a controversial hometown decision, then defeated him handily in a New York rematch. A few more impressive victories set Ross apart in his division and set up probably the most intense ethnic rivalry in modern boxing history: three title fights with the Jewish nemesis, Irish welterweight champion McLarnin.

Both fighters were good and both were popular, and New York, with its heavily Jewish and Irish population, was divided, and tense. On the night of the match, few New Yorkers were indifferent. Harold U. Ribalow, author of *The Jew in American Sports*, recalled the evening with clarity. "I remember that at this time I was living in a section in New York where many European Jews—all young men—were attending *yeshiva* in the city. These boys knew little about boxing, but they could not miss the excitement throughout the city. And the fact that McLarnin had beaten many Jewish fighters made the event even more important to them. It was odd, watching these boys, with skullcaps on their heads, taking time out from their Talmudic studies to listen to a fight on the radio. And no matter how long I shall remember the famous trio of Ross-McLarnin fights, I shall recall the intense faces of the Jewish students who listened to each blow-by-blow account as though it were the most significant thing in the world."

All three battles went the fifteen-round limit. Ross won the first on a split decision and achieved fistic immortality by becoming the first boxer to win both lightweight and welterweight titles. McLarnin unanimously recaptured the crown in a rematch, but Ross took it back with an unequivocal victory in their final meeting in 1935.

Despite the fiercely overt ethnic pride and prejudice that prizefighting engendered, some boxers were willing to surrender their heritage for what they perceived as a more marketable background. Thus, the success of the Irish led a black fighter to become Shamus O'Brien, two Jews to become Mushy Callahan and Al McCoy, and Andrea Chiariglione, the only man who knocked out Jack Dempsey, to become Jim Flynn. And in the 1930s, when Jewish pugilists were in style, a non-Jew named Max Baer won the heavyweight championship with a Jewish star appended to his trunks. Such transformations occasionally occurred in the public mind alone. Jews supposedly were so convinced that a popular boxer named Harry Greb was Jewish they created the legend that "Greb" was an anagram of his "real" name, Berg.

Even if apocryphal, the story suggests the intensity surrounding group feelings and the need for ethnic and racial heroes, particularly when they disprove stereotypes or slurs. Positive role models as both an inspiration and as an aid to refuting bigotry have served New York's minorities since colonial times. The city's history has demonstrated repeatedly the value of popular culture in providing opportunities for talent to surface, regardless of background, and for disparate groups to share in its appreciation. Yet, popular entertainment, arts, and sports have exploited and aggravated racial and ethnic differences, often hindering mutual understanding and respect. Clearly, the maintenance of pluralism and diversity has not proved painless.

Ethnic groups in New York traditionally have yearned for ring heroes, and few were more lionized than Benny Leonard, a Lower East Side Jew who dominated the lightweight division for a decade, holding the title from 1917 through 1925.

Native sports are among the hardiest of the customs that immigrants have brought to New York. Occasionally, they have gained widespread popularity; soccer, for example. But more often they have remained a cherished remnant of a traditional culture, kept alive by diverse ethnic groups, and sometimes passed along to their children. In season, a wide variety of ethnic sports are on display around the city, including West Indian cricketers of the Wembley Cricket Club at Vans Cortlandt Park in the Bronx (above), Gaelic football and hurling, sponsored by the Gaelic Athletic Association of New York (opposite center and above), at Gaelic Park, and bocce at the Italian-American Bocce Courts at Dyker Heights in Brooklyn (opposite below). For blacks, basketball seems to dominate at city playgrounds, reaching a crescendo during the annual tournament at the Holcombe Rucker Memorial Playground at 155th Street and Eighth Avenue (right).

By century's end, the best estimates indicate that New York City's population will be increased by the addition of another one million immigrants—most of them from the Caribbean and Far East. For the first time in the city's history, a majority of New Yorkers are likely to be nonwhite. Such a citizenry will provide a stern test for a city that has shown a marked affinity for European stock.

There is ample documentation of this bias. No major groups have been subjected to discrimination for so long nor with such impact as have blacks and Latinos. As New York's newest newcomers, they have become the principal victims of the city's neglect, unable to get decent—let alone equal—housing, jobs, health care, education, and protection.

Their lot, sired by racial and ethnic prejudice and fed by differences in language and culture, has been compounded by an insidious factor that distinguishes them still further from prior immigrants. According to the Commission on the Year 2000, a panel of experts formed by Mayor Edward I. Koch in 1984 to peer ahead, "Earlier impoverished New Yorkers had something that many of today's poor lack: They had faith that their own work would pay off for themselves and their children, that their descendants would have a better life." Thus, hopelessness has been added to the unconscionable assortment of ills that New York, like a malevolent Welcome Wagoner, seems to dispense to these most recent immigrants.

Despite a determinedly upbeat approach overall (its report was entitled *New York Ascendant*), the mayor's commission envisions an even more ominous future for that growing underclass. In effect, they have been doubly afflicted by an uncaring economy that shifted from manufacturing to such fields as finance, information, communications, and services. Just when blacks and Latinos entered the manufacturing sector—that traditional ladder of opportunity for previous immigrants from Europe—New York left it. Deprived of jobs in the contracting garment industry, for example, they found themselves ill-prepared to benefit from the expanding (and booming) white-collar market.

The prognosis, therefore, appears all too clear: While the city prospers, the well-being of most of its people will decline. Yet, such a consequence is not only immoral and undesirable, it is unnecessary. Like their namesakes from Gotham, England, New Yorkers have demonstrated that ingenuity and resourcefulness can overcome adversity. The Commission on the Year 2000 repeatedly invokes the city's dramatic response to its fiscal crisis of the 1970s as evidence of that capacity.

As trying as were the days of near-bankruptcy, those fiscal problems lent themselves to pragmatic solutions: reduce spending, exercise discipline, find new sources of revenue. The social dilemmas of today and tomorrow are far more complex; they are crises of the heart and soul. And they will demand of New Yorkers an unparalleled degree of open-mindedness, an unequaled commitment to justice and compassion.

A significant beginning would be to discard the misconception that the success or failure of immigrant groups was and is based solely on their inherent qualities and not subject to the economic and political vagaries of the times. It is from such simplistic notions that destructive racial and ethnic stereotypes develop. And the composition of the future city suggests that there will be little tolerance for the bigotry-bred strife that has scarred the past. That the burgeoning nonwhite population will produce an electoral majority should not evoke fear among whites. Power achieved through the ballot is not only in the best democratic tradition but in the best immigrant tradition, having provided successive waves of newcomers with the most effective response to the hostility they had encountered.

There must be a recognition that immigration is an ongoing process to be approached realistically, with understanding and resources, not simply an historic phenomenon to be celebrated. For New York is a city constantly undergoing transformation, responding to the presence of an ever-new influx of "outsiders": New Yorkers with new needs, new vitality, new dreams.

Introduction

Bayor, Ronald H. *Neighbors in Conflict: The Irish, Germans, Jews, and Italians of New York City, 1929–1941*. Baltimore: Johns Hopkins University Press, 1978.

Bernstein, Iver, University of Chicago. Interview with Rob Snyder regarding New York City draft riots of 1863. December 1985.

Billington, Ray Allen. *The Protestant Crusade*. New York: Macmillan, 1938.

Cook, Adrian. *The Armies of the Streets: The New York City Draft Riots of 1863*. Lexington: University Press of Kentucky, 1974.

Dinnerstein, Leonard. "The Funeral of Rabbi Jacob Joseph," unpublished manuscript, University of Arizona.

———; Nichols, Roger L.; and Reimers, David M. *Natives and Strangers*. New York: Oxford University Press, 1979.

Headley, Joel T. *The Great Riots of New York, 1712–1873*. Indianapolis and New York: Bobbs-Merrill, 1970.

Higham, John. *Strangers in the Land: Patterns in American Nativism, 1860–1925*. New Brunswick, New Jersey: Rutgers University Press, 1963.

New Yorkers at Home

Anderson, Jervis. *This Was Harlem: A Cultural Portrait, 1900–1950*. New York: Farrar, Straus and Giroux, 1982.

Badillo, Herman, former congressman. Interview with Rob Snyder. May 1987.

Brinkley, Alan. *Voices of Protest: Huey Long, Father Coughlin, and the Great Depression*. New York: Alfred A. Knopf, 1982.

Carro, Judge John. Interview with Rob Snyder on Puerto Rican life. May 1987.

Coleman, Terry. *Passage to America: A History of Emigrants from Great Britain and Ireland to America in the Mid-Nineteenth Century*. Harmondsworth, England: Penguin, 1976.

Dickens, Charles. *American Notes for General Circulation*. Harmondsworth, England: Penguin, 1972.

Dolan, Jay P. *The Immigrant Church: New York's Irish and German Catholics*. Baltimore: Johns Hopkins University Press, 1975.

Ellis, David M.; Frost, James A.; Syrett, Harold S.; and Carman, Harry F. *A Short History of New York State*. Ithaca: Cornell University Press, 1957.

Ernst, Robert. *Immigrant Life in New York City*. New York: King's Crown Press, 1949.

Fitzpatrick, Joseph P. *Puerto Rican-Americans: The Meaning of Migration to the Mainland*. Englewood Cliffs, New Jersey: Prentice-Hall, 1971.

Foster, George. *New York in Slices*. New York: W. H. Graham, 1849.

Gartrell, Leland. Telephone interview with Rob Snyder on the religious composition of New York City. December 1985.

Griesinger, Karl Theodor. From *Land und Leute in Amerika*. In Still, *Mirror for Gotham*.

Howe, Irving. *World of Our Fathers*. New York: Harcourt Brace Jovanovich, 1976.

Joselit, Jenna Weissman. *Our Gang: Jewish Crime and the New York Jewish Community, 1900–1940*. Bloomington, Indiana: Indiana University Press, 1983.

Kessner, Thomas. *The Golden Door: Italian and Jewish Immigrant Mobility in New York City, 1880–1930*. New York: Oxford University Press, 1977.

La Sorte, Michael A. *La Merica: Images of Italian Greenhorn Experience*. Philadelphia: Temple University Press, 1985.

Lewis, David Levering. *When Harlem Was in Vogue*. New York: Alfred A. Knopf, 1981.

Metzker, Isaac, ed. *A Bintel Brief: Sixty Years of Letters from the Lower East Side to the Jewish Daily Forward*. Garden City, New York: Doubleday, 1971.

Muffs, Judith Herschlag and Cole, Bruce, Anti-Defamation League. Interview with Rob Snyder on the present state of interfaith relations in New York City. December 1985.

Osofsky, Gilbert. *Harlem: The Making of a Ghetto*. New York: Harper and Row, 2nd ed., 1971.

Pitkin, Thomas. *Keepers of the Gate*. New York: New York University Press, 1975.

Pratt, John W. *Religion, Politics, and Diversity: The Church and State Theme in New York History*. Ithaca: Cornell University Press, 1967.

Quinn, Bernard, et al. *Churches and Church Membership in the United States, 1980: An Enumeration*. Atlanta: Glenmary Research Center, 1982.

Riis, Jacob. "Feast Days in Little Italy." *Century Magazine,* August 1899.

Rosenwaike, Ira. *Population History of New York City*. Syracuse, New York: Syracuse University Press, 1972.

Sanchez Korrol, Virginia E. *From Colonia to Community: The History of Puerto Ricans in New York City, 1917–1948*. Westport, Connecticut: Greenwood Press, 1983.

Smith, Willie "The Lion," with Hoefer, George. *Music on My Mind: The Memoirs of an American Pianist*. Garden City, New York: Doubleday, 1964.

Still, Bayrd. *Mirror for Gotham: New York as Seen by Contemporaries from Dutch Days to the Present*. New York: New York University Press, 1956.

Strong, George Templeton. *Diary*. Allan Nevins and Milton Halsey Thomas, eds. New York: Macmillan, 1952.

Thomas, Piri. *Down These Mean Streets*. New York: Vintage, 1974.

Vega, Bernardo. *Memoirs of Bernardo Vega: A Contribution to the History of the Puerto Rican Community in New York*. César Iglesias, ed. Juan Flores, trans. New York: Monthly Review Press, 1984

Wittke, Carl F. *The Germans in America*. New York: Teachers College Press, 1967.

WPA Guide to New York City. New York: Pantheon, 1982.

New York Politics

Bridges, Amy. *A City in the Republic: New York and the Origins of Machine Politics*. New York: Cambridge University Press, 1984.

Callow, Alexander B., Jr. *The Tweed Ring*. New York: Oxford University Press, 1966.

Caro, Robert A. *The Power Broker: Robert Moses and the Fall of New York*. New York: Vintage, 1975.

Connable, Alfred and Silberfarb, Edward. *Tigers of Tammany*. New York: Holt, Rinehart, and Winston, 1967.

Costikyan, Edward. *Behind Closed Doors*. New York: Harcourt, Brace and World, 1966.

Countryman, Edward. *A People in Revolution: The American Revolution and Political Society in New York, 1760–1790*. Baltimore: Johns Hopkins University Press, 1981.

Dubofsky, Melvyn. "Success and Failure of Socialism in New York City, 1900–1918: A Case Study." *Labor History* 9: 361–375.

Elliott, Lawrence. *Little Flower: The Life and Times of Fiorello La Guardia*. New York: William Morrow, 1983.

Hammack, David. *Power and Society: Greater New York at the Turn of the Century*. New York: Russell Sage, 1982.

Handlin, Oscar. *Al Smith and His America*. Boston: Little, Brown, 1958.

Josephson, Matthew and Josephson, Hannah. *Al Smith: Hero of the Cities; A Political Portrait Drawing on the Papers of Frances Perkins*. Boston: Houghton Mifflin, 1969.

Kammen, Michael. *Colonial New York: A History*. New York: Charles Scribner's Sons, 1975.

Kaufman, Herbert and Sayre, Wallace S. *Governing New York City*. New York: W. W. Norton, 1965.

Lowi, Theodore. *At the Pleasure of the Mayor*. New York: Free Press, 1964.

Mandelbaum, Seymour. *Boss Tweed's New York*. New York: Wiley, 1965.

McManus, James, Democratic District Leader, 64 AD, Part B. Interview with Rob Snyder. July 1986.

Moscow, Warren. *Politics in the Empire State*. New York: Alfred A. Knopf, 1948.

———. *What Have You Done for Me Lately?* Englewood Cliffs, New Jersey: Prentice-Hall, 1967.

———. *The Last of the Bigtime Bosses*. New York: Stein and Day, 1971.

Mushkat, Jerome. *Tammany: The Evolution of a Political Machine*. Syracuse, New York: Syracuse University Press, 1971.

O'Dwyer, Paul. *Counsel for the Defense: The Autobiography of Paul O'Dwyer*. New York: Simon and Schuster, 1979.

Perkins, Frances. *The Roosevelt I Knew*. New York: Viking, 1946.

Remini, Robert V. *Martin Van Buren and the Making of the Democratic Party*. New York: Columbia University Press, 1959.

Riordon, William L. *Plunkitt of Tammany Hall*. New York: E. P. Dutton, 1963.

Schafer, Alan. *Vito Marcantonio*. Syracuse, New York: Syracuse University Press, 1966.

Shefter, Martin. *Political Crisis/Fiscal Crisis: The Collapse and Revival of New York City*. New York: Basic Books, 1985.

Spann, Edward K. *The New Metropolis: New York City, 1840–1857*. New York: Columbia University Press, 1981.

Wilentz, Sean. *Chants Democratic: New York City and the Rise of the American Working Class, 1788–1850*. New York: Oxford University Press, 1984.

Young, Alfred. *The Democratic Republicans of New York: The Origins, 1763–1797*. Chapel Hill, North Carolina: University of North Carolina Press, 1967.

Zinn, Howard. *La Guardia in Congress*. Ithaca: Cornell University Press, 1959.

New Yorkers at Work

Albion, Robert G. *The Rise of New York Port, 1815–1860*. New York, 1939.

Banks, Gil, Harlem Fightback. Interview with author describing discrimination against blacks in construction industry. January 1987.

Barnes, Charles B. *The Longshoremen*. New York: Survey Associates, 1915.

Bernhardt, Debra E. *New Yorkers at Work: Oral Histories of Life, Labor and Industry*. New York: Robert F. Wagner Labor Archives, New York University, 1985.

Chin, David. Interview January 1981, with Jack Tchen of the New York Chinatown History Project.

Clark, Sue Ainslee and Wyatt, Edith. "First Morning of the Strike." *McClure's Magazine*, November 1910. In Stein, *Out of the Sweatshop*.

Deer, Louis. Local 40, International Association of Structural Machinery Movers, Erectors, Riggers and Iron Workers. Interview with Rob Snyder on Native Americans in the construction industry. February 1987.

Dickens, Charles. *American Notes for General Circulation*. Harmondsworth, England: Penguin, 1972.

DiDonato, Pietro. *Christ in Concrete*. Indianapolis: Bobbs-Merrill, 1937.

Dreiser, Theodore. "The Color of the City." In Stein, *Out of the Sweatshop*.

Ernst, Robert. *Immigrant Life in New York City*. New York: King's Crown Press, 1949.

———. "The Economic Status of New York City Negroes." *Negro History Bulletin*, March 1949.

Fitch, Lyle C. and Walsh, Annmarie Hauck. *Agenda for a City*. Beverly Hills, California: Sage Publications, 1970.

Foerster, Robert. *Italian Emigration of Our Times*. Cambridge, Massachusetts: Harvard University Press, 1919.

Freedman, Marcia. "The Labor Market for Immigrants in New York City." *New York Affairs* 7, 1983.

Freeman, Rhoda G. "The Free Negro in New York City in the Era Before the Civil War." Ph.D. dissertation, Political Science, Columbia University, 1966.

Friedman, Saul. "A New Era of Sweatshops." *New York Newsday*, August 18, 1985.

Frowne, Sadie. "Days and Dreams." *Independent*, September 25, 1902. In Stein, *Out of the Sweatshop*.

Gambino, Richard. *Blood of My Blood: The Dilemma of the Italian-Americans*. Garden City, New York: Doubleday, 1974.

Gerard, Karen. "New York City's Economy: A Decade of Change." *New York Affairs* 8 (1984).

Herbstein, Judith F. "Rituals and Politics of the Puerto Rican 'Community' in New York City." Ph.D. dissertation, Anthropology, City University of New York.

History Task Force, Centro de Estudios Puertoriquenos, Hunter College, City University of New York. *Labor Migration Under Capitalism: The Puerto Rican Experience*. New York: Monthly Review Press, 1979.

Howe, Irving. *World of Our Fathers*. New York: Harcourt Brace Jovanovitch, 1976.

Jordy, William H. *American Buildings and Their Architects: Progressive and Academic Ideas at the Turn of the Century*. Garden City, New York: Doubleday, 1972.

Kessner, Thomas. *The Golden Door: Italian and Jewish Immigrant Mobility in New York City, 1880–1930*. New York: Oxford University Press, 1977.

Kim, Ilsoo. *New Urban Immigrants: The Korean Community in New York*. Princeton: Princeton University Press, 1981.

"Labor in New York: Its Circumstances, Conditions and Rewards." *New York Tribune*, September 5 and 9, and November 11, 1845.

Levine, Louis. *The Women's Garment Workers*. New York: B.W. Huebsch, 1924.

MacFayden, J. "Exploring a Past Long Locked in Myth and Mystery." *Smithsonian*, January 1983.

Maldonado, Gloria, International Ladies Garment Workers Union Local 89-22-1 official. Interview with author describing Puerto Rican work experiences in the garment industry. January 1987.

New York Chinatown History Project. "Washing and Ironing: Chinese Laundry Workers in the U.S."

Oral History Task Force, Centro de Estudios Puertoriquenos, Hunter College, City University of New York. "Continued Exclusion: Puerto Rican Women in the Garment Industry." Unpublished manuscript.

Orsi, Robert. *The Madonna of 115th Street: Faith and Community in Italian Harlem, 1880–1950*. New Haven: Yale University Press, 1985.

Reimers, David M. *Still the Golden Door: The Third World Comes to America*. New York: Columbia University Press, 1985.

Scilipoti, Vincent. Interview, Covello Papers (Box 67/1), Balch Institute for Ethnic Studies, Philadelphia, Pennsylvania.

Shepherd, William G. "Eyewitness at Triangle," *Milwaukee Journal*, March 27, 1911. In Stein, *Out of the Sweatshop*.

Sheridan, F. J. *Italian, Slavic and Hungarian Unskilled Immigrant Laborers in the United States*. Washington, D.C.: U.S. Bureau of Labor Bulletin 72, 1907.

Stansell, Christine. *City of Women: Sex and Class in New York, 1789–1860*. New York: Alfred A. Knopf, 1986.

Stein, Leon, ed. *Out of the Sweatshop: The Struggle for Industrial Democracy*. New York: Quadrangle/The New York Times Books, 1977.

Vernon, Raymond. *Metropolis 1985: An Interpretation of the Findings of the New York Region*

Study. Cambridge, Massachusetts: Harvard University Press, 1960.

Walker, George. "The Afro-American in New York City, 1827–1860." Ph.D. dissertation, Political Science, Columbia University, 1975.

Wilentz, Sean. *Chants Democratic: New York City and the Rise of the American Working Class, 1788–1850*. New York: Oxford University Press, 1984.

New Yorkers at School

Berube, Maurice and Gittell, Marilyn, eds. *Confrontation at Ocean Hill-Brownsville: The New York City School Strikes of 1968*. New York: Praeger, 1969.

Clark, Kenneth. *Dark Ghetto: Dilemmas of Social Power*. New York: Harper and Row, 1965.

Covello, Leonard, with D'Agostino, Guido. *Teacher in the Urban Community*. New York: Littlefield, 1970.

Drachsler, Julius. *Democracy and Assimilation: The Blending of Immigrant Heritages in America*. New York: Greenwood, 1920.

Fantini, Mario; Gittell, Marilyn; and Magat, Richard. *Community Control and the Urban School*. New York: Praeger, 1970.

Gittell, Marilyn. "School Governance." *Setting Municipal Priorities, 1981*. Raymond D. Horton and Charles Brecher, eds. Montclair, New Jersey: Allanheld, Osmun 1981.

Howe, Irving. *World of Our Fathers*. New York: Harcourt Brace Jovanovich, 1976.

Kaestle, Carl F. *The Evolution of an Urban School System: New York, 1750–1850*. Cambridge: Harvard University Press, 1973.

Kazin, Alfred. *A Walker in the City*. New York: Harcourt Brace Jovanovich, 1951.

Pratt, John W. *Religion, Politics, and Diversity: The Church and State Theme in New York History*. Ithaca: Cornell University Press, 1967.

Ravitch, Diane. *The Great School Wars: New York City, 1805–1973*. New York: Basic Books, 1974.

Ravitch, Diane and Goodenow, R., eds. *Educating an Urban People: The New York Experience*. New York: Teachers' College Press, 1981.

"Report of the Special Committee from the Board of Aldermen of New York City Appointed to Investigate the Ring Frauds," January 4, 1878.

Rodgers, David. *110 Livingston Street: Politics and Bureaucracy in the New York City School System*. New York: Random House, 1968.

Simon, Kate. *Bronx Primitive: Portraits in a Childhood*. New York: Viking Press, 1982.

Stokes, Anson and Pfeffer, Leo. *Church and State in the United States*. Westport, Connecticut: Greenwood, 1975.

Tyack, David B. *The One Best System: A History of American Urban Education*. Cambridge: Harvard University Press, 1974.

New Yorkers at Play

Adams, John. In Still, *Mirror for Gotham*.

Adelman, Melvin L. *A Sporting Time: New York City and the Rise of Modern Athletics, 1820–1870*. Urbana, Illinois: University of Illinois Press, 1986.

Anderson, Jervis. *This Was Harlem: A Cultural Portrait, 1900–1950*. New York: Farrar, Straus and Giroux, 1982.

Bender, Thomas. *Toward an Urban Vision: Ideas and Institutions in Nineteenth-Century America*. Lexington: University Press of Kentucky, 1975.

Bernard, John. *Retrospections in America, 1797–1811*. Mrs. Bayle Bernard, ed. In Still, *Mirror for Gotham*.

Buckley, Peter George. "To the Opera House: Culture and Society in New York City." Ph.D. dissertation, Department of History, State University of New York at Stony Brook, 1984.

De Sille, Nicasius. May 23, 1654, letter to Maximiliaen van Beeckenke. In Still, *Mirror for Gotham*.

Foster, George G. *New York by Gas-Light: With Here and There a Streak of Sunshine*. New York: Derwitt and Davenport, 1850.

———. *New York Naked*. New York: no publisher, no date.

———. *New York in Slices*. New York: W. H. Graham, 1849.

Gorn, Elliot J. *The Manly Art: Bare-Knuckle Prize Fighting in America*. Ithaca: Cornell University Press, 1986.

Grimsted, David. *Melodrama Unveiled: American Theater and Culture, 1800–1850*. Chicago: University of Chicago Press, 1968

Haswell, Charles. *Reminiscences of New York by an Octogenarian*. New York: Harper, 1896.

Hentoff, Nat and Shapiro, Nat, eds. *Hear Me Talkin' To Ya'*. New York: Rinehart, 1955.

Kasson, John. *Amusing the Million: Coney Island at the Turn of the Century*. New York: Hill and Wang, 1978.

Lambert, John. In Still, *Mirror for Gotham*.

Lewis, David Levering. *When Harlem Was in Vogue.* New York: Alfred A. Knopf, 1981.

Mezzrow, Milton and Wolfe, Bernard. *Really the Blues.* New York: Random House, 1946.

Moody, Richard. *Ned Harrigan: From Corlear's Hook to Herald Square.* Chicago: Nelson-Hall, 1980.

Page, Charles H. and Talamini, John H. *Sport and Society.* Boston: Little, Brown, 1973.

Paine, Albert Bigelow. "The New Coney Island." *Century Magazine* 68, August 1904.

Peiss, Kathy. *Cheap Amusements: Working Women and Leisure in Turn-of-the-Century New York.* Philadelphia: Temple University Press, 1985.

Ribalow, Harold U. *The Jew in American Sports.* New York: Bloch Publishing, 1948.

Roberts, John Storm. *The Latin Tinge: The Impact of Latin-American Music on the United States.* New York: Oxford University Press, 1979.

Snyder, Robert William. "The Voice of the City: Vaudeville and the Creation of Mass Culture in New York Neighborhoods, 1880–1930." Ph.D. dissertation, Department of History, New York University, 1986.

Toll, Robert C. *Blacking Up: The Minstrel Show in Nineteenth-Century America.* New York: Oxford University Press, 1974.

———. *On With the Show: The First Century of Show Business in America.* New York: Oxford University Press, 1976.

Tucker, Sophie. *Some of These Days: The Autobiography of Sophie Tucker.* Garden City, New York: Garden City Publishing, 1946.

Weinberg, S. Kirkson and Arond, Henry. "The Occupational Culture of the Boxer." *American Journal of Sociology*, March 1952.

Acknowledgments

The creation of this book has involved the cooperation of many people; their contributions deserve recognition.

No author has been the recipient of greater dedication, loyalty, and productivity from a researcher than have I. Without Rob Snyder, whose involvement infuses every page, this would have been a far lesser work.

My editor, Eric Himmel, was a constant source of erudition and encouragement, and his input, while necessarily unidentified, is hardly unappreciated.

By contrast, the work of Harvey Weber, both a former colleague and collaborator, is self-evident. Yet his fine photographs can barely suggest the extent of his participation.

There were a number of friends, old and new, whose assistance surely exceeded my hopes, but none was more giving nor more helpful than Mike D'Innocenzo. I would like also to express my thanks to Ralph Wilcox and Dick Zander, who responded unhesitatingly to my calls for aid.

For the opportunity to write this book, I am grateful to *Newsday* Publisher Bob Johnson, retired Editor Tony Insolia, Editor Tony Marro, Managing Editor Howard Schneider, and Assistant Managing Editor Rich Galant. They were responsible either for committing *Newsday* to the project or enabling me to take part in it. Once again, I am appreciative of the support of *Newsday* Vice President Stan Asimov, for his confidence, and for the independence he gave me.

AP/Wide World, New York: 80, 81, 85 bottom. Avery Library, Columbia University, New York: 119 (Louis Hine photo). Bettmann Archive, New York: 59. The Bronx Community History Institute, Herbert H. Lehman College, New York: 18, 105 bottom, 139. Brooklyn Historical Society, New York: 156, 157 both. Brown Brothers, Sterling, Pennsylvania: 31 top left, 40, 41 both, 42 bottom, 68–69, 70–71, 106 top right, 106 bottom right, 107 left, 108, 109, 110, 111, 112, 113, 165 bottom. Centro de Estudios Puertorriqueños, Hunter College, New York: 51, 88 right, 168, 169 both, 172. George Cohen, New York: 91, 118 left, 120 both. Andreas Feininger: 166. Greenfield Village and Henry Ford Museum, Dearborn, Michigan: 36–37. Hunter College, New York: 136, 137. Institute for Research in History, New York: 8, 12 both, 13, 14 both. Fiorello H. LaGuardia Archives, LaGuardia Community College, New York: 29, 31 top right, 31 bottom right, 84, 131 center. Library of Congress, Washington, D.C.: 15 top (Walker Evans photo), 15 bottom (Jack Delano photo), 16 left, 32 bottom left (Marjory Collins photo), 33 top right (Gordon Parks photo), 38 (Marjory Collins photo), 45 (Gordon Parks photo), 107 top right, 165 top (Gordon Parks photo). Leonard McCombe, *Life* Magazine © 1947 Time Inc.: 121. Metropolitan Museum of Art, New York: 63. Museum of the City of New York: 6, 17 bottom left, 32 bottom right, 33 bottom, 62, 67, 75, 105 top, 115, 149, 151, 159 both. Museum of the City of New York, Jacob Riis Collection: 17 top left, 19, 31 bottom left, 33 top left, 39 right, 77 bottom, 104, 106 left, 128, 129, 130 all, 132. New-York Historical Society: 22, 58, 64, 65, 77 top, 94, 97 bottom, 98–99, 127 bottom. City of New York, Parks & Recreation: 78–79. New York Public Library, Astor, Lenox and Tilden Foundations: 20, 55, 66, 86 (Marcantonio Papers), 126, 127 top, 143 (Marcantonio Papers), 148, 153. Timme Rosenkrantz, courtesy Duncan Schiedt: 164. Schomburg Center for Research in Black Culture, New York: 42 top, 43, 116, 163 both. Staten Island Historical Society, New York (Alice Austen Photographs): 16 right, 17 right, 32 top left, 32 top right, 95. Staten Island Institute for Arts and Sciences, New York: 24 bottom. Tamiment Institute Library, New York University: 117. Teachers College, Columbia University, New York: 131 bottom. Transport Workers Union, New York: 118 top right, 118 bottom right. UPI/Bettmann Archive, New York: 73, 83, 85 top, 87, 88 left, 90, 161, 170. Harvey Weber: 2–3, 24 top, 24 center, 25, 26 all, 28, 35, 39 left, 46, 47, 49, 52, 56, 57, 89 both, 92, 96, 97 top, 100–101, 107 bottom right, 124, 135, 138 top left, 138 bottom left, 154, 155 both, 167, 171, 174 all, 175 all. Yivo Institute for Jewish Research, New York: 9 (both), 10–11, 27, 131 top, 138 right, 160 both.

This book is dedicated to Joe, Ron, and Jack

Editor | Eric Himmel
Designer | Judith Michael

LIBRARY OF CONGRESS CATALOGING-IN-PUBLICATION DATA

Bookbinder, Bernie.
City of the world: New York and its people / by Bernie Bookbinder; with photographs by Harvey Weber; research by Rob Snyder.
p. cm.
"A New York/Newsday book."
Bibliography: p. 177
Includes index.
ISBN 0–8109–1363–1
1. New York (N.Y.)—History—1865-1898. 2. New York (N.Y.)—History—1898-1951. 3. New York (N.Y.)—History—1951-   4. New York (N.Y.)—Emigration and immigration—History. 5. Ethnology—New York (N.Y.)   I. Weber, Harvey.   II. Snyder, Rob.   III. Title.
F128.47.B69   1989
974.7′1041—dc19   89–292

Published in 1989 by Harry N. Abrams, Incorporated, New York
All rights reserved. No part of the contents of this book may be reproduced without the written permission of the publisher

A TIMES MIRROR COMPANY

Printed and bound in Japan